THE ART OF PRODUCING GAMES

THE ART OF
PRODUCING GAMES

David McCarthy, Ste Curran, and Simon Byron

THOMSON

™

COURSE TECHNOLOGY

Professional ■ Trade ■ Reference

First published in the United States in 2005
by Course PTR, a division of Thomson Course Technology

For Course PTR:
Publisher: Stacy L. Hiquet
Senior Marketing Manager: Sarah O'Donnell
Marketing Manager: Heather Hurley
Associate Marketing Managers: Kristen Eisenzopf, Jordan Casey
Associate Acquisitions Editor: Megan Belanger
Manager of Editorial Services: Heather Talbot
Editorial Services Coordinator: Elizabeth Furbish

ISBN: 1-59200-611-6

5 4 3 2 1

Library of Congress Catalog Card Number: 2004111629

Educational facilities, companies, and organizations interested
in multiple copies of this book should contact the publisher for
quantity discount information. Training manuals, CD-ROMs, and
portions of this book are also available individually or can be
tailored for specific needs.

COURSE PTR,
A Division of Thomson Course Technology
(**www.courseptr.com**)
25 Thomson Place
Boston, MA 02210

This book was conceived, designed, and produced by:
ILEX
Cambridge
England

Publisher: Alastair Campbell
Executive Publisher: Sophie Collins
Creative Director: Peter Bridgewater
Managing Editor: Tom Mugridge
Project Editor: Ben Renow-Clarke
Design Manager: Tony Seddon
Designer: Jonathan Raimes
Junior Designer: Jane Waterhouse

Printed and bound in China

For more information on this title please visit:
www.web-linked.com/gandus

CONTENTS

01   **02**   **03**   **04**   **05**

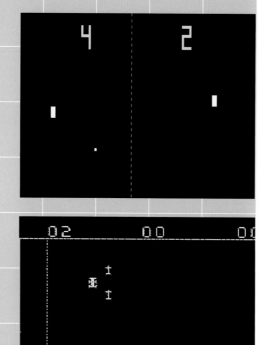

THE ART OF PRODUCING GAMES

We have come a long way in 40 years. From room-sized machines with paper input, to sleek boxes of silicon; from the backrooms of universities and bedrooms of hobbyists, through to multimillion dollar operations; from simple concepts sketched on the back of envelopes and then written in binary, to sprawling, multigenre epics whose marketing budgets are often considered as crucial as their development costs. Videogaming is now a global, multibillion dollar industry, and it is still growing.

As the industry grows, the way that games are developed also becomes more sophisticated. *The Art of Producing Games* aims to give the reader an insight into that process, a disparate, multitiered art that is now as diverse and sophisticated as the movie industry, and that has budgets to match. Those who wish to get involved in the business of making games—and more and more people are finding

it an attractive and lucrative form of creative expression—should look no further for a guide to the skills that are required.

After all, this is no longer a medium where success requires a computer science degree, a collection of death metal records, and a fear of the outside world—a stereotype all but eliminated today.

The Art of Producing Games has five broad sections, and four of those offer opportunities for those who have never touched a line of code, much less devoted their lives to it. Programmers are still in demand, but the games industry today requires much, much more.

Following a look at the history of game design, the book begins with a look at the preproduction phase, where concepts are settled, budgets defined, tools chosen, and pitches produced. Production follows preproduction—presuming the pitch is accepted, of course—and here the programmers really are required, along

THEN...
Opposite page,
clockwise from top left:
Pong, Atari, 1972
Manic Miner, Bug-Byte, 1983
Spacewar!, MIT, 1962
Death Race, Exidy, 1976

NOW...
Clockwise from top left:
Virtua Tennis 2K2, Sega, 2001
Super Mario Sunshine,
Nintendo, 2002
Eve Online: The Second Genesis,
Crucial, 2003
Grand Theft Auto: Vice City,
Rockstar, 2003

with artists, writers, level designers, and audio experts. Milestones need to be hit, too, which means employing a producer, and adding another set of skills entirely.

Postproduction is next, which involves localizing the game for different countries, and proves not just a technical challenge, but a cultural one, too. This chapter of the book also looks at sequels and expansions, and the difficulties inherent in producing them. Finally, the business and financing side of the games industry is covered with chapters on marketing and PR, and the alternative models that are emerging for games development.

Interviews with leading games industry figures complement the chapters, and paint a comprehensive picture of videogame construction in the 21st century. Those people already involved in making games will find *The Art of Producing Games* provides

a succinct overview of the work that surrounds them every day demonstrating just how crucial a role they play in this vast, intricate constantly evolving machine. Those people who aren't will be shown the expertise that they will need to get into the games industry.

And who wouldn't want to do that? With the budgets for blockbuster games now approaching those of their Hollywood rivals and the sales figures exceeding them, rewarding positions are on offer for workers across the employment spectrum. All this, and there is still so much creative space left to explore—it's an exciting place to be. *The Art of Producing Games* shows why. We hope you enjoy it.

A BRIEF INTRODUCTION TO GAME DEVELOPMENT

01

**PART 01. A BRIEF
INTRODUCTION TO GAME
DEVELOPMENT**

CHAPTER ONE

IN THE BEGINNING

If there is one place that everything in videogaming can be traced back to—one single point, genesis, the birthplace of the first videogame—then it is a computer laboratory at the Massachusetts Institute of Technology in 1962, home to four long-haired coders in their mid-twenties, and a PDP-1. The PDP-1 was, in essence, the first personal computer, albeit one the size of a room that required input in the form of reels of punched paper tape. The coders—Martin Graetz, Wayne Witaenem, and Stephen Russell—were pulp science fiction fans out to create a demonstration program that pushed the system to the limit. In an interview with *Edge* magazine, Graetz recalled the group's first conversation on the matter. "Wayne said, 'Look, you need action, and you need some kind of skill level. It should be a game where you have to control things moving around on the scope like, oh, spaceships.' 'Spacewar!' we shouted."

Some (what would prove to be typically slacker, coder-led) procrastination later, the game was born. Two player-controlled torpedo-laden spaceships could battle around a vector-sketched sun,

that pulled ships toward it with its gravity field, against a background of a correctly plotted solar system in realtime using a control system based on the PDP-1's switches. The switches were cumbersome, to the point of being physically painful, and that led to gaming's first peripheral: push-button boxes were acquired from the university's model railroad club, and wired into the system. The first gamers could now play for hour upon hour, and they did. Eventually, as hardware costs fell, the first computer game became the first arcade machine. *Computer Space* was developed by Nolan Bushnell, who produced 1,500 cabinets in 1971, but the game was too complicated for an uninitiated audience, and was largely ignored by the public.

Bushnell found more success the following year with *Pong*, the bat and ball game that became videogaming's first icon. Programmed by Al Alcorn, *Pong* started as a working demo of the coder's abilities, but became a worldwide smash—so popular, in fact, that many attribute the success of gaming's first console, the Magnavox Odyssey, released that same year, to the way that *Pong*

the greatest TV show on earth ... with over 1,000 game variations

Far left: **A family enjoy electronic entertainment in the mid-80s thanks to the Magnavox.**
Left: **A PDP-1, a far cry from the games machines of today.**
Above: **The Fairchild Channel F was rebranded the Grandstand in the UK.**
Below: **Odyssey: The ultimate videogame system...for a short time, at least.**

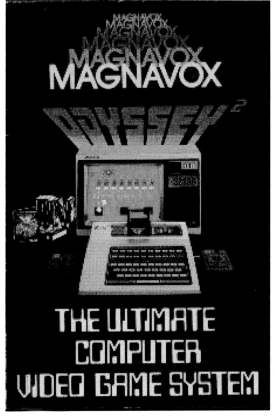

had so effectively infiltrated the public consciousness. Gaming as a mainstream pursuit was born, arcades boomed, and a host of home systems followed. Notably, 1976 saw the release of the Fairchild Channel F, the world's first cartridge-based game console, which led to the Atari VCS in 1977. But, while hardware was increasing in sophistication, the videogame development model remained broadly the same: one person, one idea, one game.

Which isn't to say that game design stood still. Innovation flourished in the arcades, and nowhere more effectively than with Taito's *Space Invaders*. A cultural phenomenon in its native Japan, it was imported by Midway in 1978, and contained one notable improvement on its predecessors: a high score. Now games players had a target to aim for, and the industry reaped rewards out of competitiveness. In 1979, Atari's *Asteroids* took that principle one stage further. This best-selling arcade game owed its popularity to its high-score table. Successful players were rewarded with three initials alongside their hard-won score.

SEMINAL VIDEOGAMES FROM THE PERIOD

Below: **SPACEWAR!**
MIT (1962)
The father of all videogames, *Spacewar!* laid the ground rules for game design: make something that's technically impressive, always different, and always fun. Despite this, its transition to the arcade was unsuccessful. Would-be players found the controls too complex, and waited for something simpler.

Bottom: **PONG**
Atari (1976)
Pong was that simpler game. Players grasped the bat-and-ball concept with enthusiasm, partly due to the one-line mission statement: "Avoid Missing Ball For High Score." The design survives today in the form of tennis games, which cover the same elegant principle in layers of modern game design.

Below: **GUN FIGHT**
Midway (1975)
The first game released by Midway, the new videogame division of pinball manufacturer Bally, *Gun Fight* was the first arcade game to use a microprocessor. Again, it was a two-player competition. Gamers played cowboys on opposite sides of the screen, shooting each other and hiding behind cacti.

Bottom: **BREAKOUT**
Atari (1976)
Included here not because its designer, Steve Jobs, went on to cofound Apple Computers, but because it was the first successful example of iterative game design. In *Breakout*, *Pong*'s bat-and-ball principle became bat-and-wall, the ball speeding up as bricks at the top of the screen were eliminated.

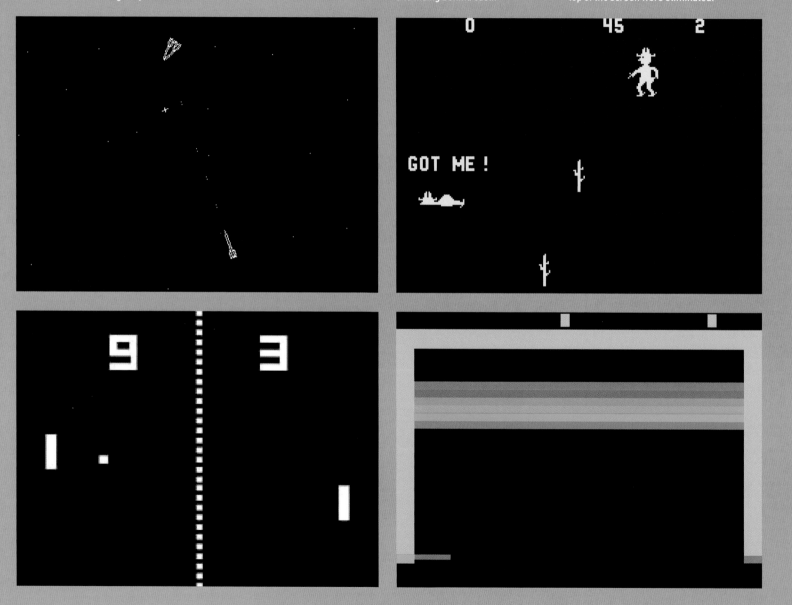

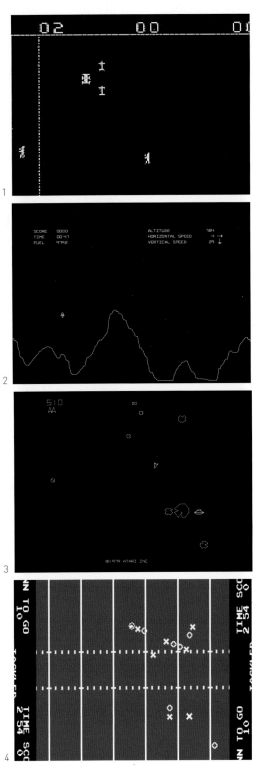

1. DEATH RACE
Exidy (1976)

If you thought controversy over violent videogames was a new thing, think again. *Death Race* was banned in 1976 for its gruesome gameplay, which featured a tiny white car trying to run over tiny white goblins. Inspired by the movie *Death Race 2000*, it set the bar for several decades of weak, controversy-packed cash-ins.

4. ATARI FOOTBALL
Atari (1979)

Atari Football wasn't the first game to cash in on the enormous desire to recreate sports in a lazier fashion, but it was the first to use a trackball as a method of input. Xs and Os on the playfield defined the football players' locations, and players spun the trackball hard and fast to make them move around. The input method would return a quarter century later, for the worldwide success *Golden Tee*.

2. LUNAR LANDER
Atari (1979)

Though the principle behind *Lunar Lander* is hardly revolutionary—take a spaceship, and park it neatly on the planet surface before your fuel runs out—the technology was. This was Atari's first vector graphics game, a feature which allowed the game to "zoom in" as the player approached the planet surface, and brought a different kind of style to videogaming.

COMPUTER OTHELLO
Nintendo (1978)
(No images exist)

Notable because it represents Nintendo's entry into the arcade market, *Othello*'s graphics may have been simple—the black and white pieces were portrayed on the monochrome screen by plus and square symbols—but its appeal was broad. *Othello* was built into a cocktail cabinet, allowing players to sit down while they played.

3. ASTEROIDS
Atari (1979)

Asteroids' main input into gaming's creative pantheon was the high-score table that finally gave players show-off rights. Other elements stick just as long in the memory, though, like developing strategies to "fish" for the high-scoring UFOs, or the intimidating two-tone music that upped the game's tension as the playfield was cleared.

5. SPACE INVADERS
Taito (1978)

In this case, videogaming's lore is true: *Space Invaders* really did create a shortage of coins when it was released in Japan. It has proved to be a huge influence culturally, but also in design terms, creating the high-score system which was to draw players back to various strands of arcade gaming for many, many years.

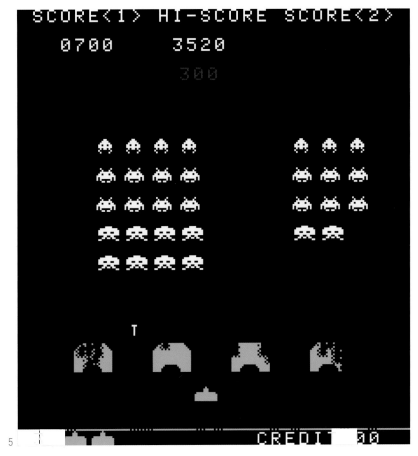

Left: "Those were the days," they say. They weren't, although for those involved at the time, Sinclair's initial wave of home computers must have felt like science fiction. Compared to today's computers and consoles, their power is laughable. However, developers like nothing more than a challenge and, despite their limitations, these machines permitted the kind of experimentation only possible nowadays with languages like Java. A generation of coders grew up on these machines. Sadly, few remain in the business to this day.

**PART 01. A BRIEF
INTRODUCTION TO GAME
DEVELOPMENT**

CHAPTER TWO

GAME DESIGN IN THE 1980s

Anyone reflecting on the early 1980s videogame landscape today would be forgiven for assuming it was made entirely from Lego. Crude, blocky graphics bearing little association to their real-life counterparts were as high as artists could aspire. Which was fairly fortunate, as the artists of the day had other things to be concerned with such as programming, sound, and game design.

While early home consoles were already fairly popular, thanks to Atari's VCS, it wasn't until the advent of affordable home computers around the turn of the decade that independent game design became a reality.

Sinclair's ZX80 and ZX81 computers—the last two digits reflect the year they debuted—were ambitious for their day, but that didn't stop developers from trying to squeeze every drop of power for their games. One of the more astonishing achievements of the time was a chess program that ran in 1K, meaning that the whole code was less than 1,024 characters long. It played a competent game but you needed to combine a real chessboard with it, as it had no graphics to speak of.

While the ZX series of machines proved popular with hobbyists, it was the color home computers that really permitted inexperienced and aspiring developers the freedom to experiment on

their own. In 1982, Sinclair released the Spectrum, with its rubber keys that still evoke such strong memories. Commodore retaliated with the VIC 20 (1982) and the Commodore 64 (1983), with an astonishing 64 kilobytes of RAM. By now, developers had enough memory to begin coding relatively sophisticated games.

Initially, many home computer and videogames were representations of popular arcade titles. Given the technology of the day, games in both the arcade and at home needed to be simple. Forget the complicated button configurations of the modern videogame. *Pac-Man* (1980) and *Frogger* (1981), for example, were driven by a four-way joystick, *Donkey Kong* (1981) used a stick and a "jump" button, and while *Defender* (1980) was admittedly more complicated, even its two-way stick and four buttons were nothing compared to the current PlayStation DualShock gamepad.

This simplicity is no more evident than in one of the most seminal games of the 80s. To date, Alexei Pajitnov's *Tetris* (1985) remains the most perfectly designed piece of games software. Its development, distribution, and subsequent legal ramblings also form one of gaming's most interesting background stories, yet one that is too interesting to be dismissed in a couple of paragraphs here.

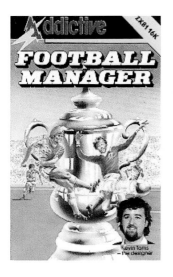

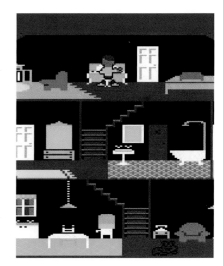

Above: **The game that started it all.** Running in 16K, the ZX81's *Football Manager* was more smoke and mirrors than a sophisticated soccer management sim. Its limited size obviously restricted the statistics permitted within the game, resulting in it attempting to create the illusion of realism rather than emulate it.

Above: **One of the more ambitious games for the humble ZX81 was** Psion's *Flight Simulation*, which required the 16K RAM pack. While it was hardly sophisticated, it offered a basic illusion of flight in just a few pixels.

Above: *Game Over*, **by David Sheff,** covers the extraordinary story of *Tetris* and its part in Nintendo's history in greater detail than possible here—and comes highly recommended. What it doesn't mention, however, is the atrocious marketing—clearly influenced by the "Aren't they clever, those foreigners?" positioning of the Rubik's Cube a few years earlier.

Above: **Activision's 1985 title** *Little Computer People* was arguably the forebear of *The Sims*. A simple game more popular for its novelty value than its in-depth gameplay, it encouraged users to entertain and play games with a virtual friend. Of course, more vindictive users would soon derive pleasure from starving their virtual chum.

Another influential title of the era was David Braben and Ian Bell's *Elite* (Acornsoft, 1983). The game originally appeared on the BBC Micro and Acorn Electron computers, but it was ported onto many other home formats, both computers and consoles. The game was rightly lauded at the time for its excellent 3D wireframe graphics and expansive universe, but perhaps its most lasting contribution to game design was its freeform play style. Its simple premise of space trading, combat, and a universe within which the player is free to chart their own course is perhaps one of the earliest examples of the "sandbox" method of game design—one which is most recognizable in the *Grand Theft Auto* series of games today.

THE MID-EIGHTIES

Following the resurgence in popularity of home computers, the mid- to late 80s were to start a trend in which dedicated games consoles would become the electronic entertainment platform of choice. Atari and Commodore did their best to support more sophisticated computers, with the release of the Amiga and ST series, but, ultimately, they would be beaten by industry heavyweights Nintendo (NES, 1985) and Sega (Master System, 1986).

Unlike the early days, which saw the prominence of developers in the USA and UK, it was the Japanese developers that really began making waves from the middle of the decade. As in subsequent decades, Shigeru Miyamoto was an influential figure. Buoyed by the success of *Donkey Kong*, Miyamoto exported the game's hero into his own unique videogame—and *Super Mario Brothers* (1985) subsequently went on to sell more than 40 million copies in North America alone.

Sega's superstar developers also began to emerge. Yu Suzuki oversaw development on *Hang On* (1985) and *Space Harrier* (1985), but it was *Outrun* (1986) that made his name. It turned heads with its smooth racing, varied routes, glorious soundtrack and the inclusion of a moving Ferrari Testarossa body as part of the grander displays.

The 80s are fondly remembered by the more mature gamer, as the decade that pioneered the medium. And while that's true to some extent—practically all current genres were invented by the start of the 90s—most games that are revisited now through emulation or antique hardware obtained on eBay provide extremely short-term interest. The fact remains that the charm of these games ultimately proves their undoing. They were brilliantly simple. But the games of the next decade and a half changed tastes forever.

Left: **GAUNTLET**

Hard on the heels of the successful *Marble Madness* and *Paperboy* came this staggering arcade adventure. Its 13-strong team worked hard to push coin-op gaming further than any game prior to it—with four concurrent players, over 200 digitized sounds and a limitless playfield. Shame they didn't spend more time considering design; it was a little too close to the Spectrum game *Dandy* for its author's liking, who threatened to sue. Atari settled cheaply, by giving Jack Palevich an arcade cabinet.

Left: **FINAL FANTASY**

The *Final Fantasy* games may have evolved over time to embrace improving technology, but the turn-based combat and party system remains central to its heart. The original's primitive design was nonetheless ambitious for the time, although some may argue that more recent FF titles have relied too much on impressive cut-scenes than gaming mechanics. Hironobu Sakaguchi—the driving force behind the original—has been credited on 38 other videogames.

Left: **TETRIS**

Nothing could illustrate the minimalism of 80s game design better than the design for the seminal *Tetris*, released in 1985. Its perfect symmetry and simplicity—move, rotate, drop; that's all—surely makes it the most perfect videogame ever devised. Despite numerous attempts at pseudo-sequels and variations, no developer has come close to equalling Alexei Pajitnov's incredible achievement.

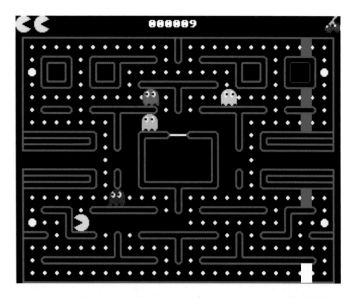

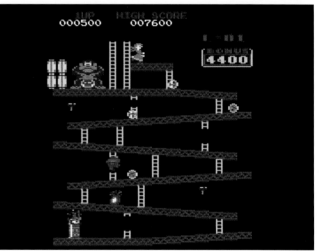

Top: **PAC-MAN**

Inspired by a piece of pizza with a slice missing—good thing Toru Iwatani wasn't musing while tucking into meat and potatoes—*Pac-Man* holds the record for best-selling arcade game of all time. Given the decline of coin-operated gaming, this is a record it's likely to retain indefinitely. The game took eight people 15 months to design—four working on the hardware, four on the software.

Above: **DONKEY KONG**

The great ape boasts two significant videogame records; it was the first to feature movable objects that must be avoided by leaping, and also the first to boast multiple playfields. And while it's generally thought that Mario is the lead character, in 1981 he was simply called "Jump Man."

Right: SUPER MARIO BROTHERS
Widely considered to be the first side-scrolling platform game of its kind, Mario had actually featured in no fewer than seven previous computer and arcade titles between *Donkey Kong* and *Super Mario Brothers*. The game's eight worlds—each with four subworlds—occupied just 32K of program code and 8K of graphics.

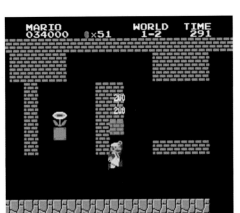

Below: DEFENDER
A project completed almost solely by Eugene Jarvis, *Defender* was essentially the result of a bet by manufacturer Williams. After working on a succession of pinball titles, the young engineer—a huge fan of the original *Spacewar!* and *Space Invaders*—badgered his superiors into allowing him to design a videogame of his own. They gave him until the upcoming arcade expo, expecting nothing. The rest, as clichés go, is history.

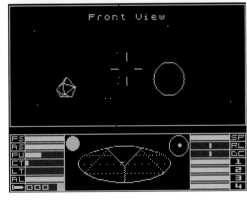

Above: **ELITE**
Despite the limited host hardware, *Elite* managed to create the illusion of a living, breathing universe thanks to the mathematical genius of authors David Braben and Ian Bell. Development started in 1982, with the game emerging in 1984—although a well-publicized spat between the authors would eventually see Braben continue development alone on a couple of sequels to date.

Above: **THE LEGEND OF ZELDA**
A top-down adventure with primitive graphics; none could predict that Shigeru Miyamoto's childhood exploration fantasies would translate into such a seminal title, let alone one with such staying power. Despite numerous attempts, no other game or series of games has managed to replicate the mix of combat, exploration, and puzzle-solving with which the series is synonymous.

Below: POPULOUS / SIM CITY
Developed entirely separately but released in the same year (1989) both titles pioneered the "God" sim in different ways. *Populous*, with its fantasy setting, was markedly different from *Sim City*'s regimented conurbation simulation (*Sim City 2000* shown). Both titles benefited from a number of expansion packs, which boasted reduced development times and a lower suggested retail price, while requiring the original game to run. While these were not the first to attempt to drive loyal, follow-on sales, the popularity of both *Populous* and *Sim City* expansion packs encouraged many others to replicate the model.

Left: **FROGGER**
Various iterations of the original *Frogger* have appeared on upward of 20 formats, making this one of the most widely ported games of all time. A seemingly harmless game which, unusually, appealed to girls as well as boys, this Konami/Sega title did manage to find itself in the headlines when religious fundamentalists called for the splattered frog sprite to be redrawn, as they felt it resembled Christ on the cross.

Left: **OUTRUN**
Defying the tradition of aiming for realism (or as realistic as you could get at the time), Sega's *OutRun* could be described as the first boy racer videogame. The glamor of the Ferrari, the accompanying blonde, and the smooth bilinear parallax scrolling held many adolescents in awe. In an early example of ego, pressing the "Start" button when passing a checkpoint shows the message "Created by Yu Suzuki" on the screen.

This didn't stop the PC from introducing perhaps the most influential title of the 90s, when a little-known shareware title was released in 1993. An evolution of the previous year's *Wolfenstein 3D, Doom* was a true phenomenon; refreshingly simple yet utterly addictive. It was also the first PC game to be widely networked, almost single-handedly responsible for the "Deathmatch" games that remain today.

SONY STYLE WINS OUT

Games moved out of the bedroom and into the nightclub in September 1995, as Sony released its PlayStation console in North America. This was the defining moment of videogaming to date, as its combination of extraordinary graphical capabilities, sleek design, simple operation, and most importantly, smart marketing dragged gaming from the ghetto of the geeks and into popular culture.

PlayStation was an instant success, dismissing earlier, seemingly rushed, hardware launches from rival manufacturers in the previous years. Commodore made their final entry into home gaming with the CD32, and Sega peppered the market with confusing technology in the form of the Mega CD, the 32x, and the Saturn.

GAME DESIGN IN THE 1990s

Home consoles began to emerge as the dominant formats in the early 90s, as Sega's Mega Drive and Nintendo's SNES completed their global rollout. Although home computers such as the Amiga and the ST enjoyed a dedicated following in Europe and North America, Japan's obsession with cartridge-based gaming would ultimately win out, forcing Commodore into bankruptcy and Atari to concentrate solely on its software business.

An unforeseen consequence of the introduction of more mainstream consoles was the death of the bedroom programmer. The ability to experiment with all aspects of game design was restricted to formats that did not require approvals from their manufacturer. As the open formats declined, so, too, did the commercial opportunities for those keen to design and publish any type of game. Development teams of ten and above ceased being the exception—and throughout the decade this figure often increased tenfold.

Nonetheless, until the middle of the decade there were healthy markets for both computer and console games. And, despite its numerous and complicated hardware configurations, the PC gaming market also took off—although often gamers needed the technical knowledge of a hacker in order to get their games up and running.

Microsoft wisely introduced the DirectX API in the mid-90s, to enable PC owners to theoretically enjoy the "plug and play" gaming that their console brethren were boasting about. This gave developers a stable platform, enabling them to concentrate on designing their titles rather than worrying about the hardware configuration.

The relative stability of the Windows platform and its derivatives resulted in an unusual alliance at the end of the decade as Sega opted to team up with Microsoft and hardware acceleration company NEC to drive its Dreamcast console. This, in theory, offered developers a platform similar to PC, making ports from computer to console relatively simple and, crucially, cheaper. But despite innovating in many areas and beating PlayStation 2 to market, the console would enjoy only limited and brief success.

The 1990s were the most exciting era for games and games development. The explosion of people playing games across the world put the medium firmly on the entertainment map. But the arrival of the mainstream or casual gamer often resulted in poor games that were heavily marketed, topping the charts ahead of what the hardcore gamers deemed "better" titles. This debate continues. For modern formats, a game that plays well is often no guarantee of chart success.

Above: In 1988, staff at Nintendo HQ appeared dismissive when Sega announced that it would release its 16-bit Sega Mega Drive (Genesis in America) the following year in an effort to steal a march on the rival NES. However, when the Mega Drive quickly took over the market in North America and Europe in the early 90s due to its superior processing power, Nintendo quickly decided to begin development on their own system. The two consoles would battle it out during the early stages of the decade in a war which would establish territory for years to come, dominating the home computer market outside of the emerging PC platform.

Open   Walk to   Use
Close Pick up   Look at
Push   Talk to   Turn on
Pull   Give   Turn off

Left: The idea for PlayStation began in 1988 when Nintendo and Sony partnered to develop the Super Disc—a CD-ROM add-on that was intended to be part of Nintendo's future hardware plans. However, Sony and Nintendo parted ways during its development and the Super Disc never made it to market. In 1991, Sony used a modified version of the Super Disc as part of its new game console, "PlayStation." Research and development for the PlayStation had begun in 1990, headed by Sony engineer Ken Kutaragi. Launched in 1995, it was to shape the videogaming landscape forever— for both consumers and developers.

Above: Released by the then-called Lucasfilm Entertainment, a game developer and publisher set up by George Lucas in 1982, *The Secret of Monkey Island* (1990) remains perhaps one of the most fondly remembered adventure games. Its combination of wit and production values was streets ahead of the competition at the time, and started a series that was to continue for 10 years. Perfectly preserved through the SCUMMVM emulation program, it remains a joy to this day.

Top: A triumphant move to 3D for the series that began on the NES, *Metal Gear Solid* broke fresh ground in the way games could become self-referential. For starters, an essential radio frequency was listed on the back of the packaging, with the game asking players to check the back of the box in order to progress. Smart gimmicks such as recognizing other saved games on the PlayStation memory card—and commenting on them in cut-scenes—reinforced creator Hideo Kojima's credentials as one of the most innovative designers in videogames.

1

3

5

1. TOMB RAIDER [1996]

While *Tomb Raider*'s success was no doubt mainly down to its breathtaking visuals and memorable heroine, its design was built on solid 2D platform foundations. A team of 16 started development in 1994, led by Toby Gard, whose goal was to create a female version of Indiana Jones. He succeeded— and then some. The first gaming icon to appear on the cover of British style magazine *The Face*, Lara almost single-handedly transformed the image of games, despite the best attempts of the industry and the litany of disgraceful, clichéd characters that followed.

2. DUNE II [1992]

Humble beginnings for what would subsequently evolve into one of the most popular franchises of the decade. *Dune II* is commonly referred to as the first "realtime" strategy game, and while this

isn't strictly true, there's no doubting it was the first to achieve widespread popularity. At the heart of the game was the *Command & Conquer* interface, which offered players incredible freedom to develop bases, build armies, and defeat rogue factions. The series subsequently evolved into *Command & Conquer*, and was followed up with numerous spin-offs. However, it's an example of how easy it is to take your audience for granted. The series has rarely repeated the success of the original iterations, and has been overtaken in almost every area by its competitors.

3. CHUCHU ROCKET [1999]

A clever, if sometimes impossibly chaotic puzzle game, *ChuChu Rocket* was original in both design and execution. Developed by Sega's Sonic Team, its place in gaming history is assured, as it was

the first console game to be playable online. Sega gave this game away to encourage Dreamcast owners to use its visionary, but ill-fated and underpowered Dreamarena online network. In its enthusiasm to make the console Internet-ready, Sega opted to include a dial-up modem rather than wait for Broadband to take off. The result was a service unable to handle significant traffic. *ChuChu Rocket* is an example of a game developed with external technological restrictions in mind, with a minimal amount of data exchanged between consoles.

4. ALONE IN THE DARK [1992]

The original survival horror game, *Alone in the Dark* may not have boasted the gore of its imitators, but it remains one of the greatest examples of how to scare a player. Inspired by gothic horror writer H.P. Lovecraft, it combined realtime 3D graphics

over pre-rendered scenery, which resulted in a unique look and feel at the time. *AITD* was developed by Infogrames, which was at the time a medium-sized French company. The original idea is credited to Bruno Bonnell, who was then in product development for the firm. In an unusual series of events, which combined the affection of the French stock exchange for its native developers and the predatory nature of its management team, Infogrames has risen to become one of the world's largest publishers, operating under the current guise of Atari. There, surely, is hope for us all.

5. WOLFENSTEIN 3D

With hindsight, the similarities are obvious, but in 1993 *Wolfenstein 3D* was an unexpected glimpse of the future. Developed by the same core team that went on to program the seminal *Doom*, *Wolfenstein* was

a remake of the top-down game *Castle Wolfenstein*, available for the Apple II and the C64. Developer id Software couldn't think of a better name, so licensed it from Muse Software. *Wolfenstein*'s view wasn't unique, but its implementation was, and it's the game that was to kick-start a genre.

6. GRAND THEFT AUTO [1997]

Although it was the subsequent move to 3D in *GTA III* that encouraged the industry to break free from the shackles of linear level design, this was evident in the first title—albeit a simplified top-down version of what was to follow. GTA's original concept was to place players in the role of the cop, rather than the criminal. The inspired decision to switch perspective, offering a series of missions that could be attempted almost ad-hoc, resulted in a breathtaking title that courted controversy on its

2

4

6

8

10

release. Indeed, then publisher BMG even hired the services of notorious publicist Max Clifford to promote the game through hysterical tabloid stories. *GTA III*'s *Liberty City*, *Vice City*, and *San Andreas* have remained true to the original game, which boasted these locations as part of its three-stage story.

7. FINAL FANTASY VII (1997)
Inexperienced players introduced to the medium by PlayStation must have wondered what all the fuss was about. Indeed, on paper, one baffles at the reason why *FFVII* tops many "best game of all time" lists. It's bizarrely Japanese in places, boasts a ridiculous amount of dialog and—worst of all—relies on turn-based combat, when the gaming world had moved on. But that's missing the point. It's an astonishingly emotive piece of software which—harsh ending aside—is a joy to play for

every minute of its average 70-hour playtime. A huge game—but with over 90 people involved in its production, it should be.

8. DONKEY KONG COUNTRY (1994)
Donkey Kong Country put Rare firmly on the map, following seven years of original titles and conversions of variable merit. Cleverly, Nintendo didn't discourage the original reporting of the game, when hacks assumed it was running on Nintendo's subsequent hardware. The game employed Advanced Computer Modeling (ACM) techniques to produce its distinctive visuals, and serves as an example of how developers often get the best out of consoles when they're past their peak. Rare was acquired by Microsoft for over $300 million in 2002 as the firm seeks to bring the developer's expertise to their current and next generation of consoles.

9. DOOM (1993)
Don't believe the hype; U.S. soldiers were never trained to kill on *Doom*, despite what flamboyant lawyers will claim. But there's no doubting that a generation of gamers playing id's guttural shooter were trained to love the first-person genre. The game is perhaps the most successful shareware title of all time, distributed for free on magazine cover discs and the bulletin boards. This limited version was digital dope; once it had been sampled, it was difficult to resist. *Doom* also gave many their first taste of multiplayer gaming, as PCs the world over were networked together specifically to play *Doom*. Indeed, following its release, a number of companies began offering specific dial-up gaming services—the precursor to Xbox Live and PlayStation Network. The game was also one of the first to encourage user modifications, where levels

and graphics were supplied by players. A flood of imitators followed—some good, many awful—but for many, the original remains the purest form of combat to date.

10. SUPER MARIO 64 (1996)
Every new console should ideally boast an exclusive title so impressive it encourages consumers to buy the system just to play it. *Super Mario 64* is one such example. Drawing on the rich history of the previous games, *SM64* reunited the central characters in a beautiful 3D world. Released the same year as *Tomb Raider*, and with a roughly similar development time, it's interesting to see how both games—which were among the first platform games to move into 3D—differed in terms of control. Lara was restricted almost to a system of grids, whereas Mario could go anywhere. It remains an almost perfect example of how to do it.

11. PRINCE OF PERSIA (1990)
Released on the Apple II in 1989, it wasn't until the following year that the world first took notice of Jordan Mechner and his incredible platform game. Almost entirely the work of Mechner himself—although with help from his dad who wrote the music, and his brother who provided the animation inspiration—*Prince of Persia* was a genuine labor of love, taking four years to make. His endeavors were worthwhile: the game went on to sell over two million copies across numerous formats, and was renowned for its rotoscoped animation. The series went downhill during the middle to late 90s, when a couple of dubious sequels sucked the soul from what was a flawless title. However, French publisher Ubisoft restored credibility in 2003 with *Prince of Persia: The Sands of Time*, a truly breathtaking adventure in the spirit of the original.

9

11

HARDWARE 2000
Competition to Sony and Nintendo's dominance of the hardware sector emerged from an unlikely source: the world's largest software company, Microsoft. Thus the Xbox joined Sony's PlayStation 2 and Nintendo's GameCube in a line up of consoles that seemed to herald the dawn of mass-market online gaming—a dawn that's proved slightly longer in coming than some had expected.

**PART 01. A BRIEF
INTRODUCTION TO GAME
DEVELOPMENT**

CHAPTER FOUR

GAME DESIGN
FOR THE 21ST CENTURY

If the end of the 1990s saw small, independent teams driven to the brink of extinction, then the start of the 21st century saw developments that would place those few remaining teams under even more pressure. It was a time when the gaming public put its wallet away and began its wait for the "Next Generation." March 2000 brought the first of these, the PlayStation 2, to Japan, and it proved to be a difficult system to develop for. That, and increased public expectations for huge, Hollywood-style experiences, brought bigger budgets, larger teams, and the growing feeling among some that the games industry was spiraling out of control. Microsoft's announcement that it would soon enter the console market didn't help matters, either.

The biggest loser was Sega, whose Dreamcast games console quickly took on the air of a dying platform. In 2001, the manufacturer first announced it would start developing games for other platforms, and then that it was to drop out of the hardware business entirely. The next generation console wars would be fought between Microsoft, Nintendo, and Sony—but even in September 2001, the launch month of Nintendo's GameCube, it was clear who the

winner would be. Sony's headstart meant its domination was assured; developers might have complained about the console's architecture, but the number of systems in living rooms across the globe meant publishers had little choice.

Spurred on by the increased complexity of hardware in general, middleware took on a new level of importance. An increasingly popular model of game development saw third parties employed to deal with the low-level aspects of the game engine—physics components, for example, or AI routines—while the developer concentrated on the core aspects of the game's design.

Microsoft's first console, the Xbox, made its debut in November 2001, and it soon found itself locked in a heated battle with Nintendo for second place. While Microsoft's titles were almost entirely targeted at videogaming's core demographic, males in their late teens and early twenties, Nintendo continued to focus the majority of its attention at younger, family-oriented gamers. Each manufacturer met with only limited success, and the next "Next Generation" will prove crucial for both.

Below: **ICO** (SCEI 2001)
Few games have been as undeservedly neglected by the mainstream as SCEI's *ICO*, a glorious fairytale which takes narrative videogames to a minimalist, elegant new level. The boy must save the girl, of course—we've been doing that since *Donkey Kong*—and the mechanics are just levels and ladders in 3D. Some call it a triumph of style over substance, but oh, what style.

Ⓨ Finger of Death!
29 Combat Points

Left: **GALLEON** (SCI 2004)
Tomb Raider designer Toby Gard left to form his own company, Confounding Factor, in 1997. It took seven years for its first and only game, *Galleon*, to be released to little fanfare—at which point Gard joined Crystal Dynamics to work on the next *Tomb Raider* game. An extreme case, perhaps, but it shows that independent developers have little opportunity to produce vanity projects in the 21st century.

Above: **DEUS EX** (EIDOS 2000)
Deus Ex is the logical conclusion of several design trends that began to appear toward the end of the 1990s; its conspiracy-laden setting is home to a richly multilayered, emergent game universe that grants unprecedented player choice and narrative flexibility. Though no game has yet matched its scope, including its own sequel, many developers have begun to emulate its systemic design.

Below: HALO: COMBAT EVOLVED
Microsoft (2001)
The launch title for Microsoft's Xbox, designed by Microsoft-owned Bungie Studios, *Halo* was still the system's best game three years later when the sequel arrived. That's not a dig at the other titles on the Xbox, but testament to the game's quality, no mean feat for a debut game on a new system. A first-person shooter, *Halo* doesn't try to do much, but everything it does it does to absolute perfection.

Below right: REZ
Sega (2001)
The shoot-'em-up, one of videogaming's core genres since *Space Invaders*, hasn't really changed since its inception. And although *Rez* represents its targets in glorious, lucid, three-dimensional space, the mission is still the same: shoot things, and don't get shot. But *Rez* is different because, in successfully taking on the concept of synesthesia in a videogame, it shows that videogames are as capable of high art as they are of low culture.

Far right: EYETOY: PLAY
SCEE (2003)
Consoles have often followed the arcade sector's penchant for bespoke controllers to make games feel more approachable. *EyeToy* took this principle still further, using a webcam to evolve the party-game genre to the extent that no contact with peripherals is necessary at all. The minigames in this collection all work by detecting the player's motion, resulting in an experience that looks as ridiculous as it is entertaining.

Right: **GRAND THEFT AUTO III**
Rockstar (2001)
In all the tabloid-inspired furore over *Grand Theft Auto*'s questionable content, it's easy to lose sight of why it's such a successful game in the first place. People don't play it for the violence; they play it because it affords the opportunity to do whatever they please. The camera is horrible, the combat is (literally) hit and miss, but GTA's toy set is equal parts bewitching and influential.

part 01. a brief introduction to game development

THE FUTURE OF ELECTRONIC ENTERTAINMENT

Prophecies are almost always doomed to failure, and the temptation to leave nothing but a huge question mark here is huge. That said, some things seem inevitable. As the PlayStation 2 enters middle age, Sony appears increasingly intent on wooing nongamers over to their hardware, with titles like *EyeToy*, *SingStar*, and *DJ: Decks and FX* attracting players from outside traditional demographics. Those demographics must be included as part of the company's PS3 (and PSP) strategy, and if that strategy is successful, its impact will be immense; videogame companies who want to thrive will be forced to cater for people they've never considered before, with enormous design implications.

Technically, while the code behind games will get ever more intricate, the trend toward middleware will continue, with even more components of games being freelanced out to specialist agencies. Middleware has the benefit of making the production of cross-platform software easier, and its proliferation will lead to console manufacturers offering increasingly similar portfolios of titles. First-party games will become more crucial than ever.

The conglomeration of third parties, meanwhile, will continue. Minor publishers will be consumed by major publishers, and only the largest independent developers will survive. Cost is key: the videogame industry cannot support the production of major titles at current rates, let alone if the production of the titles

is to increase still further in complexity. It will increase, and so will the conservative nature that a stellar budget makes inherent. Innovation will come from home-coded games, from the Internet and "mod" community.

And this: those who invest in the videogame industry and try to second-guess its future either will end up very rich, or looking very stupid. That's the only thing that's absolutely certain to be as true tomorrow as it is today.

Above left: **PHANTASY STAR ONLINE**
Sega (2001)
Though PC gamers had online titles for an age, *Phantasy Star Online*'s status as the first console RPG was guaranteed to make it some kind of landmark. It turned out to be an exceptionally beautiful one. The four-player experience was simple but frighteningly compelling, and just one more reason to mourn the death of the Dreamcast.

Above middle: **SUPER MARIO SUNSHINE**
Nintendo (2002)
Warranting its place here for not entirely positive reasons, *Super Mario Sunshine* is a very good platform game that falls short of Nintendo's high, self-set standards. Glitchy and often half-hearted, the game reveals a more modern company, pressured by imposing deadlines and competition from Microsoft. The disappointing *Mario Kart: Double Dash* would only confirm those fears.

Above right: **ADVANCE WARS**
Nintendo (2001)
If Sunshine disappointed, *Advance Wars* proved that Nintendo is still more than capable of producing the finest entertainment. A strategy title for the GameBoy Advance based on an old Famicom title, it's digital proof that games don't have to have huge budgets, massive development times, or spectacular visuals to be perfect.

PREPRODUCTION
- Design document drawn up
- Playable proof of concept/ Vertical-slice demo created
- Technology and tools initiated
- Art direction finalized
- Funding and materials (e.g. Dev kits) obtained

PRODUCTION
- Team scaled up to full-size
- Producer oversees scheduling and logistics
- Programmers create tools and finalize technology: Physics, AI, Renderer etc.
- Artists create and animate characters, textures, backgrounds, vehicles etc.
- Level designers create levels and missions
- Sound designers work on background music, audio etc.
- Playable game is tested by testers
- Console approval met

POSTPRODUCTION
- Playable game is localized for foreign territories
- Planning for sequels and expansions
- Game is advertised and distributed

PART 01. A BRIEF
INTRODUCTION TO GAME
DEVELOPMENT

CHAPTER FIVE

HOW MODERN GAMES ARE MADE

THE PROCESS The production model currently employed by the vast majority of the world's videogame developers has evolved out of the trends outlined in the preceding chapters. Specifically, the increasing emphasis on movielike production values has required larger teams and greater specialization of the roles played by team members. Of course there is no single way of making a videogame, and recent years have seen the rise of gaming on cellphones and interactive TV services, and both of these facilitate a return to small-team development (see section 5.02). Equally, the creation of certain genres can force very different demands onto developers, but the majority of videogames share a similarly broad approach to the development cycle.

Perhaps one of the biggest changes wrought by the rising scale of development costs is the increasing importance of the preproduction phase. Since full production in today's development environment requires large teams and a significant financial investment, it is essential for a smaller-scale team to originate and test the initial game design ideas and technology before full production can start. It is also during this phase that independent developers need to seek funding, and publishers' in-house development teams

seek approval. It's a measure of the evolving demands made on videogame developers that there is still some debate about how best to utilize the preproduction stage—and even whether it should be a formalized stage at all.

Whether or not a preproduction phase does take place, when a game goes into full-production mode, the team is scaled up, with additional artists, programmers, and designers coming on board. By now, a clear design should be in place, with an unambiguous direction in mind for visual style and the like. It's at this point that programmers write the code that drives the game. Using special development kits—scaled up versions of the target console that feature increased memory and a hard drive—they write engines and tools; while the game engine generates polygons, shadows, and textures, code is also required to simulate lifelike physics and the AI behavior of characters in the game.

During this process, the programming team works in tandem with artists, sound artists, and level designers, who between them create the visual appearance of the game, and populate it with enemies, objects, and sound effects. Toward the end of production, a quality assurance (QA) department will test playable versions of

Above: **The sequel to Microsoft's groundbreaking first-person shooter, *Halo 2* boasts cinematic sensibilities and extensive online multiplayer modes that had to be thoroughly tested before the game could be released.**

the game to make sure that they function properly, and throughout the process, a writer or writers will create any necessary dialog or important background information.

Finally, the cycle moves into postproduction. Although the game itself is created by this stage, the marketing and distribution efforts nowadays are as important to the commercial success of a videogame as any other part of the development process. So it's essential for a game to be localized effectively to take advantage of the now global market for videogames—text needs to be translated, and tailored to local customs and tastes, and even legal regulations. Indeed the game itself now needs to be submitted to any necessary ratings boards, such as the ESRB, and put through any approval processes required by hardware manufacturers. And finally, the game is publicized via large-scale marketing campaigns across print magazines, Internet sites, and TV advertisements.

THE TEAM As with the overall production cycle, there's more than one way to organize a development team. But there is a widely used division of roles across the industry. Broadly speaking, there are four main types of team member: design, art, programming, and testing. Depending on the size of the team, these are further broken down into even more specialized roles, outlined below.

PRODUCER

The producer is perhaps the most important member and sits at the head of the team. Although principally concerned with the logistics of the process—making sure the game is developed on time and to budget—many producers also provide creative input. In any case, the producer manages the overall process, so needs a broad understanding of the technical skills used by all the other members on the team.

WRITER

Although there's some overlap with the designer, increasingly, professional writers are brought in to work on story, dialog, and scripts for cut-scenes, as well as any incidental text that will be featured in the game, such as tutorials and the like.

DESIGNERS

PROGRAMMERS

LEAD DESIGNER

Although the overall blueprint for the finished game needs to be pinned down reasonably early during the development cycle, the lead designer continues to contribute throughout the process, reacting to any changes and fine-tuning the design. And while theoretically it's possible for anyone to become a designer, good designers need to have a sufficient technical background to know what will be possible for the rest of their development team to implement.

LEVEL DESIGNER/ MISSION DESIGNER

Level, or mission, designers typically create the overall architecture of game missions or levels, and populate them with objects, goals, and enemies. This requires close collaboration with the lead designer, as well as the programmers responsible for AI, and the background artists.

LEAD PROGRAMMER

On balance, the lead programmer is probably the most important team member, apart from the producer, leading the efforts of a team of specialized programmers (most of whom are outlined opposite) who are responsible for implementing the game designer's ideas, creating the tools for art and sound to be implemented, and the development of a game engine that can produce the game's AI, graphics, and sound. The most commonly used programming language for creating all of this is C++, although the best programmers will also have a good knowledge of Assembler.

CHARACTER ARTIST/ANIMATOR

Like programmers, the art team is divided into specialized roles. And while game artists don't need to know how to program, like designers, they do need to have some technical skills in order to understand the capabilities of their target hardware. Character artists create the visual look and animate the characters used in games (or vehicles in a racing game, for example).

TEXTURE ARTIST

Texture artists create textures used by the rest of the art team, either generating them by hand or using digital photography. Some texture artists are also responsible for placing the textures in the game world.

BACKGROUND ARTIST

Background artists create environments. Increasingly these days, the raw layout will be generated by level designers using abstract blocks. These environments are then brought to life with objects, textures, and lighting.

ARTISTS

SOUND DESIGNER

Sound designers are responsible for everything from background music to voice-acting and sound effects that add atmosphere to the game. Consequently they need to be able to create sounds, or use libraries or orchestras to create them.

GAME TESTER

Game testers play through the game repeatedly, recording every glitch, crash, or bug, and compile them into a report that allows the programming team to fix them. They may also assist the design team by providing feedback about difficulty and gameplay issues.

LOCALIZATION MANAGER

Converting games for audiences across the globe is an essential part of most modern game development, and is overseen by a localization manager.

TOOLS PROGRAMMER

The tools programmer creates the tools used to create the game, which can vary from project to project, and encompasses scripting, importing or converting art, and building levels. While some tools are commercially available, building custom tools allows greater flexibility or focus. Increasingly, PC games make their tools available to the public after release to elongate the game's lifespan.

ENGINE PROGRAMMER

The game engine provides the framework within which the rest of the programming team operate to create a believable world. It generates the polygons or patches used to create 3D worlds, provides the means for characters and objects to be animated, generates visual effects, and simulates physics.

AI PROGRAMMER

The AI programmer is responsible for making sure that entities within a game behave and respond to the player's actions in a believable and consistent manner by using pathfinding and logic techniques.

GRAPHICS PROGRAMMER

With advances in hardware requiring increasingly specialized techniques, programmers who focus on developing and modifying complex 3D graphic renderers are assuming an ever greater importance.

PREPRODUCTION

02

02.01

PHASE ONE

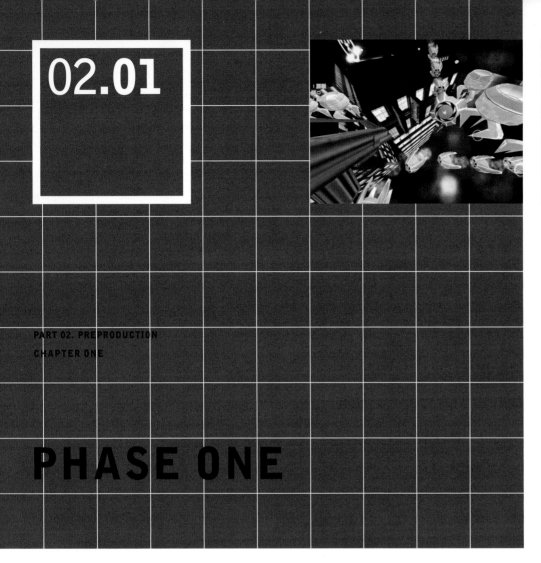

3D GAME STUDIO

There are many tools options available to independent developers that allow prototyping and development for a relatively small cost. For simple prototyping, *3D Game Studio* offers a decent solution—and is so easy to use that it claims that novices can create a simple action game in an afternoon by following a step-by-step tutorial. It combines the C-Script programming language with a high-end 3D engine, a 2D engine, a physics engine, a level, terrain and model editor, and huge libraries of 3D objects, artwork, and pre-made games. It is available in four versions, ranging from $49 to $899, and over 75,000 developers have bought versions, producing a diverse range of titles to date.

Before anything else, there is the idea; that magic spark that has the potential to be coaxed and nurtured into a successful game. The idea can appear at any moment and can range from an overall feel for the design, the setting, the characters, or the story, right down to a simple defining game mechanic. What is important is that the idea can support a fully fledged title—and that's something the preproduction process aims to test.

While games can still be commissioned on the strength of a design and pitch document, this is very much the exception rather than the rule. Opinions differ wildly on the appropriate budget for the preproduction stage. Some, such as Mark Cerny, argue that a million dollars is the ideal figure, venturing that the investment during this crucial stage can be repaid many times over by identifying potential problem areas when the team is relatively small.

To date, no game has had the luxury of a million-dollar budget set aside solely for the preproduction stage. Indeed, a budget of this size would cover the entire development cost of a typical single-format title. Experience and vision in these early stages are as crucial as money, along with the ability to be patient and get things right before embarking on full development.

How quickly a game moves into full production can vary, but the goal is a working prototype, with budgets and milestones set as rigidly as possible. This can take weeks or, in extreme cases, months. Many games fall at this hurdle—which is by no means itself a failure. Provided the team learns from the experience and identifies problems (and their solutions) that can benefit future development, it's money well spent. Far better to waste a relatively small amount of money than invest heavily in full production only to discover the concept will fail, for whatever reason.

Preproduction teams are usually relatively small. Broadly, this stage of development will involve a director, a producer, a designer, a programmer, an artist, and a writer—although the suggested scale and investment of the proposed finished title will sometimes require a larger or smaller initial team.

THE FIVE TYPES OF DESIGN IDEAS

Broadly speaking, games fall into five typical design ideas. The most obvious is an entirely original game concept—the Holy Grail of development design. However, these are risky ventures and rarely meet with commercial success at the beginning of their life cycle—publishers will usually frown upon them, particularly if they are being developed by a new, unknown outfit. Sequels are less creatively rewarding, but more financially viable, and will often stand a better chance of being published. However, sequels are usually the exclusive domain of the original developer—unless, as we've seen in recent years, franchises such as *Tomb Raider* and *Stuntman* are taken from the originator as punishment when expectations are not met.

Character spin-offs—or licensed games—are usually proposed to take advantage of an existing fanbase. They tend to be less commercially risky, although the freedom of working within an existing intellectual property can prove detrimental to innovation. Simulations of other forms of entertainment—such as card or board games—are usually easier to design, though often the temptation can be to over-complicate the original idea. Simulations of real-world events—from historical periods or events (war and sport remain fertile subject matters) to vehicle simulators—can prove popular, and benefit from being easily explained to publisher and, eventually, consumer. Finally, development concepts can come from taking specific advantages of a platform—be that the Internet or a format—or a narrow demographic, such as the younger gamer.

Of course, each can have its creative and commercial merits. However, each must undergo a strict preproduction process to ascertain its viability—both from a technical and a business point of view.

PREPRODUCTION 2 While the game concept, vision, and direction are the responsibility of the director, the producer needs to monitor the business side of things, creating a budget which exactly identifies the finances needed to fund development through to the gold master disc. Producers can be internal or external and their role will change throughout development from one of empowerment to one of restriction as overspending and slippage in one area leads to cuts and compromises in another. For this reason it's a tough job, often resulting in conflict with other areas of the team.

The background information is created and finalized as much as possible during the preproduction phase. The artist will produce a range of illustrations that visualize the game's central characters and models. The writer will develop extensive background notes fleshing out the main characters and motivations, and historical and geographical references, which will be referenced throughout development.

The game's structure should be outlined first, identifying the theme, the narrative setting, the characters, and any other key features. Technology demands should be decided at this stage, so the appropriate tools can be reused, developed, or bought in. It is vital that when developing custom-made tools, they are stable prior to moving into production—and today's middleware solutions are at a stage where they compete reasonably with proprietary technology, offering perhaps the best option.

A roadmap or flowchart of the game is required, listing the main sections that the player will experience, and the possible routes through to completion. Depending on the nature of the title, this can be a straightforward, linear path or it can occupy dozens of sheets of paper taped together where player freedom is offered.

With these factors decided, the game moves to storyboard stage. A game's storyboard is no different to that of a movie or TV show, although the nonlinear nature of the medium can lead to a complicated layout. Any full-motion video sequences are also identified at this point, and sample sequences or placeholders are defined for the sections that will be relevant to the preproduction phase. These can be expensive to render, so they are not always necessary for this stage of development.

In the past, games would go into full production purely on the strength of these documents. But as development costs have increased, so has the need to be commercially sensitive. Publishers and financiers need to see evidence at these early stages that the idea can recoup its development, marketing, and the cost of goods, and turn in a healthy profit. Therefore, the extent to which any subsequent development is classed as preproduction can vary. Each facet of the final game should be up and running in its most basic form—so the number of different sequences that need to be produced at the preproduction stage will depend on the genre and technical aspirations. Put simply, it's until there is sufficient material available to judge the viability of the final game. At the very least, untextured test levels are necessary to illustrate core gameplay components. Some developers opt to produce a trailer, piecing together elements from the final game into a polished, linear movie—although this is an expensive luxury only a few can afford.

The preproduction stage can have a series of false dawns. The prototype will be revised and improved until it's clear whether or not the game should enter full production. A revised design document will be produced for the first milestone, drawing on the experiences learned through the initial stages. When the developer is happy, the title will be judged by those holding the purse strings. And once the game concept, design, budget, and proposed milestones are agreed by the financiers, the game moves into full production. It's then that the really hard work begins.

Left: **TORQUE**

The *Torque Game Engine* from Garage Games currently retails for $100, and is royalty-free under certain conditions. Boasting multi-platform functionality, it started life as the technology behind Dynamix/Sierra/Vivendi´s products *Tribes*, *Starsiege*, and *Tribes 2*, and is an industry-proven engine. It is currently being used by thousands of developers around the world for titles such as *Marble Blast*, *Orbz*, and *Think Tanks*. It also includes excellent online support.

Mark Cerny was a team leader, designer, and graphics programmer for Atari's Marble Madness before the age of 20. His career is littered with blockbusters such as the *Crash Bandicoot* and *Spyro the Dragon* series, and more recently with work on *Ratchet and Clank* and *Jak and Daxter*. As founder of Cerny Games, a game design consultancy, Cerny continues to offer his expertise in the areas of production, design, and technology. His "Cerny Method" is an explorative, risk-taking preproduction period, based on the belief that the best ideas require a period of creative freedom free from rigidly scheduled deadlines. Cerny also asserts that the ultimate success or failure of a game can be determined by its first playable level. His ideas are interesting, yet radical—and few developers are in a position to "invest" a million dollars in preproduction.

Above: **REALITY FACTORY**

Reality Factory is another efficient and effective prototyping solution, offering a complete suite of tools that provide game developers with an extremely customizable game engine for creating commercial or noncommercial games. Complete with editors, actor converters, terrain generators, "gamebuilder" pack tools, and more, *Reality Factory Pro* licenses begin at $149, although support beyond the first year requires an extra subscription.

Left: **VIRTOOLS**

Virtools offers a PC, LINUX, and Xbox engine which, according to Xbox tools manager Drew Angeloff: "enables Xbox game developers to prototype in weeks rather than months, and concentrate on the quality of both graphics and gameplay." It incorporates a high-level graphical user interface and an extensive library of over 450 ready-to-use behaviors, combined with all the low-level access that programmers need to create custom features.

02.02

THE PITCH

Conceptually, it might seem a little odd to consider the pitch—the highly commercial act of securing funding for development—as a full-blown component of the otherwise artistic process of creating a videogame. But the pitch is where art meets commerce. It's an essential—arguably the most essential—stage in the course of game development, because, to put it simply, without a successful pitch, there will be no game development.

Although practice varies widely among titles, the creation of a commercially viable videogame typically costs upward of $3m at the time of going to press. With new consumer hardware on the horizon, such as the PlayStation 3 and Xbox 2, this figure looks set to rise even further; in all likelihood toward the region of $10m to develop a single game—less than a Hollywood blockbuster, but still a lot more than most games companies are used to. To transform a promising first concept into viable playable code, somebody needs to provide the money to pay the salaries of increasingly large teams, as well as the associated office overheads, the costs of any software and hardware used, the marketing and distribution of the finished product, the licensing fees that are charged by console manufacturers for the right to release a game for their system, as well as a plethora of other expenses.

Recouping these costs, however, is increasingly difficult, with industry estimates suggesting that as few as one in ten titles will break even. For this reason, videogame development has historically been funded by publishers who have sufficient scale to offset the commercial failure of one title against the success of another, and who have access to distribution and marketing networks and expertise. Nevertheless, given the escalating costs of this hit-driven industry, it's essential that developers make the best case possible for the development of their game, because publishers, like anyone else, are reluctant to lose money.

A BRIEF HISTORY OF VIDEOGAME PUBLISHING

The publisher-developer relationship that sits at the heart of current videogame development is a bit of a historical accident. Having come about during the early days of bedroom coding, when development costs were low and potential profits relatively high, it has survived into the modern era of escalating costs because there is no more obvious solution to the problem of financing development.

Modeled on the book-publishing system, the way it works is that the publisher pays the developer an advance from the royalties that are expected to be earned by the finished game. Frequently, this money is given to the developer in a series of stages as the developer meets a series of contractually agreed development milestones. In return, the publisher, which is taking on the substantial share of the financial risk, receives a large share of the profit, and frequently also control over the resultant technology and/or intellectual property that is generated by development.

What this means in practice is that the publisher has to feel confident that by financing the development of a game, it will make a greater return on its investment than if the money had simply been left in a bank to accrue interest. Which means that a developer will, at some point, have to convince a publisher that this is the case. This can be a frustrating process, but there are things that every developer can do to minimize the pain and maximize their chances of success.

Getting an appointment to show
your idea to a publisher isn't always
easy, but attending the various trade
shows and industry events that take
place throughout the year can reap
significant dividends. E3, which
takes place in Los Angeles every May
is undoubtedly the most important.
Others include the annual Game
Developers' Conference, the Tokyo
Game Show, and, in Europe, the
European Games Network.

THE PERFECT PITCH Pitches can take place at various points during the development cycle. Sometimes a developer's reputation along with a sketched-out initial concept will be sufficient to persuade a publisher to provide funding for the development of a prototype, with an option to finance full development; at other times, a publisher might require a fully-fledged paper design document, or a playable gameplay demo, or even a finished game before they can be convinced of a game's merit.

A PUBLISHER'S PITCH WISHLIST

Although it was once possible to secure funding for development on the basis of some scribbles on the back of an envelope, it's increasingly rare in the modern era of videogame development. These days, you need to make sure you tailor your pitch to a publisher's submission guidelines. Ideally, a developer pitching an idea should try to prepare most, if not all, of the following materials:

SALES SHEET
This should sum up the game, as succinctly as possible, providing basic information such as genre and target platform, general gameplay details, and any new technology, as well as identifying any key features that will help market the finished title.

DESIGN DOCUMENT
(See 2.04, Game Design) This should be a comprehensive overview of the game, providing greater detail than the sales sheet, and offering a breakdown of characters, setting, levels, etc.

INTERACTIVE DEMO
Ideally this should be more than just a technical demonstration, and should provide an example of how finished gameplay will work, and what the completed game will look like. It's also useful to provide a walkthrough to minimize frustration.

TECHNICAL DESIGN DOCUMENT
This should provide an overview of how the game will be built, detailing things like backup procedures and version control.

RISK ANALYSIS
Developers should be able to show publishers that they have identified things that can go wrong, and convince them that they have plans to cover such contingencies and manage risk.

PROJECT PLAN
This should outline the development schedule (and any software used to manage that), and demonstrate that the developer has a realistic grasp of how long development tasks will take to complete.

COST FORECASTS
Perhaps the most essential part of the pitch. This needs to be drawn up on the basis of the project plan, and needs to be as realistic as possible.

Regardless of the stage at which the game is pitched, the process of greenlighting videogames is fairly consistent across publishers—albeit with enormous variation as to the extent to which it is formalized. Essentially, the idea for the game and any materials produced by the developer will be recirculated within the publishing company, and presented to all of the major departments that will eventually be involved in the release of the game. Every one of these will have a say in the final decision whether to publish the title (or at the very least will need to contribute to the eventual success of a game), so developers need to convince every part of the organization from the outset. Consequently, any pitch materials need to satisfy the sales and marketing team as much as the finance and legal departments.

Part of any successful pitch is indisputably the use of "soft" skills; the ability to network, for example, or an instinct for knowing which member of an organization is most likely to champion your idea, or has most say in the final decision. But there's also a set of hoops that any developer can jump through to maximize their chances without curtailing their creative instincts, because, though a good design is the basis of any successful pitch, persuading a publisher that this is matched by the professionalism to produce a finished game is equally important. While developers need to display some sort of awareness of the commercial realities of the market, for example, this doesn't mean that they need to inhibit their imagination. Contrary to popular belief, most publishers are not looking for a tired remake of an existing successful game; rather they're looking for developers to demonstrate the commercial case for their original ideas. If a developer can sum this up concisely, in a form that can be handed out to members of the publisher's marketing department, then that's one less hurdle to leap.

Similarly, providing documentary evidence that contingencies have been planned for, that schedules are realistic, and that the game will be fun to play, is a fundamental part of any pitch.

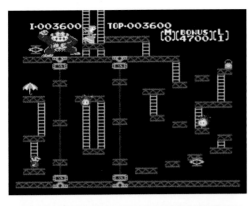

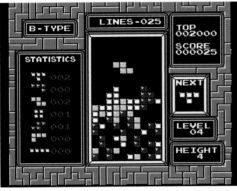

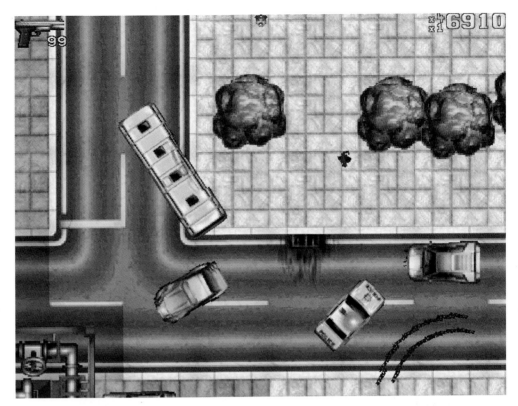

When preparing to pitch your game to the hyper-attenuated attention spans of videogame publishers, one useful exercise is to try to sum up the appeal of the game as concisely as possible. Here's how some classics might have fared....

Above right: *Grand Theft Auto*: Crime and criminals in a big city.

Top: *Donkey Kong*: Plucky hero takes on giant gorilla, saves the day, and wins the girl.

Right: *Tomb Raider*: Indiana Jones meets Bruce Wayne meets Barbie.

Above: *Tetris*: Um...bricks. Lots of falling bricks.

EFFECTIVE NEGOTIATION Of course, any pitch meeting is about more than just one-way negotiation. Although any developer needs to impress potential publishers, they also need to make sure that they're getting a good deal for themselves and aren't edged into making promises that they can't keep. And they also need to make sure that any contractual or legal documents that they sign don't contain clauses that could come back to haunt them later.

Indeed, since one of the first steps of any negotiations will often be the signing of a Non-Disclosure Agreement (NDA), and hopefully one of the final steps will be signing a contract. One of the smartest moves a developer can make is to hire a lawyer at the outset to guide them through the minefield of contractual clauses, intellectual property rights, and so on.

It's also essential to find out as much about prospective publishers as possible. What sort of games do they publish? Have they already signed a similar game to yours? What sort of marketing budget will they provide your game with (and are they willing to guarantee it contractually)? What are they like to work with? This sort of information is pretty easy to find out by attending trade shows, talking to other developers, and monitoring videogame websites, but it will have a dramatic impact on the success of any game.

This ground work might seem mundane, but if nothing else it demonstrates a professional attitude to publishers. And it is essential to ensure that the pitch process establishes a solid working relationship between publisher and developer, because it's a relationship that will have to last for the next year or more.

Above: **Relying on publishers to stump up funds for development isn't the only option available to would-be game creators. It's also possible to finance a title using completion bonds, which can protect against the possibility of the publisher going under, as in the case of** *Juiced*, **which was originally going to be published by the now defunct publisher Acclaim.**

OTHER SOURCES OF FUNDING

Even assuming you've done all your homework, and targeted a publisher with an impeccable set of presentation materials, ultimately, every developer needs to be prepared for rejection. There are, after all, only a finite number of publishers around. In fact, after a deal has been inked there's still scope for a publisher to cancel the project midway through. So it's incumbent upon any developer who wants to continue making games to explore alternative sources of funding.

One option that's open to developers is that of self-publishing, particularly now that the Internet has opened up alternative distribution methods. The most obvious advantage of going down this route is that it provides developers with a greater share of revenue than the conventional publisher-developer model. But the obvious downside is that it carries the additional costs associated with marketing and distribution that would normally be taken on by a publisher. It's an alternative that works well for smaller budget games, which break even on smaller sales, but to recoup the costs of making a typical, high-production videogame, self-publishing is rarely a viable choice.

Nevertheless, there is still the possibility of raising money for game development through the financial markets. The most common sources of funding, outside of individual

Left: Another possibility is to obtain investment from venture capital funds. By adopting this route, UK developers Lionhead Studios and Elixir Studios have been able to protect themselves against the odd cancellation or underperforming title, allowing them to focus on creating highly original titles such as *Evil Genius*, *Fable*, *The Movies*, *Black & White*, and *BC*.

investors, are either appealing to venture capital funds, or recourse to completion bond financing. The latter is a novel financial instrument that sees an insurance company guaranteeing, or "bonding" interim milestone payments, with a publisher stepping in to pay the bond, plus interest and fees, when the development of a game is complete. For the publisher this reduces the risk (but increases the cost), while for a developer it guarantees that their game won't be canceled on a whim.

In the case of both venture capital and completion bonding, developers need to be aware that they'll have to provide a much greater level of disclosure than they would under the conventional publishing model. Due diligence teams from investors will need to see a comprehensive list of materials, including (where applicable) a detailed company organization and history, a list of employees and details of their salary, financial statements (and projections), including details of loans, assets, insurance, tax history, ownership details, and so on and so forth.

And, of course, venture capital still won't provide the manufacturing, marketing and sales, customer and technical support, and QA resources that a good publisher will.

A DEVELOPER'S PITCH TO-DO LIST

HIRE A LAWYER
Unless you have a history of negotiating IP rights, or you understand the implications of obscure points of contract law, it's probably best to get a professional to take care of such things.

FIND OUT ABOUT THE PUBLISHER'S PORTFOLIO
There's no point pitching a kiddie platformer to a publisher that specializes in historically authentic wargames, or to a publisher that already has a surfeit of kiddie platformers scheduled.

FIND OUT WHO YOU'LL BE WORKING WITH AT THE PUBLISHER
Does the publisher have sufficient production resources? Will you be working with a well respected or experienced production team? There's nothing worse than your game getting bogged down by internal company politics.

FIND OUT WHAT SORT OF DEADLINE THE PUBLISHER HAS IN MIND
Does it coincide with your own schedule? There's no point accepting a commission for work that you can't complete on time if it's going to saddle you with a reputation for unprofessional behavior.

ASK FOR MARKETING REASSURANCES
And, if possible, guarantees, to protect your game from falling foul of a publisher's change of heart.

FIND OUT WHAT THE PUBLISHER IS LIKE TO WORK WITH
Talk to other developers to see what their experiences have been. Do your research.

JEREMY CHUBB, BUSINESS DEVELOPMENT MANAGER, EA PARTNERS

Having gained valuable experience of videogame A&R at now defunct publisher Acclaim, Jeremy Chubb went on to join Electronic Arts, in its EA Partners division, a new business unit established in 2003 from which the company's distribution and copublishing deals are now managed. Among the developers it has worked with are, Digital Illusions, C. E., Krome Studios, LEGO Interactive, IO Interactive, Warner Brothers Interactive, Lionhead Studios, and Free Radical Design.

Could you give a brief overview of the pitch process from a publisher's point of view? Who initiates any contact?

Most parties pitching to games publishers are experienced developers and they have games that they wish to make. They get in touch, we see whether what they are offering matches what we are looking for, and will eventually go into partnership to build the thing. We don't look at ideas pitched by the general public.

By "pitch," I guess you mean the process of pitching any of the following: original IP, developer-owned franchise or license, development resource for possible future license-based opportunities, or specific publisher-owned licenses.

First contact depends on who you are and who you're talking to. If you divide developers into three types, you get a clearer picture of how most successful pitches come about. The "Triple-A" Developer is in constant touch with

Below: **TIMESPLITTERS: FUTURE PERFECT**
Published by EA Partners, and created by Free Radical Design, a developer made up of some of the minds behind Rare's earlier hit N64 game, *GoldenEye*.

Right: **FREEDOM FIGHTERS**
Another EA Partners title, *Freedom Fighters* was developed by IO Interactive, the developer behind the popular *Hitman* series.

publishers. We'll track specific teams and try to get something lined up with them long before they finish the games they're working on. The "Upcoming Talent" might be fresh off the back of completion or great publicity for a surprise hit, so these guys might have something awesome to talk about. "Unknown" developers need to make contact and show something dazzling in terms of tech, design, or concept.

What meetings need to take place?

Loads! Developers need to be ready to spend time on this. Pitching for new IP can take anything from three to fifteen months as game designs are refined and deals are negotiated. Smart developers will try to avoid balancing their income statement on the assumption that a couple of months after first showing a game, there will be cash rolling in from a publisher. Developers typically need to satisfy A&R, Production, and Marketing departments that gameplay, technology and process, and concept will combine to make a groundbreaking and commercially viable game, before the project finally goes before a senior executive group.

How widely do acquisition processes vary across publishers? Some publishers seem to have more focused A&R departments than others, for example.

You can meet anybody and everybody at trade shows, visit developers on location, and invite anyone to present, but you'll probably waste a lot of time on projects that just won't happen. We've found only a handful of developers worldwide capable of delivering benchmark quality on multiple platforms and next-gen systems. The result is greater focus on those developers from larger A&R teams comprising production and marketing staff as well as dedicated A&R.

How can a developer increase their chances of conducting a successful pitch?
Think bigger! The current business model (high cost of development into a hit-driven market) takes no prisoners. Developers need to show they can make a great, revolutionary game, as well as a commercial one.

What are the most common mistakes that developers make when pitching to publishers? What sort of things give you second thoughts?
Bad preparation of demonstrable game assets is the most common. PowerPoint presentations that won't run video, bringing the wrong leads or the wrong game builds, forgetting memory cards, using untested code, etc. They're minor inconveniences, but publishers will be unwilling to invest millions of dollars on complex development projects with teams that get this wrong. Developers also frequently fail to bring the right people to a pitch. There's little point CFOs and MDs demonstrating code that they don't know how to use. Bring the designers: they can always be banished to the corridor if the conversation turns uncomfortably toward company finances.

What sort of materials do developers ideally need to produce?
There's no ideal here, and developers can turn up with anything on a sliding scale through: the initial high concept; a production resource schedule; deal terms; some concept art; a movie-based atmosphere piece; a storyboard; game script; a demo covering a few minutes of gameplay; design docs; technical design docs; in-game cut-scenes; prerendered cut-scenes; character and environment work-in-progress models; a gameplay prototype; vertical-slice demo; all the way up to a complete game.

柴田軍　柴田勝家

材木庫の敵部隊を撃破せよ！

115討

上杉軍　突忍

墨俣城を奪還し、正門を守れ！
185討

Above: **SAMURAI WARRIORS**
The EA Partners unit also covers distribution deals, such as the one which saw the company release *Samurai Warriors* in North America, on behalf of the Japanese publisher Koei.

Above: **ODDWORLD STRANGER'S WRATH**
The follow up to the Xbox hit videogame *Munch's Oddysee*, *Oddworld Stranger's Wrath*, is another EA Partners title.

02. preproduction

Q&A JEREMY CHUBB

How important is it for developers to possess "soft" skills—such as identifying and negotiating the political hierarchies at a target publisher, for example?

It shouldn't be, but I'm sure there are plenty of cases where it's not what you know but who you know. If you realize that the European division of a big Japanese or American publishing group is just a satellite operation, you're clearly better off going directly to the source.

Publishers are constantly being accused of risk aversion; how far do you think these accusations hold water? Or do you think that it's a misleading impression that encourages developers to pitch conservative ideas?

The videogame industry has an unfortunate heritage. Publishers operate in a market largely defined by hobbyist consumers, creators, and opinion formers. It's tough to do anything radically different and still satisfy this hardcore. Graphics have a benchmark, control systems have a default, and $40 price tags should equal voluminous content.

Set this against a backdrop of rapidly and relentlessly advancing hardware tech, the inherent production risks of development, and spiraling art overheads and you can see the difficulty for publishers and developers. The issue is that developers very often think this means pitching derivative, low-risk designs. Many developers rein in their ambition to ensure that what they have is achievable. The reality is that within obvious commercial parameters, publishers like EA need to justify big budgets with ambitious, break-out designs.

Developers need to think more comprehensively about their consumer. Many strong developers have traditionally made games defined by a combination of new technology and their own passion for a particular game type. To meet the demands of the current market and establish enduring franchises, we all need to consider concept and consumer first and technology second.

How important is the pitch? Do you think the majority of developers ascribe enough importance to it?

The pitch? The single meeting, where the game is presented? Less important than the concept, the talent, or an understanding of the audience.

How important is it for developers to investigate alternative sources of funding, outside the traditional publisher advance? How easy are these to come by?

Increasingly, convincing a publisher to part with $10m for an Xbox 2/PS3 project isn't like snagging a SNES development deal. Developers that can find ways to invest more in the game, before approaching publishers will be able to better illustrate what they're trying to create, and address some of the early risk through preproduction. The development cost is a small component part of the cost of bringing a game to market.

Do you have any memorable experience of pitches— good or bad?

There's one memorable experience that still haunts me to this day, in which an entire room of senior execs for a major publisher began to assemble in an LA hotel boardroom, and the developer said "Well, I sure hope this disk works. We didn't have time to check before we got on the plane." Obviously, it didn't.

How does the approval process compare between internally developed and externally developed products?

It's mixed. On one hand, EA's internal teams are probably judged more harshly, because they're burning company money and resources to create their pitches. On the other, they have the luxury of greater resources to devote to pitches than most independent developers budget for.

THE TYPICAL PREPRODUCTION PROCESS

The current norm is for developers to use a small-scale team during the preproduction phase; to originate the design of the game, and to take the key decisions about its ultimate vision and direction. By the end of the process, this vision will be embodied within a variety of materials, such as design documents and technical demos, which will help the developer pitch the idea to publishers, and help keep the direction consistent even after the development team has geared up to go into full-scale production. By using a small team, costs are reduced, and projects can be started concurrently with other projects that may be drawing to a close.

During this formal preproduction process, the team will draw up a fully featured design document. The advantage of producing a written document that embodies all the features of a game's design is that the underlying game mechanics and principles will be apparent to every member of the team for the duration of the development process. Indeed although a playable demo is typically produced, its function is usually to demonstrate a rough impression of the finished visual style of the game and the key technical features of the engine.

PART 02. PREPRODUCTION

CHAPTER THREE

APPROACHES TO PREPRODUCTION

While there is a considerable degree of consensus over the importance and purpose of preproduction, there is less certainty about how exactly it should be managed and structured—or even whether it merits being formally distinguished from the rest of the videogame production process. Every developer knows what they need to have achieved by the end of preproduction: they need to have made key decisions about a game's technology, design, art direction, and audio. But there's less certainty about the way these conclusions are reached, or by what point in the process they need to be pinned down.

Historically, the preproduction process has been a fluid and organic part of a relatively unstructured development practice. While this worked well back in the days when development teams were small and the resources required to create a videogame were low, it is more tricky to get this to work in the current era of higher production values and rapidly-escalating budgets. Indeed the rising cost of producing videogames has increased the significance of the preproduction phase to the extent that it's assuming ever greater importance, and consequently developers are increasingly formalizing the process.

So by the end of the process, the majority of tools will be in place and middleware will be bought in if required (see section 2.05), or alternatively, an internally developed game engine will be largely complete. A combination of written documentation and a technical demo will be enough to convey the essence of the title to the rest of the development team as well as potential publishers.

The advantages of such a system are that there's a pretty clear guideline in place, which is flexible enough to add new features or rework the design in the coming months, and the whole thing is a relatively low-cost process. But the disadvantages are that a game may go into full development before the core gameplay concepts have been tested sufficiently, and with technology that's not prepared for the tasks that will be assigned to it during the subsequent refinement of the game's mechanics.

Even a cursory glance at these screenshots of classic videogames and their modern updates demonstrates the enormous progress that has been made since the early days of videogame development—particularly with regard to the increase in production values. Consequently, it's simply not possible to adopt the same chaotic "bedroom-coding" practices of yesteryear when it comes to preproduction.
Top: *Castlevania* by Konami
Bottom: *Ninja Gaiden* by Tecmo

THE ORGANIC PROCESS Perhaps because of these disadvantages, some developers eschew this formal process, and continue to evolve the design of a game over the course of the entire development process, taking technical decisions along the way. Nintendo's celebrated design guru, Shigeru Miyamoto (the brains behind *Donkey Kong* and *Mario*) famously develops a game up to a playable point before throwing everything out and starting afresh, retaining and reusing only the best elements of the assets that are thrown away.

Metal Gear Solid creator, Hideo Kojima famously uses Lego bricks to conceptualize playing areas. Both he and Shigeru Miyamoto are examples of a more elastic, less structured approach to preproduction.

They're not the only developers who don't formally distinguish a preproduction phase, choosing to employ a more organic approach instead. Zoonami's Martin Hollis recently gave a talk at the European Developers' Forum in 2004 about the gestation of the seminal N64 title, *GoldenEye*, which he created while at UK developer Rare. The initial design that he drew up for the game, which went on to sell more than 8 million copies, was only nine pages long. What's more, at this stage, there was still some vagueness about the design concept itself. "The first sentence of that design was: 'The game will be similar to *Virtua Cop* in terms of gameplay.' For those not familiar with *Virtua Cop* it is an old classic—an on-rails shooter, made by Sega, and released first in the arcades. So for the first months, *GoldenEye* was partly envisioned as a simple on-rails shooter only with no lightgun. But I also wanted it to be a FPS. At this point the team was happy to contemplate making two modes for the game, an on-rails mode and a FPS mode. Yes, there was some vagueness here. You have to understand, we didn't know what the controller of the N64 would be like, so it made designing the control system difficult at such an early stage."

Indeed one of the advantages of adopting a more organic philosophy toward preproduction is the flexibility that it affords developers—which can evidently be particularly useful when contemplating the switch to a new hardware platform. Hollis and his team spent much of the initial development period simply creating the game engine and tools and art assets, only moving to fleshing out the mission design and refining the AI at a later stage. This somewhat chaotic process therefore moved into full production without the need to formalize it, providing the opportunity for an extended preproduction phase that ultimately proved to be creatively fruitful.

Other developers to employ the organic approach include Intrepid Games, the developer of Xbox title *BC*, which is on record as describing its way of working as an iterative process with no formal distinction between pre- and full production. Thus, gameplay concepts are conceived of throughout the development process, and tested using placeholder technology. Nevertheless, there are disadvantages to the organic process: particularly the fact that in the hands of an undisciplined developer it creates the potential for delays as unforeseen problems arise, and the desire to create new content and features overtakes the need to finish development on time.

Variations of the organic approach to preproduction have been employed since the earliest days of the videogame industry, typified by *GoldenEye* (top and above right), conceived by its creator, Martin Hollis, as a cross between *Doom* and *Virtua Cop*. Although it's a method that continues to be followed by developers, it'll be more difficult to justify in the future due to the demands of new hardware and larger team sizes. Thus, Shigeru Miyamoto's well documented use of post-it notes and the trash can may have reached their apogee in *The Legend of Zelda: The Ocarina of Time* (right) and *Super Mario 64* (above), while Hideo Kojima may even begin to find that Lego bricks might have found their limit in *Metal Gear Solid 2: Sons of Liberty* (left).

THE MOVE TO THE VERTICAL SLICE
Since developers not finishing development on time is just about the biggest headache a publisher can have, many are increasingly favoring developers who adopt yet another approach to preproduction; the production of a fully featured demo. This is known as a "vertical slice" because it is designed to offer a cross-section view of all the gameplay elements that will be present in the finished game.

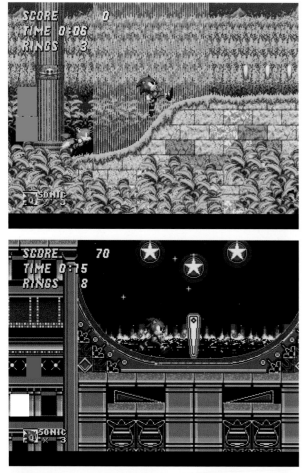

Consequently, a growing number of developers are eschewing the laborious process of creating written documentation and technical demos, choosing instead to pursue the more streamlined approach of the vertical-slice demo. Instead of creating a written design, which may become superfluous, the focus is on creating a working demo that encapsulates all the features of the finished game, and which will be used as a consistent reference point throughout production.

Although the vertical slice model "front loads" a lot of the development effort, requiring considerable effort to be expended during preproduction, it can pay off in a number of ways. Chief among these is that the most important technical systems are up and playable by the end of preproduction, allowing developers to devote their resources to the arguably more important task of honing gameplay elements during the production phase. Another is that by pinning down features early, and getting them working, there is little scope for the sort of feature creep that can stall or derail the production process.

Finally, one other advantage to publishers is that the vertical-slice model makes it easy for an initiation team to handle the game conception and technology creation before handing the project over to an execution team who will transform the demo into a finished game. Although the creative merits of such practice may be open to question, the financial benefits of this "factory" approach are convincing more and more publishers to seriously consider adopting it.

THE CERNY METHOD
Speaking at GDC Europe in 2002, industry veteran Mark Cerny outlined one final alternative approach to preproduction. Based on his extensive experience with the likes of Sega and Atari (where he created the seminal coin-op, *Marble Madness*), the "Cerny Method" is almost an attempt

Mark Cerny's extensive experience in the industry encompasses such games as *Marble Madness* (left), *Sonic the Hedgehog 2* (above), *Ratchet & Clank*, and *Jak and Daxter* (both opposite), and inspired his "Cerny Method" approach to preproduction.

to distill the creative chaos of the organic approach, while pinning it down into the more organized framework provided by the vertical-slice model. As with the latter, it increases the up-front costs of development, by increasing the duration and intensity of the preproduction phase, and by encouraging experimentation and risk-taking within it. But by adopting a more ruthless approach with concepts that aren't working, and canceling titles during preproduction if necessary, the Cerny Method aims to save money in the long term.

If proof is needed of the efficacy of this approach, one only need look as far as *Jak and Daxter* and *Ratchet & Clank*, both critically acclaimed and commercially successful platform titles on the PlayStation 2.

And while the Cerny Method is certainly not the only possible approach, its formulation is a measure of the importance that escalating development budgets and a more ruthless marketing environment have thrust upon the preproduction process.

THE KEY PRINCIPLES BEHIND THE METHOD ARE AS FOLLOWS:

1. Preproduction is chaotic; at least $1 million needs to be set aside to create iterative prototypes during preproduction
2. Preproduction requires throwing away a lot of work; Cerny estimates that in order to create 20 usable levels, 80 need to be thrown away
3. Use prototype technology; gameplay concepts can be tested without finished technology, so there's no need to create cutting-edge tech unless absolutely necessary
4. No milestones should be imposed during preproduction
5. A first playable demo is required before alpha stage; essentially a vertical-slice demo. This needs to consist of one or two levels that contain all of the game's global features
6. Cancellation saves time and money
7. No lengthy design document is required at this stage; it just creates unnecessary labor
8. Listen to your consumer; focus test core game mechanics and level design extensively

02.04

GAME DESIGN

One of the industry's most sought-after positions, the role of Game Designer may soon earn "classic crushed childhood dream" status, alongside Racing Driver, Astronaut, and International Playboy Quarterback. Superficially at least it seems like an enviable position: the designer comes up with an idea for a videogame, then puts his or her feet up and lets the production team do the work. As ever, though, the superficial view misses out on the less than glamorous majority of the job description.

Game designers conceptualize videogames, it's true. But the days of a single sentence sufficing as a commercial game design are as dead as those of the bedroom coder. Designers, who generally work as part of a design team, produce large design documents to specify absolutely everything that will be produced over the course of the game's development. This includes almost absurdly specific details of the gameplay, which defines the experience, but also detailed consideration of elements the casual designer might consider part of someone else's remit: the menu design, the plot, the aesthetic, the animation style, and so on. The document will prove a crucial part of the pitch to publishers, as will the design team who created it, so good presentation skills are crucial.

Game designers are also responsible for keeping that document current as the design evolves throughout the game's production, an essential task that ensures all of the design team are working to the same goal. Also to that end, game designers must maintain a constant dialog with other sections of the development team, not simply to create a coherent, one-world vision, but also developing a two-way feedback system that allows, say, the lead artist to offer their expertise to the document. A good designer has a broad understanding of all of the disciplines that are involved in creating a game.

Finally—if there can be a finally in such a flexible role—the game designer must work closely with the producer to establish realistic milestones, and to make sure the team manages to hit them. This can involve brutal cuts to the feature set. It's part of the designer's responsibility to work out which parts of their team's grand plan can be most efficiently sacrificed with the least damage to the overall design, and then explain those changes, and the motivations behind them, to their team. Game design is as much about communicating original ideas as it is about coming up with them.

Though there's no clearly defined career path to becoming a game designer, it's not an entry-level position, and those chasing that childhood dream can expect to spend some time working their way up the game-development food chain, perhaps beginning as a tester. Though it may not be the most financially rewarding career path the games industry has to offer, edification comes in different ways. It's certainly one of the most creative, and fame and fortune await those who design multimillion dollar successes for their publishers. The best designers' reputations precede them like those of movie directors, and some—Sid Meier, for example, or Hideo Kojima—carry enough weight to warrant putting their names on the front of game boxes.

FIRSTPERSON SHOOTER

Some will say id software's *Doom* kick-started the FPS genre; others will go back still further and say *Wolfenstein 3D*, or maybe even *3D Monster Maze*. Whatever, the principle is simple and constant. The player sees the action through the eyes of their avatar, and fires the hero's arsenal of weaponry at just about anything that moves.

Key titles: *Halo*, Microsoft, 2002 (Far left)
Half-Life, Vivendi, 1998 (Left)

REALTIME STRATEGY

Evolving from the God-game trend of the mid-eighties, the RTS places the player in a strategic military conflict, and challenges them to defeat their opponent. Balancing defense and attack is usually the key, and good realtime strategy games offer the player more than just one way of approaching each battle. Arcade skills are only sparsely required. This game's about thinking.

Key titles: *Command & Conquer*, EA, 1996
Rome: Total War, Activision, 2004 (Below left)

SPORTS GAME

Games have emulated sports for decades—the earliest consoles contained variants of *Pong* labeled "football," "squash," and so on, depending on the number of bats on screen. As gaming's technical capacity increases, so the sports game's limited ambition means they approach real life faster than most genres. The genre is less limited by technology than it is by traditional computer input systems.

Key titles: *Winning Eleven 8*, Konami, 2004
Rocky Legends, Ubisoft, 2004 (Above)

PUZZLE

Though the genre seems to be considered a kiss of death by many publishers these days, an excellent puzzle game can be produced on a shoestring budget and has the potential to reach many more people than, say, an excellent firstperson shooter. There are very few people who don't know what *Tetris* is. The key, of course, is finding a balance of reaction and intellect just as sublime.
Key titles: *Tetris*, Nintendo, 1989
Puzzle Bobble, Taito, 1994 (right)

ROLE-PLAYING GAME

All videogame RPGs owe their existence to the pen-and-paper version of *Dungeons & Dragons*, and much of that heritage is still visible today. Players take the role of an adventurer and embark on a series of quests that ultimately lead to the narrative's resolution. Combat in an RPG can be based on arcade-style reactions, but more often than not it's a mathematician's delight, the computer rolling a hundred dice to decide who wins.
Key titles: *Baldur's Gate*, Interplay, 1998
Knights of the Old Republic, Activision, 2003 (below)

THIRDPERSON ADVENTURE

A very flexible genre, TPAs usually show their protagonist from a perspective fixed just behind them. The most famous example is *Tomb Raider*, which neatly illustrates how the genre has evolved from humble roots in early eighties platform games. TPAs range from beautiful, benign, child-friendly fare (*Super Mario 64*, say) to much darker places (*Manhunt*).
Key titles: *Tomb Raider*, Eidos, 1996
Grand Theft Auto 3: Vice City, Rockstar, 2003 (right)

RHYTHM ACTION

The newest of the genres listed here, rhythm action games require the player to accompany an in-game tune using their pad or some kind of musical peripheral. The popularity of games like *Dance Dance Revolution* in noncore demographics has seen publishers flock to the genre over the last two years, although the market for the titles in Japan, the genre's home, seems to be flagging.
Key titles: *Dancing Stage Euromix*, Konami, 2000
Samba de Amigo, Sega, 2000 (opposite, top left)

DRIVING GAME

The driving genre encompasses a range of subtypes, from the verging-on-simulation stylings of *Gran Turismo*, to the unreal excitement of *F-Zero GX*. All have the same thing in common, though: go faster than your opponents and you win. Driving games have been part of videogaming's hardcore for as long as arcades have existed, and they show no sign of decreasing in popularity.

Key titles: *Super Mario Kart*, Nintendo, 1992
Gran Turismo, SCEI, 1998 (below right)

MANAGEMENT / SIMULATION

The most sedate of genres, the management game gives gamers a chance to play God, or at least the head of a medium-to-large organization. Good management games manage to involve the player in what could, superficially, seem like the gaming equivalent of spreadsheet software. In other words, play down the bureaucracy and play up the humanity, hide the math and give the player plenty of feedback.

Key titles: *The Sims*, EA, 1999 (bottom right)
Championship Manager, Eidos, 1992

MASSIVELY MULTIPLAYER

Massively multiplayer games require a decent Internet connection and a desire to play games with strangers, two things that automatically exclude a good percentage of gamers. Those that remain participate in one of gaming's newest forms, and one whose experience is almost entirely dictated by the players themselves. Many new challenges await those who would design a massively multiplayer experience.

Key titles: *Everquest*, Ubisoft, 1999 (bottom left)
Phantasy Star Online, Sega, 2001

DESIGN DOCUMENTATION If the designer's job is to communicate a vision to a team, then the design document lies at the core of that. It is central to everything, biblically revered, updated throughout the project, and provides a comprehensive guide to every detail of every aspect of the game. If a team member has a question, he or she refers to it first. They should not have to refer to anything (or anyone) else. The design document is a concrete guide to what happens where. A kind of navigational chart, without which the design team are lost at sea.

As with all maps, the first thing to get right is clarity. Design documents must be expressed coherently, in concise, well-written English, clearly set out and, ideally, properly bound. The idea is to convey that this is a document people must respect. It's difficult to take instructions from an easily-lost pile of crumpled paper. Just as important is preserving the document's accuracy. All evolutionary changes must be recorded, new copies of the document produced, and old ones destroyed. Everyone must be working from the same set of pages.

The design document must be absolutely exhaustive. A short, simple, attention-grabbing summary at the start of the document may help with pitching to publishers, but if a developer can't show afterward that it's considered every aspect of every part of the game, and provided a written answer to any and every situation that a gamer might face, then the design will appear incomplete. Picture the document as a textual representation of the collective imaginations of the design team; the less imagination of their own the reader has to use, the less chance they have of introducing foreign, unconsidered ideas into the plan, and the more effective the design document is. If the reader's brain never has to fill in any gaps at all, never fails to find an answer to the question, "But what if...?" then the document is complete.

But the design document must also be flexible, and the writer(s) must be able to accept suggestions from other members of the team. To that end, some game designers mark sections in the document with codes ranking their importance. This helps direct external queries and suggestions to those

Game design

The game-design document is an essential part of every game, and should be tied down as soon as possible in the project's life cycle. Although a design document should be flexible, this is not an invitation for feature creep— the addition of new features throughout production—and any new suggestions should be justified thoroughly before they are added to the document.

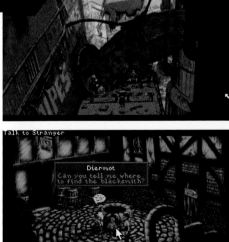

Revolution Software's games are renowned for their in-depth design documents. Titles such as *Broken Sword: The Sleeping Dragon* (above), *Beneath a Steel Sky* (left), and *Lure of the Temptress* (bottom left) have all benefited from a tightly-defined game concept and design at an early stage.

parts of the document that need it most, while elsewhere in the document, a full list of previously rejected ideas, recorded alongside the reasons why, prevents the same suggestions from appearing time and time again.

Crucially, the final point made here is also the most difficult to pin down. The perfect design document fulfills all the above criteria, but also possesses something else: passion. A lifeless document will never inspire, and even if it (miraculously) finds itself in production, the chance of it motivating a team enough to produce something more than functional is minimal. The design document isn't just a team's map, it's a statement of intent, a vibrant, rousing description of something wonderful. In other words, it should aspire to the same high level of entertainment as the media it hopes to create.

chapter 04. game design

DEBATES IN MODERN GAME DESIGN

Left above: **Dogma 2001: Ernest Adams' list of rules are a simple, but controversial, framework...**
Left: **...while the 400 Project attempts to be comprehensive.**

Right above: **When *The Getaway* fell short of its realism target, players were distracted by the unnatural...**
Right below: **...but there's nothing natural about Sega's beautiful *Jet Set Radio Future*.**

PLAYING BY THE RULES

In February 2001, Ernest Adams introduced the idea of "Dogma 2001," a set of ten rules inspired by Lars von Trier's "Dogme" film manifesto. Rules like, "There shall be no knights, elves, dwarves, or dragons," and "There may be victory and defeat, and my side and their side, but there may not be Good and Evil." The rules were intended to steer videogame design in a different direction, away from the standard (predominantly fantasy-based) thinking that had governed it since its inception, and toward a wider audience.

While Adams' rules seem driven more by polemic than theory, "The 400 Project" is a community project devoted to coming up with 400 hierarchical rules to help make better games. It's an admirable aim, and one that's sure to produce some good ideas. But can game design really be reduced to decisions on a flowchart, or should the rules exist only to be broken?

NARRATIVE VS. PLAY

Should videogames try and tell stories, or leave that to media more suited to linearity? Games like Konami's *Metal Gear Solid 2* blur the line between cinema and videogaming, but not necessarily in a positive fashion: some players were bored by the seemingly interminable cut-scenes that advanced the story. THQ's *Broken Sword 3* also takes the narrative route, offering the player a prescribed beginning, middle, and end, but always entertains. Games like *Tetris*, *Everquest*, and *The Sims* sit on the other side of the border, either entirely abstract, or allowing players the freedom to write their own stories.

The conclusion is, sensibly, that gaming is broad enough to encompass both of these ideals, but if you want to tell a story you need to make sure it's either compulsive enough to keep the player involved from beginning to end (as seen in the best adventures), or that it has enough freedom to allow players to go off and do their own thing (offered by the best RPGs). Games will always have plots, but they should never interfere with the entertainment, only enhance it.

THE PROMOTION OF EMERGENT GAME DESIGN

Strict game design gives players a series of problems, and one or two prescribed solutions. Emergent game design provides the same problems, but offers a toy box rather than a set of solutions. Players experiment inside the box, combining objects and methods to find their own answers. The most famous recent example is *Grand Theft Auto III*, a toy set so complete that it's as enjoyable to set your own goals as it is to follow those set by the designers.

But emergent gameplay also works on the side of the developer. *Halo's* simple firstperson shooter outlook was made exponentially better by the neat enemy AI and weapon design. Levels were simple, but their contents combined to throw up a near-infinite range of situations players could find themselves in. Since tackling each one was different, combatants had to think on their feet, and "learned" routes through the game were useless. Nor is the usefulness of emergence limited by setting or genre: Eidos' narrative-heavy *Deus Ex* used emergent gameplay to enhance a narrative-driven adventure.

ABSTRACTION VS. REALISM

Gaming hardware gets ever closer to providing gamers with a facsimile of reality, but is that really the way the industry should be moving? Videogames are capable of so much, visually, yet their creators rarely stray from playing their appearance completely straight. When the industry reaches a graphical plateau, a day that's fast approaching, everything will look the same. Will it be style, rather than technical merit, that consumers buy into?

Perhaps, and not just for superficial reasons. While polygon models of humans look far better today than they did ten years ago, there's a long way to go before they look convincingly real enough to fool the human eye. The flaws in faux-real representations of human life in EA's *Medal of Honor* Series are more jarring than the human caricatures in Eidos' *TimeSplitters 2*. It's the game designer's job to draw players into their world, and a consistent, abstracted world can do that better than a realistic one with obvious visual flaws.

Top: *Metal Gear Solid 2*, by Konami, has been accused of wanting to be a film...
Above: ...but Namco's *Katamari Damacy* could only ever work as a videogame.

Left: *Halo* is a perfect example of emergent combat in game design...
Far left: ...the opposite of EA's *Medal of Honor*, which takes a stricter approach to combat.

BEN COUSINS, LONDON STUDIO, SCEE

Ben Cousins is a senior designer in the online team at the London studio of Sony Computer Entertainment Europe. He previously worked for three years as a lead designer at Lionhead Studios, on the prehistoric management game *BC*. He began his career as a tester at Acclaim's London studio in 1999.

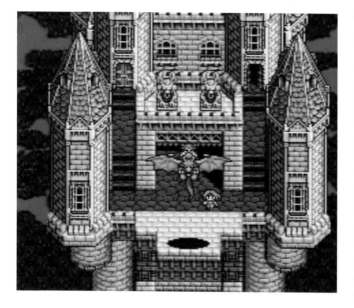

How would you describe the role of the game designer in modern game design?

The modern designer's responsibilities are twofold—the first is a duty to the customer, making sure that the experience of playing the software is as enjoyable as possible. The second is to the product, to make sure that it sells as many copies as possible.

How has that changed while you've been in the industry?

In the past, video and computer games were a hobbyist pursuit. Customers were more likely to invest time in discovering products and also in discovering the fun in a game. Nowadays we are operating in a much more crowded marketplace, with an audience which has less time to invest. This means that our products have to be designed in a way that is immediately compelling and different from the (vast) competition, as well as meaning that our games have to be more forgiving in terms of difficulty, be fun from the very outset, and set in a world that is easier to understand.

What qualifications does a good game designer need—not necessarily academic, but in terms of skills and experience?

You need to be able to put yourself in the mind-set of a consumer, to be able to forget your experiences as a hardcore gamer and developer and learn to look at your game and the competition's products in the same way as a customer. You then need to be able to add features to the game in as disciplined a manner as possible. Everything you add to the game needs to be carefully considered so that it is technically possible, can be implemented to a strict schedule and budget, and work within the context of the genre and the IP (intellectual property). You need to be a good communicator, have strong writing skills, and have a logical mind with a passion for understanding and analyzing complex systems. If you are involved in any aspect of IP development you need to have an understanding of marketing and of the market you are developing for.

How important is the design document to the design process?

High quality documentation is vital. Your documentation may not be under very much scrutiny from the team (because they are more likely to favor face-to-face communication), but people outside, such as managers, directors, and publishers, need to see that the design team have a well thought-out, considered vision for the high-level and low-level details of the game. They also need to see that the people responsible are able to communicate this vision effectively.

Right: **AMPLITUDE**
Developer: Harmonix
Platform: PlayStation 2
Designing a music game requires not just a good sense of rhythm, but also an idea of how to visually represent that rhythm and allow the player to interact with it.

Left: **FINAL FANTASY 5**
Developer: Square
Platform: Super Nintendo
The RPG might be a well-established genre, but a good designer will know how to innovate within its boundaries. Change is good...

Right: **TOMB RAIDER: THE ANGEL OF DARKNESS**
Developer: Core Design
Platform: PlayStation 2
...but too many changes can hurt. Lara's reinvention for the PlayStation 2 alienated the character's fanbase, and failed to attract new players.

What's the most important thing a game designer has to get right from the start?

It depends on the extent of the designer's responsibility. If they have overall responsibility for the game (IP, character, or setting development) they need to start with a concept that will sell. Too many games are dead from the outset because they simply do not choose a setting or character which is appealing to the market.

If the game designer is only responsible for gameplay, they need to concentrate on making the lower-level interaction as fun, polished, and robust as possible. Examples of lower-level interactions would be character control, car handling, weapon feedback design, interface, etc.

Do genres kill good game design, or help to define it?

Limitations are always a gift to a disciplined creative person. Having clear limits and focus to a project can only help the team keep a consistent end vision for the game. It is also possible to merge existing genres in a creative way, but that discipline and clear end vision has to be retained.

Has big-budget gaming killed design freedom? Do big teams make it harder for individual expression?

I think it's true that an individual in a general team role on a big team has less room for expression than on a smaller team. However many people feel comfortable in that kind of role, being able to concentrate on making the work they are responsible for as good as possible without worrying about the direction of the project as a whole. For people higher up the hierarchy in a team, bigger teams make it easier to express things creatively, because you have more resources available to help prototype, take chances, and solve problems.

What are the benefits of emergent game design, and what are the benefits of systemic? Which do you favor?

Depends on which definition of emergent you use. A truly emergent game (of which there are only very few) gives the player a sense of greater control and freedom within the game world. As games are about control at heart, having a greater breadth of possible objects and systems to control can make the game more enjoyable. It is however also possible to make a smaller, tighter set of features equally enjoyable, by making each individual interaction as strong as possible.

There are two main benefits of systemic approaches. Firstly, it is more efficient from a developmental point of view, because you are able to reuse assets and technology in different instances. The fewer special cases you have in a game, the less developmental time you need to implement things. The second benefit of systemic approaches is that the player experiences a greater consistency in the world. This consistency helps them construct strategies and make assumptions in a way that makes them feel more powerful.

Are there fixed rules for game design, and, if so, can they be broken? Do you have any rules for yourself?

I want the player to avoid failing as much as possible, while always being aware of the threat of failure.

I try to make low-level gameplay elements as enjoyable and polished as possible.

I try to keep a strong disciplined image of the end product in my mind all the time.

I try to work upward in a hierarchy in the course of the project. For instance, working on low-level elements (e.g. control) and trying to lock them down, then moving to mid-level elements (e.g. combat) and trying to lock them down, finally moving to work on higher level elements (e.g. missions) and trying to lock them down. You should try not to move to another level in the hierarchy until you are absolutely satisfied you have solved all of the problems in the previous level.

What are the biggest battles a game designer has to face, from the initial concept through to the last stages of production? Do they have to be won, or do great game designers know when and where to compromise?

Designers have to get used to the experience of being under close scrutiny. This is the price you pay for being in a very powerful position. This means you (rightly) will have to justify many of the decisions you make to people on the team, and people outside of it. This is a battle that involves being confident in your ideas, having the communication skills to transmit those ideas to others, and also being acutely aware of what everyone else individually wants from the project.

Another battle a designer has to get used to is being flexible within the development process. Often you are asked to refactor things, move schedules around, and possibly re-design elements of the game or IP. This battle is about making sure your game is carefully designed so that if the unexpected occurs, you are able to react to it in a way that does as little damage as possible. If you expect change, you will be better prepared for it when it comes along.

What advice would you give to someone looking for a career in game design?

This has changed since I started in the industry as a tester a few years ago. Nowadays I would say that aspiring designers need to do four things.

Firstly, they need to play vast amounts of games in all genres and across all platforms, they need to be skilled in the analysis of those games and they also need to understand the market conditions that the games were created in.

Secondly, designers need to have some technical skill. More and more companies expect some coding or scripting skills from designers—I think the days of "ideas men" with little technical experience (like me) getting hired into jobs as first-timers are over.

Thirdly, designers need to become knowledgeable in the language and academia of games. This would include reading magazines like *Game Developer*, *Develop*, or *Gamasutra*, attending conferences like GDC, and keeping up to date with the various blogs that developers keep on the net.

The final thing I would expect a designer to have is some good personal projects under their belt that they have done in their spare time. This could be for instance a mod or a small self-coded game. This kind of experience tells employers you are self-motivated, but it also teaches the creator important skills about the process of development that a book cannot teach.

Opposite: Approaches to game design will differ according to the intellectual demands they place on the player.

Top left: Capcom's *Devil May Cry* series requires a design that promotes free-flowing, instinctive combat over careful planning...

Top middle: ...while the design in Bungie's *Halo* encourages the player to think, then shoot.

Top right: In Ion Storm's *Deus Ex* franchise, thinking first is absolutely imperative to progress.

Below right: Lionhead's *BC*; cutting-edge game design in a prehistoric world.

02. preproduction

TOOLS AND MIDDLEWARE

WHAT ARE TOOLS?

One of the key tasks that need to be undertaken during preproduction is the creation of technology that will be used to construct and power the finished game. When Robbie Bach unveiled Microsoft's XNA suite of tools at the Game Developers' Conference in 2004 (*see page* 68), he estimated that game developers spend 80% of their time creating technology and assembling the game, and only 20% implementing and refining game features and artwork. So it's clear that choosing or creating the right tools, and making sure that they are stable and efficient, is of the utmost importance to the quality of the finished game. Making the wrong decisions during preproduction can produce far-reaching complications that disrupt the entire development cycle.

Creating a game requires the use of a wide-ranging variety of tools across the entire team. As the name suggests, they're essentially applications that are used to help each team member to do their job, allowing artists to integrate art content into a game, or testers to communicate bugs and glitches to the programming team, for example, and a typical production process might require as many as fifty different instances of such software. Each tool that's used allows an aspect of development to proceed more smoothly and quickly than it otherwise would, which, over the course of creating a game, can save considerable time and effort, allowing it to be used more profitably on improving the game itself.

Although it's possible for a specialist programmer or team of programmers to create every necessary tool from scratch, many developers choose to utilize at least some development software that has been created by an external software development house, which is known as "middleware." There are currently middleware solutions for almost every development need, ranging from process management and scheduling all the way to fully featured game-engines. Nevertheless, even if this route is the one that's chosen, specialist programmers will still be required to customize, and to get the most out of, any technology or software that is brought in.

WHAT TOOLS ARE NEEDED?

The tools used by a typical development team can be divided into various areas. The core programming tools are perhaps the most important, and essentially consist of applications that allow programmers to compile their code into a working program: the compiler, assembler, and linker are each essential, as is debugging software. Programmers can also

Left: EA/Criterion's Renderware middleware has powered an incredibly diverse set of videogames, from the company's own *Burnout 3: Takedown*, to Rockstar's *Grand Theft Auto: San Andreas*, and Vivendi's *Cold Winter*.

Opposite left, and below: **The importance of tools and technology was emphasized at GDC 2004, when Microsoft unveiled its XNA suite.**

benefit from optional tools, such as software performance analyzers, which can scan code and highlight any inefficiencies in the way that it utilizes the hardware.

Art and design tools principally consist of programs that process large amounts of data, and allow it to be converted into an efficient format to store the game world, so that artists can create art assets using a commercially available software package and then convert them into a format that's compatible with the game engine. Other art tools might process the facial data of characters to merge it onto 3D models, or allow artists to preview the in-game appearance of their creations, while tools that directly edit the game world allow level designers to go to work.

Perhaps the least glamorous set of tools are those that allow the logistics of development to run smoothly; asset management tools allow the team to track the various art assets and so on, while scheduling software allows producers to track each team member and spot any potential resource bottlenecks. And if a development team does opt to use an entire middleware game engine, or middleware physics or AI, these frequently come with their own toolsets that allow programmers to get the best use from them.

WHY CHOOSE MIDDLEWARE? One crucial decision concerning tools and technology is whether to develop them internally, or to consider buying in those that have been developed by specialist thirdparty vendors. It's a question that divides the development community because it has no definitive answer. The best solution is simply to use the preproduction as productively as possible to weigh up the benefits of both options, and to carefully determine which features are needed from any engine or tools.

before they commit to a particular suite of technology. Choosing tools that don't support the right set of features, for example, can end up compromising the design effort, or eliminating any cost savings as programmers are forced to adapt the tools to their needs. In addition, critics of middleware point out that games developed using the same engine can end up graphically indistinct from each other. In any case, the tools that are chosen will only ever function as effectively as those who use them.

Consequently, many developers continue to create and refine their own technology, investing the extra time and effort that this requires to achieve a more focused suite of tools, or to develop their own internal "middleware," which can be used by several teams across various genres. The obvious merit of such an approach being that, since they wrote it themselves, adapting the technology, or fixing it if something goes wrong, is so much easier than it is with externally created tools.

LET THE PLAYER DO THE WORK

One advantage of creating in-house tools for a PC title is that they can be shipped with the game to enhance their appeal on store shelves (*see page* 157). By allowing users to create their own content the replay value of a game is enhanced, which makes it a more attractive purchase. But the discipline of creating tools with a nonprofessional user-base in mind can also be beneficial. Probably the most desirable characteristic of any development tool is a user-friendly interface, and designing tools that are going to be released to the public forces tools programmers to address this issue of usability. This also reaps positive repercussions for their use internally by the likes of nontechnically skilled artists, testers, and so on.

Some notable examples of titles to ship with their tools in this way are *Half-Life, The Elder Scrolls III: Morrowind,* the *Unreal* series, and *Neverwinter Nights. Half-Life* in particular managed to give rise to a burgeoning mod scene made up of talented amateurs who use the existing game as their

The advantages of using off-the-shelf solutions are fairly obvious. Buying in the right tools or game engine can save an enormous amount of time and resources that would otherwise have to be used to create them in-house. Thus, the overall development process can be streamlined, saving money and allowing a greater amount of time to be spent creating and refining the game's play mechanics. Frequently, thirdparty tools are fairly versatile, which also allows their reuse across several titles, so in the long-term even more time can be saved thanks to the fact that the development team doesn't have to adapt to a new set of tools for each new project.

But choosing the wrong tools can eliminate these advantages at a stroke, so it's essential that developers do their homework core technology, modifying it to produce an entirely new product. Some popular mods even manage to attain commercial release, such as the phenomenally successful *Counter-Strike*. Quite simply, the mod scene is the closest equivalent that the videogame industry has to the independent movie scene, allowing games to be created for a fraction of the budget of full production models. Indeed it is not surprising then that many developers go on to graduate from the mod scene to find employment within fully fledged development teams.

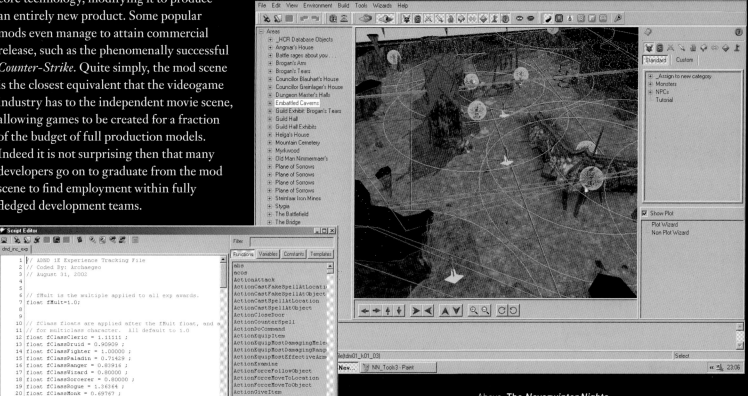

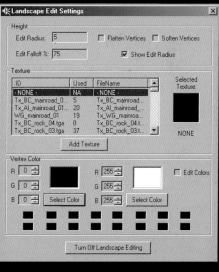

Above: **The *Neverwinter Nights* Aurora Toolset.**

Below: ***Elder Scrolls III: Morrowind* tools, and** (opposite) **a still taken from the main game.**

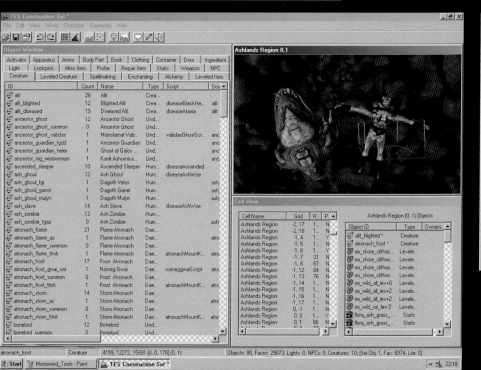

MIDDLEWARE PACKAGES
There are enough middleware solutions out there to suit every possible development need or whim. The following represents a cross-section of the most popular packages.

Left: **XNA, MICROSOFT**

Unveiled at GDC 2004 XNA is actually a suite of tools aimed at next-generation development architecture, designed to make life easier for developers. It aims to combine Microsoft's own tools with middleware and thirdparty tools by means of standardized APIs and input systems. Based on the DirectX API and Visual Studio, features include HLSL (High-Level Shading Language), PIX (a graphics pipeline analysis tool), XACT (an audio creation tool), and various Xbox Live tools.

Below: **RENDERWARE, CRITERION/EA**

With over 500 videogames based on its technology, Criterion's Renderware is one of the most successful middleware products around. It's an integrated suite covering graphics, physics, AI, and audio, and a corollary set of production tools. But it also highlights the drawbacks of using someone else's technology: when EA acquired the business in 2004, unsigned Renderware games suddenly became slightly less attractive to other publishers.

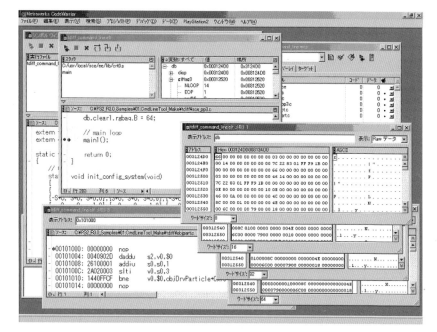

Above: **CODEWARRIOR, METROWERKS**

Codewarrior is an integrated development environment (IDE), which means that it provides a whole suite of programming tools. Available for a number of hardware platforms, such as Sony's PlayStation 2 and PSP and Nintendo's GameCube, it provides a C++ compiler and libraries, linker, and debugger, and it supports various plug-ins.

Right: **GAMEBRYO, NDL**

Based on the NetImmerse technology found in titles such as *The Elder Scrolls III: Morrowind*, Gamebryo consists of cross-platform engine technology, supported by flexible art and programming tools. It is designed to be as straightforward as possible to customize, so that programmers can add their own features with ease wherever they are necessary.

Above: **UNREAL TECHNOLOGY, EPIC GAMES**

The technology behind Epic's firstperson shooter of the same name, the Unreal engine is a widely used game engine that has now entered its third iteration. Geared toward next-generation consoles and PCs, it allows cutting-edge visual effects, such as dynamic shadows, per-pixel lighting, and volumetric lighting effects, as well as providing a rigid-body physics system and AI systems.

Below: **HAVOK PHYSICS, HAVOK**

The trend in videogame design toward emergent gameplay has heightened the necessity for featuring realistic physics, once the sole preserve of racing games, across all genres. Havok's cross-platform technology has been used in a number of high-profile titles, most notably Valve's *Half-Life 2*, to provide features such as ragdoll effects, detachable limbs, and vehicle physics. It is supported by a set of tools that are compatible with a number of other content creation packages.

Above: **ALIENBRAIN, AVID**

Used by developers and publishers across the videogame spectrum, Avid's Alienbrain is an asset management system that provides configuration management, version control, efficient workflow tools, and team collaboration support. It's designed to improve the productivity of development teams, while also increasing security.

Below: **SPEEDTREE, INTERACTIVE DATA VISUALIZATION**

Perhaps the most specialized piece of middleware yet devised, IDV's SpeedTree is designed, as the name suggests, to assist the quick and easy creation of trees within realtime environments. Essentially it consists of a modeling package and a C++ API that allow trees to be implemented within games, and supports automatic level of detail generation.

ANDY BEVERIDGE, DIRECTOR AND COFOUNDER, SN SYSTEMS

Having helped develop some of the early software and hardware accessories for the Apple II computer, Andy Beveridge cofounded SN Systems after joining a videogame developer and discovering firsthand that better software development tools were needed.

Right: Based in the UK, SN Systems now produces industry-standard console game development tools for most current hardware platforms. Activision, Atari, Capcom, Namco, EA, Sega, and Square Enix are just some of the major videogame creators drawn from across the world who use the company's tools.

What sort of skills and qualifications does someone need to be able to become a tools programmer?

Well, any actual directly relevant tools experience is always a big plus but it's very difficult to find good experienced tools people. We generally look for an excellent C/C++ programmer, a good problem solver, and someone familiar with development tools and the debugging process on their own code. Familiarity with computer architectures (not just PC) and a reasonable awareness of code efficiency is also desirable. We mostly look at programming graduates and people already in the tools or games industries. A good starting point is to show a healthy interest and understanding of the development cycle.

How important are tools to the game development process?

Well you have to have some tools of course but they can be very basic. A good programmer can make do with simpler or poorer tools, but the cost is development time and scope. Pretty much all game developers today regard it as very important to get the best tools sorted out at the beginning of the game development process.

How many people will typically be responsible for tools on an average development team?

Here at SN where we specialize in tools it may be anything from two to eight people. But within a game development studio there will also typically be tools programmers responsible for the custom tools that a game uses—model and level designers for example. Those teams can be typically one or a few people. Some game development studios have quite large teams (up to maybe 20 programmers) producing library code, which is effectively their own middleware.

How do tools programmers fit into the rest of the development process? What points of contact and interaction are there between tools programmers and the rest of the development team?

The tools programmers mainly get a pile of impossible wish lists and feature requests. To make something of that you really have to have your own underlying idea of what the tool(s) should be, and then use the feedback from others as guidance. The key is to listen

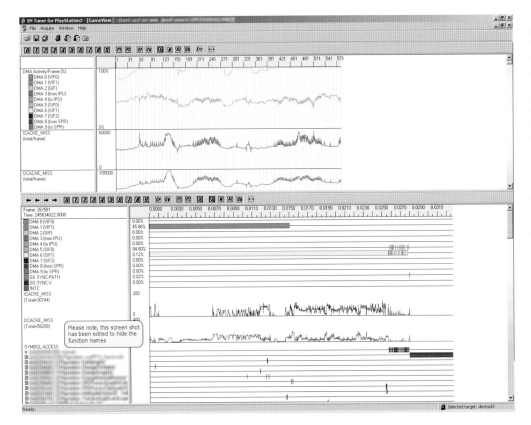

well to what the users (developers) tell you; to work out what they really want rather than what they tell you they want; and to give them early versions of things to try out rather than force your own completed opus onto them.

What sort of tools are typically used during the development process? How widely do developers differ in the sorts of tools that they use, and the functions that they require?
We mainly produce the core programming tools, which basically amounts to the compiler, assembler, linker, and debugger. We specialize in customizing those tools very specifically for the platform we are targeting. So for example our latest PSP tools know about custom relocatable file formats, graphics processor commands, floating point number formats, vector math coprocessor opcodes and registers, the machine's operating system, etc.

Further down the line a game development team's own custom tools will typically include programs that process large amounts of data to convert it to an efficient format to store the game world, or tools that process character facial data to merge it onto 3D models, or tools to directly edit the game world, for example.

What can go wrong with tools, and why? How can developers minimize the risk of upsets? What are the most common mistakes that developers make with regard to tool creation and usage?
They can of course damage important data but then every game team should have a good reliable backup procedure in place

But if tools break, they can still drag development to a halt while people try to figure out what went wrong because it is not always obvious. A common problem is not to buy or design/develop the right tools for the job early enough—it can really slow up development to put these tools and processes in place later on.

What is the fallout from using wrong or inadequate tools?
Late titles. Titles that never get finished. Titles that have to have features removed from the specification in order to deliver anything. Poor performance (bad programming tools or bad data layout tools or bad asset creation tools can all hit performance badly). Having good performance monitoring/tuning tools will allow a developer to spot those problems and hopefully do something about it, but if you don't have those performance monitoring tools or the skill to use them well, then you are stuck with poor performance and cannot find the root cause.

What is the key to creating successful tools?
Listening to the users. Being able to understand the developer's position and viewpoint and putting yourself in their shoes. An ability to see around problems—the direct route is not always the best.

How important are middleware tools to the development process? What are the advantages and disadvantages of middleware over self-created tools?
This is a very controversial issue and one that game developers often disagree over. The advantage clearly should be shorter development time (and hence hopefully lower costs) and/or more time to spend developing the gameplay rather than the background technology; but the downside can be that you end up using code that does not fit the job well and cannot be easily customized. If not used well then the overall appearance of the game can be shoddy—just a look of having rough edges because it is that little bit less easy to tweak the fine details. It's a fine balance and good middleware is no guarantee of good results—it still takes skill to use those tools wisely.

On self-created tools, it is becoming increasingly important that studios have their own reusable and customizable technology in their toolkit when they start a new game. In effect they write their own middleware but since they wrote it themselves, if they did it right, then they have a bit more control over it and an understanding of what it can do and what its limitations are.

Could you give an example of the sorts of middleware tools that are available?
Everything from game component kits that replace your code (EA/Criterion's Renderware, Havok's physics, landscape modeling systems, AI for character behavior, etc.). Then there are the more obvious tools like 3D modeling and texture editing tools, preview tools, tools to customize your graphics for the platform (color reduction and texture compression, etc.), animation tools, version control and asset management tools, and so on.

Above: **Alienbrain Studio is an asset management tool that allows developers to version, track, and store all of their game's assets during and after production. Not the most glamorous end of the middleware spectrum, but essential nevertheless.**

Right: **One of the biggest videogame releases in recent years, Valve Software's** *Half-Life 2* **is built upon Havok's physics middleware. Havok's technology provides developers with tools for content creation, tweaking, debugging, and profiling, and it allowed Valve to fundamentally redesign the core mechanics of its paradigmatic firstperson shooter.**

Do you have any informative experiences from your time working with development tools?

One of my worst memories is our first piece of substantial work on PlayStation tools, back in 1993 I think. We didn't have long to pull something together. The plan was to take our results to the CES trade show, where we would show Sony what we could do. At the end of an already intensive two-week stint with new hardware with no tools and no manuals we finished up by working for three days and nights straight to get everything ready. Already suffering from sleep deprivation we had to sit in the cheap seats on a plane for a 10-hour flight from London; then the plane from San Francisco International Airport to Vegas was overbooked so we had another six-hour wait for the next flight. By the time we got to Vegas it was past midnight and our overbooked hotel had let our rooms go so we had nowhere to stay. We could barely stay awake let alone present a coherent case to hotel staff. I remember with a grimace how I felt and heaven only knows what we must have looked like. It was all worth it in the end because Sony were impressed, but it is not something I would care to repeat. But that was one of those times that a good night's sleep really does make everything look so different—always worth remembering when you get stuck with a really knotty tools problem.

PRODUCTION

03

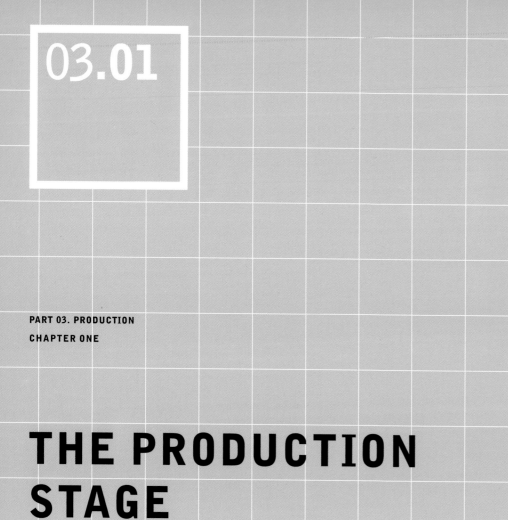

03.01

THE PRODUCTION STAGE

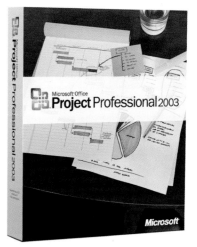

At the end of the preproduction cycle, a number of things are in place. The game has a design document, or at the very least a vertical-slice demo, on which the members of the team can base future developments. Milestones have been set and agreed upon. Above all, the game has finance. It can afford to go into full production, and it's at this point that the hard work really begins.

Hard work because over whatever time has been specified for production—generally somewhere between one or two years, though there have been many projects pushed through in time frames inside of that—the whole game has to go from concept to finished article, from a collection of ideas to something that works flawlessly on the end user's entertainment device.

Once the game has received the go-ahead, a full-size team must be assembled, and grouped into smaller teams, the roles of which are covered in greater depth later in this chapter. The programming

team must write the code that drives the game, a diverse challenge that largely depends on the type of game the team are working on. It can involve complex AI, physics components, or modifying a bought-in engine to suit.

The job of the art team is to create the substance that makes up the game, including painting textures, shaping 3D models, and creating the animations that play such an important part in defining the spirit of the game. Following the style guide in the design document, the lead artist must shape the work of several people into one consistent style. The level design team work on the individual sections of the game, building consistent worlds and crafting challenges within them. Working with tools provided by the programming team, and objects provided by the art department, their job is to interpret the design document, the whole team's bible, and make it into something solid.

Left: A good producer will be familiar with this, or something similar. Microsoft Project allows users to easily schedule events, improving communication both inside the development team and with the team's publishers.

Below: A typical project file will look something like this. The colored bars denote different stages in the project's life cycle.

CIVILIZATION 3 (developed by Firaxis, Above): The perfect producer? Excellent at resource gathering, has the ability to see the bigger picture, and willing to explore the unknown...

THE SIMS 2 (developed by Maxis, Above right): ... able to keep to a tight schedule, creates good relationships, and knows how to reap the rewards...

THEME HOSPITAL 3 (developed by Bullfrog, Right): ...has experience working with people under pressure, impressive financial acumen, and has a sixth sense that lets them tell fakers from the real thing.

Scripting must also be finished, which involves a team of writers submitting text for everything, from front-end menus and success and failure messages, to each line of dialog in a complex, branching story line. The audio team must oversee voice-acting to accompany this if appropriate, as well as looking after soundtracks, and creating and sampling spot effects. And throughout the latter stages of production, the game must be tested to within an inch of its prototyped life by a group of testers, dedicated gamers who have no issues with playing over the same section of a game again and again and trying to break it.

The people will be bound together by the design document and the lead designer in charge of that. But they will also be driven by the game's producer.

Left: The production of Valve's *Half-Life 2* took place mostly in secret. Code theft produced unforeseen problems at the end of the cycle.

Below left: Like its prequel, Bungie's *Halo 2* ran to a tightly produced schedule, and hit the stores on time.

Below: The poor production time-keeping of Confounding Factor's *Galleon* led to it becoming something of a games-industry joke.

Bottom: While Elixir's *Republic* took a long time to arrive, at least when it did it was polished.

THE PRODUCER The producer works closely with the lead designer, but while the designer's job is broadly to make sure the design document is consistent and complete, the producer's job is to make sure the work is carried out on time, to an exacting standard and within budget. They are the bad cop to the design team's good cop. They must keep the team motivated, but they must also ensure that milestones are hit, which can mean making brutal choices when it comes to the game's content.

A good producer is someone who is good at dealing with people, effective at communicating with the disparate sections of the development team, and ensuring they're working well both inside the teams, and as parts of the project. They have an understanding of each discipline; perhaps not to the same crucial degree as a designer, but to the extent that they know what's possible in what time frame. They must be a leader, inspirational, firm, and fair.

They must also be a researcher, always on the lookout for ways to save time and money in development. The complexities of modern game architecture demand a working knowledge of the middleware market. Buying in the right ready-made solution to a work-heavy part of the game can save weeks and tens of thousands of dollars. Buying in something unwieldy or inappropriate can cost just as much. Liaising with the core design team is key, here, and a good producer will have an intuitive feeling for when a process is wasteful, and how to streamline it.

Producers also compile regular reports—at least monthly, and often weekly—to keep track of the game's progress. They hold regular meetings with the team heads, and provide a brokerage service between the developers and their senior management. Project management software gives an easily-understood visual representation of a game's progress through development, and game producers will have to use that not just for their own reference, but also in progress reports to their superiors. The role is an

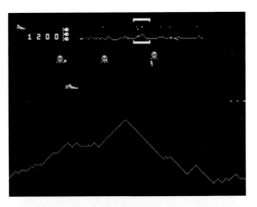

autonomous one, and carries a great degree of responsibility, but that responsibility must be quickly and efficiently justified.

Crucially, a good producer needs an excellent eye for detail so they are able to add to the things that are working in the game and eliminating the things that aren't. While even the best producer will be unable to transform a terrible concept into an excellent product, by getting the best out of a team over the course of a game's development, a good producer can make a game be the very best it can possibly be.

Top row left: *Defender* by Williams: At videogaming's dawn, one-man teams didn't really need producers.

Top row right: *Treasure Island Dizzy* by Codemasters: But as games grew in scope, so did the teams.

Above left: *Eye Of The Beholder* by Westwood Studios: RPGs with epic stories pushed the team sizes—and schedules—still further.

Above right: *Final Fantasy XII* by Square Enix: And in the present day, teams of 100+ aren't uncommon.

Above: **The Yaroze kit was released for the original PlayStation to encourage homebrew development.**

PART 03. PRODUCTION

CHAPTER TWO

PROGRAMMING

Experts in the low-level arcane, alchemists of pure logic gates, elder magicians in the dark art of C++. Making your way to the musty corner of a development studio earmarked "programming team" can be an intimidating task, particularly if you believe the only career path is from the bedroom, through Internet "leet speak" and foot-thick textbooks, and into the incomprehensible, indivisible, and absolutely individual. Maybe ten years ago; not any more. The complexity of gaming today means that programming is almost always a team task, and that means communication skills are as important as having an intimate knowledge of console architecture.

Well, almost. Of all the positions available in the games industry, jobs in programming require the most immutable set of skills, which is why these days almost all entrants into the profession come equipped with a Computer Science degree (or equivalent) and a strong grounding in one of the more popular coding languages—usually C++. A portfolio of coding projects that they have developed over the course of their education is also a must, and many would-be programmers put in the hours working on games for Internet release in their spare time as a means of honing their skills and bulking their résumés (and hopefully their incomes, too).

Increasingly a specialized art, a programmer's precise role in game creation depends on their skillset. The most "hardcore" position of all is usually considered to be the engine programmer, the man brave enough to take the machine right to its limits, and create a framework on which the game's structure and scenery can be hung. Good engine coding doesn't just require low-level assembly language, but an obscenely acute mathematical brain. Others may be more at home working on artificial intelligence routines, where an understanding of how to transfer human logic to an artificial environment is the base currency. Online specialists need to combat latency in telecommunications. Tools teams work to provide tools that enable designers and artists to work more easily, or tweak middleware to their team's requirements.

The specific area in which a programmer works will largely dictate how they spend their time over the course of the project; engine programmers will work with the art department to decide if and where visual compromises need to be made in order to preserve the game's fluency, while AI coders pay attention to the criticisms of testers and designers, and tweak their routines appropriately. Programmers are also kept together as a team by the Lead Programmer, a multiskilled taskmaster with a good head for problem-solving in all disciplines.

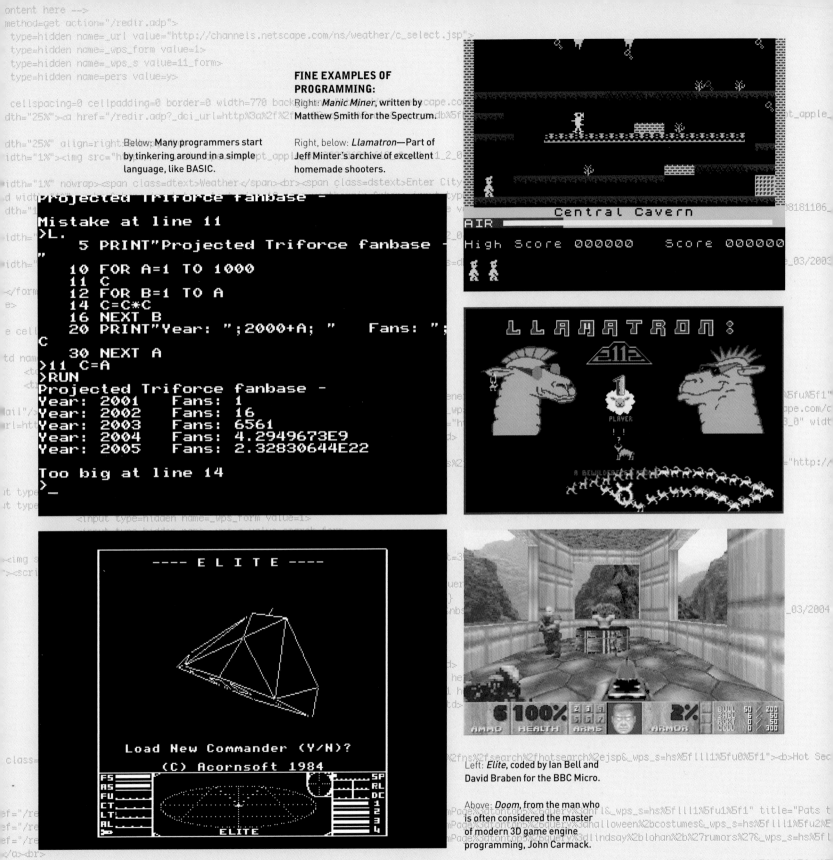

FINE EXAMPLES OF PROGRAMMING:

Right: *Manic Miner*, written by Matthew Smith for the Spectrum.

Below: Many programmers start by tinkering around in a simple language, like BASIC.

Right, below: *Llamatron*—Part of Jeff Minter's archive of excellent homemade shooters.

```
Projected Triforce fanbase -
Mistake at line 11
>L.
    5 PRINT"Projected Triforce fanbase -
"
   10 FOR A=1 TO 1000
   11 C
   12 FOR B=1 TO A
   14 C=C*C
   16 NEXT B
   20 PRINT"Year: ";2000+A; "    Fans: ";
C
   30 NEXT A
>11 C=A
>RUN
Projected Triforce fanbase -
Year: 2001    Fans: 1
Year: 2002    Fans: 16
Year: 2003    Fans: 6561
Year: 2004    Fans: 4.2949673E9
Year: 2005    Fans: 2.32830644E22

Too big at line 14
>_
```

Left: *Elite*, coded by Ian Bell and David Braben for the BBC Micro.

Above: *Doom*, from the man who is often considered the master of modern 3D game engine programming, John Carmack.

EVOLVING LANGUAGES

Below: **BLITZ BASIC**
"My First Game Designer" packages might hide much of the low-level terror from the wannabe coder, coddling them in simple WYSIWYG interfaces, but they're increasingly powerful and useful for understanding the compartmental structure of a complete game, the debugging process, and the satisfaction when an idea finally comes together.

Right: **SHOCKWAVE FLASH**
Increasingly the artist's tool of choice when it comes to putting together simple pieces of interactive media for Web-based demonstration, Shockwave Flash can be a powerful—and visually distinctive, thanks to its vector-based graphics—game creator for programmers too. Indeed, Shockwave's website sells commercial Flash games, most of which are simple puzzles, executed with panache.

Above: **MATHEMATICS**
A programmer's education begins in primary school, where he or she begins to learn the first elements of the flawless logic that will later define their lives. Mathematics is crucial to programming, and the closer coders get to the cutting edge of their profession, the more complex the equations get.

Below: **SCRIPTING**
Level designers might dabble in scripting too, but it's the budding programmer who takes their favorite game's engine to pieces completely to see what makes it tick. Playing around with id or Epic's toys can produce astoundingly fresh work; check *Quake Rally*, or the shoot-'em-ups and puzzle games constructed in UnrealEd for confirmation.

Below: **HTML AND PHP**
Hypertext Markup Language might not be the most dynamic language, but it's a good way of feeling the structure, layout, and abstraction of code. Following on and learning PHP makes things much more interesting. Both also teach the nascent programmer that structure is key, and the way you set out your code is as important as the code itself, particularly when it comes to finding the flaws in it later.

Below: **JAVA**
Java's multiplatform capabilities make it ideal for small applications that suit a variety of architectures. This is why so many developers have turned to it for game development on cell phones.

```
<!DOCTYPE HTML PUBLIC "-//W3C//DTD HTML 4.01 Transitional//EN">
<html>
<script language="JavaScript" type="text/JavaScript">
<!--
function MM_openBrWindow(theURL,winName,features) { //v2.0
  window.open(theURL,winName,features)
}
//-->
</script>
<script language="JavaScript" type="text/JavaScript">
<!--
function MM_reloadPage(init) {  //reloads the window if Nav4 resized
  if (init==true) with (navigator) {if ((appName=="Netscape")&&(parseInt(appVersion)==4)) {
    document.MM_pgW=innerWidth; document.MM_pgH=innerHeight; onresize=MM_reloadPage; }}
  else if (innerWidth!=document.MM_pgW || innerHeight!=document.MM_pgH) location.reload();
}
MM_reloadPage(true);

function MM_goToURL() { //v3.0
  var i, args=MM_goToURL.arguments; document.MM_returnValue = false;
  for (i=0; i<(args.length-1); i+=2) eval(args[i]+".location='"+args[i+1]+"'");
}

function MM_jumpMenu(targ,selObj,restore) { //v3.0
  eval(targ+".location='"+selObj.options[selObj.selectedIndex].value+"'");
  if (restore) selObj.selectedIndex=0;
}

function MM_findObj(n, d) { //v4.01
  var p,i,x;  if(!d) d=document; if((p=n.indexOf("?"))>0&&parent.frames.length) {
    d=parent.frames[n.substring(p+1)].document; n=n.substring(0,p);}
  if(!(x=d[n])&&d.all) x=d.all[n]; for (i=0;!x&&i<d.forms.length;i++) x=d.forms[i][n];
  for(i=0;!x&&d.layers&&i<d.layers.length;i++) x=MM_findObj(n,d.layers[i].document);
  if(!x && d.getElementById) x=d.getElementById(n); return x;
}

function MM_showHideLayers() { //v6.0
  var i,p,v,obj,args=MM_showHideLayers.arguments;
  for (i=0; i<(args.length-2); i+=3) if ((obj=MM_findObj(args[i]))!=null) { v=args[i+2];
    if (obj.style) { obj=obj.style; v=(v=='show')?'visible':(v=='hide')?'hidden':v; }
    obj.visibility=v; }
```

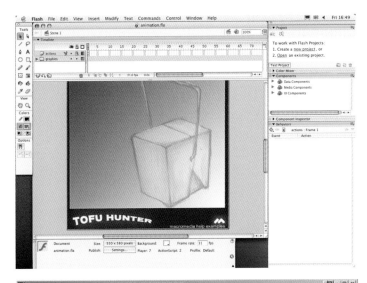

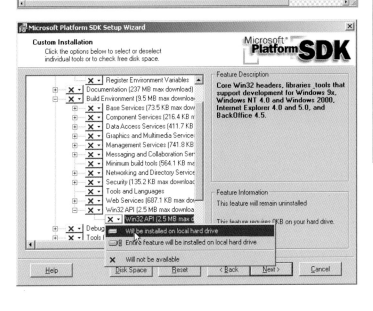

Left middle: **C++**

The most commonly used language in game development, learning C++ is just like learning a foreign tongue; the basics are relatively simple, but becoming a true native speaker, a master of the art, can take years. Those years won't be wasted, though: good C++ programmers will be in demand in the games industry for the foreseeable future.

Left bottom: **DIRECTX (AND OTHER APIs)**

An API is an Application Programming Interface—a subprogram that directly interfaces with the host system, and takes much of the hard work away from the programmer. Understanding how to use common APIs, like Microsoft's DirectX protocol for PCs and Xbox, for example, is clearly of benefit to the programmer and his studio.

Below: **MIDDLEWARE**

The job of the programmer isn't limited to writing code from scratch. Some companies license engines from specialists, but engines rarely meet a game's specifications head on, and modifying the source code to meet the needs of the design document is a difficult task. The middleware code will be well documented, but it still needs to be understood.

Bottom: **ASSEMBLER**

For the truly devoted, Assembler is the best way to get the most out of the host machine. It's also the most incomprehensible of all, and a headache to reinterpret once it's written down. A headache, that is, for mortals. Masters of Assembler rarely count themselves in that group.

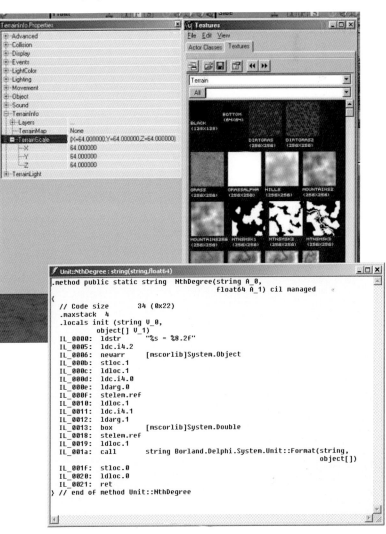

CHALLENGES A PROGRAMMER MIGHT FACE

It's not just about recreating a design document. Problems are bound to occur during game development, and it's often down to the programmer to come up with a solution.

THE CAMERA

The "camera" is the position from which the player sees the action, and getting that position right in thirdperson perspective games has become something close to an art form. And, like all art forms, there can be no correct answers, but there can certainly be things that are horribly, horribly wrong. The problem is simple. Movement in 3D games must be relative to the camera, because otherwise there is no way of mapping the control system to visual feedback; a hundred-and-eighty-degree shift of the camera will leave the controls backward, for example, and is completely counterintuitive. But a camera cannot be rigidly fixed to the back of the player—it must be flexible enough to move around objects fixed in the environment that would prove impossible for a real, solid camera to pass through, and intelligent enough to ensure that the player is visible at all times. More than that, since the player's control system shifts slightly every time the camera moves around, it must be wholly predictable, never twitchy, and never frustrating. In essence it must do what the player wants it to do, second-guessing faultlessly throughout an unpredictable adventure. And that's a challenge.

ONLINE PROBLEMS

More and more games are being shipped with online components, causing more and more headaches for programmers forced to rely on the unreliable nature of third-party communications hardware. The problems for programmers of persistent worlds start with the simple conundrum: should game data be stored on the user's local machine, or locked safely away on the server side? Well, the server side, obviously, because anything else is insecure and can lead to hacking, cheating, and devaluing the game experience for everyone. But what data gets stored, and where?

Above left: *Mario 64* from Nintendo—As close as we've come.
Left: *Blinx* from Artoon—Swinging cameras cause sudden death.

Above: *Everquest* from Verant—
Solid servers for the masses.
Above right: *Burnout 3 from EA*—
Faulty servers from the start.

Below: *Grand Theft Auto 3* from
Rockstar—Fun and flighty physics.
Right: *Trespasser*—Accurate, but
beyond dull.

Every byte transferred has to be transferred by thousands and thousands of players, and that's going to cost money. How many servers does the company need? And even then, will that system be secure against the latest console cheat devices?

And that's a slow-paced genre. Speedier things become simply impossible. If someone in London wants to race a car against someone in Sydney, data has to travel many thousands of miles. Even with the quickest route along the fastest fiber optic cable, news of a collision at one end will take a fraction of a second to arrive at the other—by which time it'll be too late, the cars will have moved on, and inconsistencies start to appear. So, how does the conscientious game programmer begin an assault on the laws of physics?

PHYSICAL WORLDS

Physics is a buzzword in game development at the time of writing, but the appearance of emergent gameplay is causing problems for the programmer. Players want worlds to behave with as much realism as possible, but computers aren't anywhere near capable of reproducing real life particle by particle. Shortcuts must be taken, but which ones? When is an approximation of a collision as good as modeling the collision itself? And when does the processing cost of real-life simulation overtake the value that simulation provides to the game?

A good physics programmer has to know the answer to questions like those when they arise, as well as developing new ways of bringing games closer to reality than ever. Above all, though, and like all members of the development team across disciplines, they must have an idea of why they're doing what they're doing, and what value it is to the game. The simplest solution to every question is to first ask if it's going to enhance the player's experience. If the answer is no, then it's probably not worth doing.

Q&A

TIM SWEENEY, EPIC GAMES

As one of the founders of Epic Games, Tim Sweeney has played a programming role in games of all shapes and sizes. Epic began as a shareware company, selling simple (by today's standards, at least) software through the Internet and mail order. Now they're a huge multifranchise operation, and specialize in making firstperson shooters.

The jewel in their crown—and Tim Sweeney's labor of love—is UnrealEngine, the powerful 3D engine series that's used by professionals and amateurs alike to create games. The latest version, UnrealEngine 3.0, will be released to the public in 2006.

How would you define the role of a programmer at a modern development studio?
Game programming is a fairly wide field now, with most programmers involved in implementing gameplay systems and features, and engine features unique to the title being developed, and doing so in close coordination with the artists and other programmers on the team. Each programmer is part of a programming team of 5-15 programmers, and part of a larger development team of 20-50 developers working on a single project.

Has middleware made the industry a better or worse place for programmers?
Middleware has hastened the end of the one-man-band game-development team, which would develop—from the ground up—every piece of technology and content required for a project. Those days really ended with the move to Windows, where system API's like Direct3D and DirectSound took over many

of the low-level programming tasks. Middleware libraries were the next logical step, enabling teams to use off-the-shelf game components like RenderWare Graphics or Havok Physics to avoid the work of developing those pieces themselves. Then, the large-scale move to game engines began, enabling teams to start with a 100% complete, fully integrated game framework, and focus on those areas of gameplay and technical features unique to their game.

Overall, middleware has been a great boon for game developers and game programmers, but it has taken some of the glory and mystique out of the do-it-yourself game programmer, who in past eras would architect all of the game's systems starting with a clean sheet of paper. The specialization that middleware has enabled, like the specialization of labor in the world economy, has been great for business and for advancing the state of the art, but it tends to reduce the role of the generalist craftsman.

The most important long-lasting attribute of a programmer now is his ability to work on a project with teammates and to work comfortably with a code base that is largely not any one person's creation. Whether that code base is a middleware engine or a team's internally developed

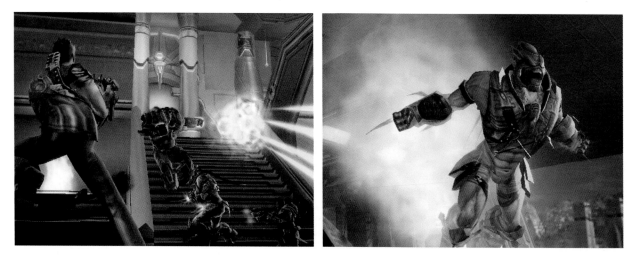

part 03. production

All images: *Unreal Championship 2*, by Epic Games.

part 03. production

All images: *Unreal Championship 2*, by Epic Games.

technology is mostly immaterial; the fact remains that it's so large and complex that it exceeds any one individual's scope.

What demands do changing technology place on the programmer?

With every generation of games, expectations increase dramatically with AI, gameplay, physics, realism, and other aspects of gameplay, so it's vital that programmers invest significant time in keeping up with the state of the art. This means changing development approaches, tools, and platforms every few years, and relearning a substantial portion of one's knowledge base. But this is good, and the fact that so many programmers do this successfully with each generation is the reason the industry has been able to move forward so quickly.

Do you consider the role of programmer to be an artistic or scientific one?

Within game programming, there is a wonderful mix of both disciplines. For example, an AI programmer's job is to create a software framework suitable for managing the movement and interaction of a diverse set of computer-controlled characters; this is a matter of engineering. But his job is to also make those characters interesting to interact with or challenging to fight; that's a creative task. When looking at the work we do, I can't help but feel lucky that we have such a mix of the two worlds. If we were writing accounting software or industrial-control programs, we would only be engineers, and not artists.

03.03

LEVEL DESIGN

THE ROLE OF THE LEVEL DESIGNER

The level designer—or level designers, because there's almost sure to be more than one of them—is responsible for creating the game world and its architecture inside a level editor. This doesn't just mean constructing the environments, but also placing every piece of interactive game furniture around the level, and defining their purpose. The level designer will define an enemy's patrol route and his range of hearing; they will determine the best place for pickups and time bonuses; and they will use sleight of hand to hide the world edges, and convince the player they're in the game world and not their own.

Which means the good level designer has to be, like so many on the development team, a multiskilled creature. Since level design tools vary from one game to the next, it helps if they're able to learn fast, but those with a good grounding in the PC mod tools bundled with many modern 3D games will find the technical aspects of creating worlds little trouble. Level designers are the architects of the game-design world, constructing environments to specifications delineated in the design document, and a fine sense of shape and dimension is an essential trait for the role.

Traditionally, most game levels are sketched out on paper before making the transition to digital media, so level designers with some draftsmanship skills have a slight advantage over their pencil-free peers. Still, getting the "feel" of three-dimensional puzzles on two-dimensional paper isn't easy, and as the complexity of environments increases along with the competence of level designers, so the in-game model becomes the swiftest way to demonstrate an idea. Modern designers can expect to draft their structure countless times before even beginning to texture or populate it. Their essential craft is the ability to coax a player through a level without ever letting them know they're being led by the hand.

Level designers also need logic. They do not construct AI, but they must understand it, and use the level design tools to frame that AI in an environment that suits the game design. They're also commonly responsible for complex scripting, tailoring the behavior of enemies to maximize the entertainment for the player. These days much of this tweaking takes place within the game engine, allowing the level designer to make changes on the fly and see how they suit the game. The level designer's sense of good game design must be as acute as the lead designer's, and communication between the two will be constant. Good level designers feed material back into the design document as well as taking it out. They follow instructions to the letter, but with enthusiasm and creativity.

Finally, with all those ideas and all of their world in their heads, level designers need to be aware of the limitations of their medium, while always disguising them from the player. The most sumptuous, well-worked level in the world is useless to the team if it runs at a handful of frames a second. A level designer with the ability to produce a rich, involving environment within a tight polygon count will be an asset to any development team.

All images taken from Epic Games'
various design tools.

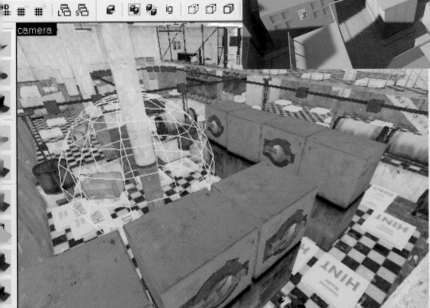

e Edit Map View Tools Window Help

camera

front (y/z)

side (

Object Properties: point_bugbait

| Class Info | Outputs | Inputs | Flags | VisGroup |

My Out...	Target Entity	Target I...	Delay	Only Once
OnBaited	laundry_glassbreak_2	PlaySound	0.00	Yes
OnBaited	laundry_glass_gibs_2	Shoot	0.00	Yes
OnBaited	laundry_window2_broken	Enable	0.00	Yes
OnBaited	laundry_window2_whole	Kill	0.00	Yes
OnBaited	laundry_window2_spawners	Spawn	0.50	No

My output named   OnBaited
Targets entities named   laundry_glassbreak_2
Via this input   PlaySound
With a parameter override of   (none)
After a delay in seconds of   0.00   ☑ Fire once only

| Mark | Add... | Copy | Paste | Delete |

Cancel   Apply

lp, press F1   point_bugbait   @910, 282   16w 16l 16h   Zoom: 1.55   Snap:

chapter 03. level design   91

FIRSTPERSON SHOOTER

Epic and id's policy of bundling their tools with their games means that there are more budding FPS designers across the globe than for any other genre. The nature of the game, too—run around and shoot just about everything—makes getting a functional level running pretty easy, but just because it works doesn't mean it's any good. Level designers working on narrative firstperson shooters must cloak their game's (almost obligatory) linearity with clever architecture. Those working on levels for multiplayer combat must create a rock-paper-scissors style hierarchy of locations for the player, so that every advantageous spot makes fighters vulnerable in another respect.

Key to both types, though, is pick-up placement. Players should often feel on the brink of running out of ammunition, but rarely actually fall completely short. Likewise, the locations of health packs must be far enough apart to cause consternation, but just within reach of the player as they brace themselves for Game Over. Checkpoints and spawn points require an equal level of thought; the smart level designer tweaks, tries, and tweaks again until it feels perfect.

Examples of excellent FPS level design: *Halo, Half-Life, Counter-Strike*

RACING GAME

Level designers of racing games have the advantage of knowing the exact route the player will take. Their challenge is to make that route as exhilarating as possible. For games where the circuit will be created from scratch, this means proper pacing. While pacing is crucial in every genre, it takes on a rather more obvious definition in the racing game. Essentially, courses aren't fun if you're going fast in a straight line, or even fast, slow, and turn, fast, slow, and turn. The track must surprise the player the first time, but there must be a logic to it, an underlying rhythm, something that the driver will eventually learn to understand.

Realistic driving games tend to use real-world tracks as their levels, which requires less creativity from the level designer, but a huge amount of attention to detail, usually using photographs and measurements taken directly from the circuit. Another of the level designer's challenges is to ensure there are no unplanned short cuts through the level—checkpoints, both visible and hidden, must be placed intelligently.

Examples of excellent Racing game level design: *Moto GP, Super Mario Kart, F-Zero GX*

THIRDPERSON ADVENTURE

The key word here is "adventure": one of the main motivations in a standard TPA is exploration, which places pressure on the level designer to create an environment worth exploring. If the player doesn't find the world aesthetically interesting, they won't explore it; equally, if they don't think there's any point in twisting along that precarious precipice because the game's never offered them rewards before, they'll be uninterested in risking their lives.

Thirdperson adventures take on the exploratory heritage of the levels-and-ladders arcade adventures of yesteryear. But while jumping in 2D is child's play, moving—and jumping, and landing—an avatar in a 3D space is much more complex. Good level design uses visual clues to make it clear which parts of the level can be reached with perseverance, and which shouldn't be of interest to the player. Thirdperson adventures that offer freedom run the risk of losing the player's interest as he or she searches for their next task. If the game design insists on genuine freedom rather than simply the illusion of freedom, then clear signposting is critical to the game's success.

Examples of excellent TPA level design: *The Legend of Zelda: Ocarina of Time, Ico, Grand Theft Auto*

Top row, left-right: *Halo* by Bungie: Intelligent pick-up placement. *Half-Life* by Valve: Exceptional set-pieces and narrative. *Counter-Strike* by Valve: Teases out strategies for team play.

Middle row, left-right: *GTA3* by Rockstar: Always something to do. *Ico* by SCEI: A solid, beautiful, and internally-consistent universe. *The Legend of Zelda: The Ocarina of Time* by Nintendo: Like going exploring on vacation.

Bottom row, left-right: *Moto GP* by Climax: Proves the real world fun. *F-Zero GX* by Nintendo: Spinning courses in three dimensions. *Super Mario Kart* by Nintendo: Brilliant traditional circuit design.

ELEGANT LEVEL DESIGN

SUPER MONKEY BALL

There is no purer example of great level design than this. The game is simple—steer a ball through a maze, taking care not to fall off the edge. *Super Monkey Ball* begins gently enough, soon becomes tricky, and then, initially, apparently next-to-impossible. But actually, the goal is tantalizingly just out of reach. When you do fall there's no one to blame but yourself, and once a level is beaten it can be beaten time and time again.

SUPER MARIO 64

A playground you never get too old to explore, *Super Mario 64's* level design is gentle and coaxing. Each of the perfectly crafted worlds hides a number of stars that must be won by performing different tasks, but it says a lot about the environments that there's a great deal of fun to be had in just running around. Even then, the player's led by design: chains of coins entice the player to where the designer wants them to go.

ICO

It's not just the bewitching narrative that drives the player in *Ico*, but also the desire to visit more of the architecturally divine castle. Few game environments feel as solid as this, a tribute to the designers who constructed them. Working the standard levels and ladders gameplay into a realistic environment without resorting to cliché shows impressive imagination.

HALF-LIFE

An object lesson in level design for those who want to create narrative-led first person shooters, *Half-Life's* genius isn't just in its set pieces, or the way that the health-restoring pickups always seem to be just within reach. It's that the level designers manage to disguise the fact that the game is essentially one long corridor, by the creative use of 3D space and cleverly nudging the player down the correct path.

COUNTER-STRIKE

There can be no greater plaudit to great level design than from the community of people who love your work, and *Counter-Strike* is the most popular online FPS in the world. Beginning life as a hobbyist mod, and ending up as nothing less than a phenomenon, the game demonstrates that you don't have to be a professional game designer to design brilliant levels; in fact, there's no better way to get into the business.

THE GETAWAY

Less a triumph of design, but more one of brute force, *The Getaway* recreates a huge area of central London, street for street, storefront for storefront. Unfortunately for *The Getaway*, London wasn't designed as a videogame, and the game suffers because of the level design dictated to it. Still, this is a phenomenal achievement, and heading on a Sony-sponsored tourist trip around the city carries a great deal of charm.

1

2

3

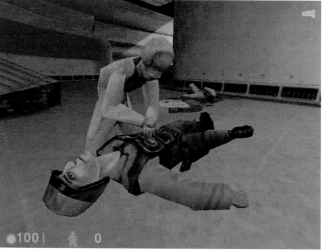

4

5

6

7

8

GRAND THEFT AUTO: VICE CITY

GTA suffered no such problems, because Vice City—the game world, and one huge level—was designed to exude entertainment at every street corner. Streets unexpectedly segue into river-jumping ramps, stairwells become routes to stupid stunts, and the airport isn't a real airport, it's just an excuse to crash lots of cars. It doesn't matter that the mission design within the world is hit and miss, because there's so much fun to be had in ignoring the challenges set for you and enjoying the rich interactivity of the game world.

DANCE DANCE REVOLUTION

It might not seem like there's a lot of level design in *Dance Dance Revolution*, but those who have played the game know that there's a good deal more to it than simply a piece of music and a random collection of arrows. Each direction is specifically tailored to the beat, each group of markers intended to shift the player's body in a certain way; to twist them, to confuse them, to make them dance. This type of level design may be more like choreography, but it's level design nonetheless, and shows the wide range of situations that level designers can find themselves in.

LEMMINGS

Fiendishly difficult puzzles marked the later level design of *Lemmings*, but puzzle design isn't simply about finding ways to hurt the brain of the player. *Lemmings* has a gentle difficulty curve, and the first handful of levels teach the player what skills their tribe are capable of, and how to use them in combination. Coming up with a way of doing that, but still keeping the levels involving and entertaining is as big a challenge as setting relatively incomprehensible problems that will stump addicts for days.

F-ZERO GX

In an article written for *Edge* magazine, *F-Zero GX's* designer Toshihiro Nagoshi compared racing game level design to writing a piece of music. *F-Zero GX's* tracks are the perfect proof of this, rolling symphonies that plead with the player to wring the very last bit of speed out of their vehicle. The courses are tough, but always fair, and the speed—along with the frame rate—rarely drops below breakneck.

1. **Super Monkey Ball**
Sega, 2001
2. **Super Mario 64**
Nintendo, 1996
3. **Ico**
SCEI, 2002
4. **Half-Life**
Vivendi, 1996
5. **Counter-Strike**
Valve, 1998
6. **The Getaway**
SCEE, 2002
7. **Grand Theft Auto: Vice City**
Rockstar, 2003
8. **Dance Dance Revolution**
Konami, 1998
9. **Lemmings**
Psygnosis, 1991
10. **F-Zero GX**
Nintendo, 2003

9

10

DARIO CASALI, VALVE SOFTWARE

Though academic qualifications rarely hurt a job application, there's really no substitute for experience. Dario Casali's first contact with professional level design was when id software, impressed with a set of single-player *Doom* levels he'd designed with his brother Milo, contacted him and asked if he'd be interested in designing 31 more for *Final Doom*.

Dario's next major project was for Valve Software, where he worked on the revolutionary, award-winning, PC firstperson shooter, *Half-Life*. More recently, he completed work on the sequel, *Half-Life 2*, which looks likely to break all the records set by its predecessor. His academic qualifications are OK too—before starting at Valve, he studied at Oxford University.

What does a level designer do on a day-to-day basis?
In the run up to completing *Half-Life 2*, we would work out of the bug database and fix as many bugs as we could day to day. Sometimes that meant fixing faulty map logic, sometimes it meant redesigning scenarios either because the solution to a puzzle is too subtle, or a combat encounter is too difficult.

When we're in the earlier stages of construction, day-to-day tasks involve working with different departments (sound, animation, art, and programming) to get the assets that our levels need to function. There is a lot of design work which several people can be involved with. Once the design is complete we begin to implement that design, we play test it, and adjust it based on feedback.

How much creative freedom does a level designer typically have? Is there a "typical" model?
The level designer is always involved in the initial design of the level. Along the road from construction to completion there is some freedom to interpret the design, but most of all, the final design will reflect the many hours of play testing and feedback we collect. The amount of freedom will vary from map to map. Usually if the level designer wants complete freedom in design, they will notice that the game needs something extra at a particular point, create the level in their spare time, and then present it to their team.

How important are basic pen and paper drafting skills to level designers?
Speaking for myself I have pretty much no artistic skills with pen and paper. There are some artistically talented members of each team who will sometimes illustrate the design we are working on either on a whiteboard or some large drawing paper. These are mainly to unify everyone's image of the level we are designing. I find sketching map layouts on whiteboards can really help me clarify a problem, but these sketches are never pretty.

Left: **Screenshots from** *Final Doom*, Dario Casali's first commercial project.

Opposite page: *Quake* deathmatch levels designed by Dario Casali. While level architecture has become more sophisticated, principles remain the same.

How have things changed over the last five years?

My job is now a lot more complicated then it ever was. As the engines and tools available to level designers get ever more sophisticated, we have to keep on top of it to push the envelope and make the best games possible.

What qualities/skills make a good level designer?

The ability to deal with feedback (this is the most important of all). A strong passion for making games (particularly, the game you're currently working on!). Being able to work with others and believe in their respective talents. The ability to work long hours and deal with stressful problems. A clear sense of what you want the player to experience. Creative problem solving. Managing a lot of resources simultaneously—a level designer is responsible for being on top of all the resources available to him (e.g., art, sound, engine features, design input, etc.).

What sort of demands does changing technology place on the level designer? How do you expect the level design process to change over the next five years?

As game systems get more complicated, so does the load on the level designer. Thankfully at Valve we have self-contained production groups such as the animation and scripts group. This group not only creates the tremendously complex animations and scripted scenes, but they also put them into the levels. This mitigates, to some degree, the amount I have to know about how it all works. This is also true of the art team. There are members of the art team who are also capable of working with the level tools, so they can carry out their work without the level designer getting involved.

As the next generation of tech becomes available, level designers are going to rely increasingly on separate production groups, and the management of information and work flow will become more important.

How crucial is "tweaking" to the level design process?

This is probably the most important element in a successful level. With so many creative talents on the team, it would be foolish not to invite and heed their input. Similarly, play testing is a crucial part of building a level. Play test as soon as you have a working model of the level, revise based on feedback, then play test again. Conduct this over and over until you're happy that the level construction is complete. Then, when the level is stable and all the elements are in, play test and tweak for another six months.

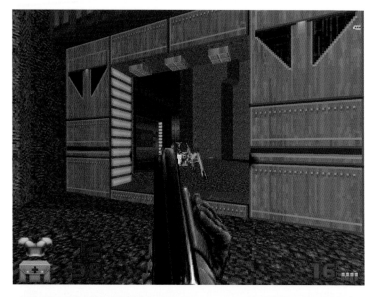

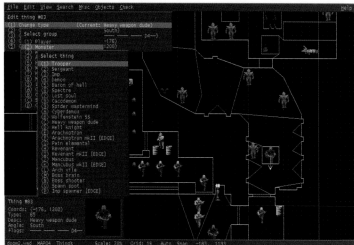

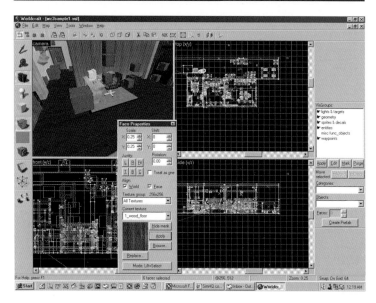

What does a level designer do on a day-to-day basis?

In the run up to completing *Half-Life 2*, we would work out of the bug database and fix as many bugs as we could day to day. Sometimes that meant fixing faulty map logic, sometimes it meant redesigning scenarios either because the solution to a puzzle is too subtle, or a combat encounter is too difficult.

When we're in the earlier stages of construction, day-to-day tasks involve working with different departments (sound, animation, art, and programming) to get the assets that our levels need to function. There is a lot of design work which several people can be involved with. Once the design is complete we begin to implement that design, we play test it, and adjust it based on feedback.

How much creative freedom does a level designer typically have? Is there a "typical" model?

The level designer is always involved in the initial design of the level. Along the road from construction to completion there is some freedom to interpret the design, but most of all, the final design will reflect the many hours of play testing and feedback we collect. The amount of freedom will vary from map to map. Usually if the level designer wants complete freedom in design, they will notice that the game needs something extra at a particular point, create the level in their spare time, and then present it to their team.

How important are basic pen and paper drafting skills to level designers?

Speaking for myself I have pretty much no artistic skills with pen and paper. There are some artistically talented members of each team who will sometimes illustrate the design we are working on either on a whiteboard or some large drawing paper. These are mainly to unify everyone's image of the level we are designing. I find sketching map layouts on whiteboards can really help me clarify a problem, but these sketches are never pretty.

Top: **Many budding level designers started by becoming hooked on** *Doom*.

Middle: **And then progressed to creating their own worlds in editors like this.**

Bottom: **These days, experience with** *Half-Life* **editor Worldcraft is likely to prove more useful.**

Opposite top: **3D level editors may look complex, but really they're just virtual block sets for kids who never grew out of Lego.**

Opposite bottom, left and right: **Dario Casali's widely respected** *Half-Life* **deathmatch level,** *Doublecross.*

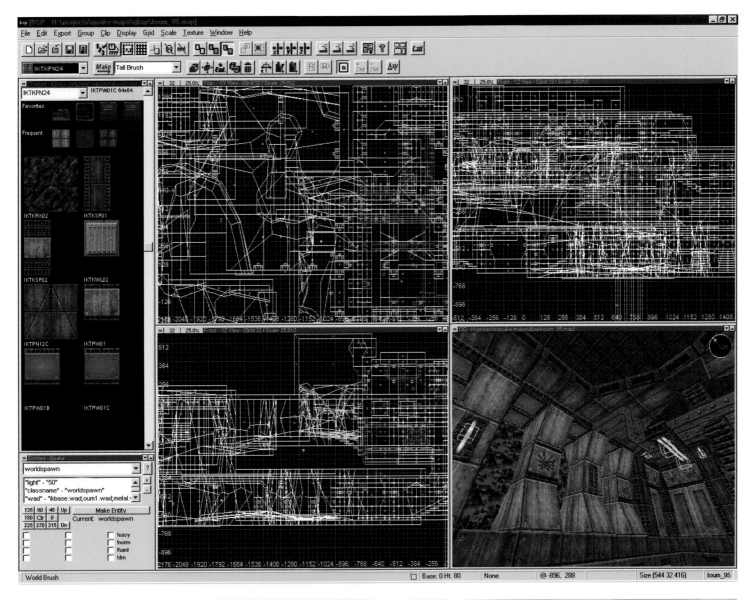

PART 03. PRODUCTION
CHAPTER FOUR

The lead artist will be responsible for the overall art direction of the game, which involves setting an appropriate mood, tone, and palette for the game's contents. Ten years ago, artists had to work within strict graphical limits, such as resolution and even the number of colors they could use, but every passing year sees these constraints evaporate further, and visuals are mostly dictated by the whims of the creatives involved, rather than restrictive hardware. That said, one part of the artist's job remains subject to current technological demands. 3D modeling involves constructing

ART AND ARTISTS

An artist's input into the game design process begins as early as the concept stage. Visual cues are often as important as anything else in the fight to get a game signed, and sketches—of everything from the lead characters through to the interface that will frame the game—can prove crucial to providing everyone involved with a "feel" for the game. It stands to reason then, that an artist's position is a creative one from the off. They are not just following orders; while visuals are often considered superficial, they define the game as much as its control system or level layout.

But the skills that they use during the progress of a project can vary wildly. Close to the idea of concept art is storyboarding— diagrammatically roughing out the camera movements and key shots—a technique that is more usually associated with film production. As narrative gaming creeps closer and closer to its cinematic cousin, so the techniques involved in its creation become more similar too, and the act of storyboarding is becoming a crucial aspect of game design. Even simpler, nonplot-based games may require moderate storyboarding, since all gaming features some sort of linear visual process, from title screen to introduction to full game to Game Over.

three-dimensional objects for use in-game, and since every visible vertex must be drawn, and processing power is limited, pressure is on artists to build things using as few polygons as possible.

Though the position barely existed five years ago, animators are now in increasing demand in the videogame industry. Responsible for making the elements of the game come to life, animators have an intuitive grasp of the physics of movement of real-life objects, and are able to create or replicate it with 3D tools detailed later in this chapter. Motion capture, the process of attaching movement sensors to a person and having them perform moves that you'd like in the game, is also heavily used in modern videogames, and animators will often have to interpret (and tidy up) the mass of data that comes with that.

Last, but not least, most videogame artists possess exceptional two-dimensional skills too, not least for providing the textures that are applied to the 3D models as "skins." Two-dimensional art is also often critical for the game's front-end and in-game interface, and good design there—a product of cooperation between the art and game design teams—can make the difference between a successful game and a frustrating one.

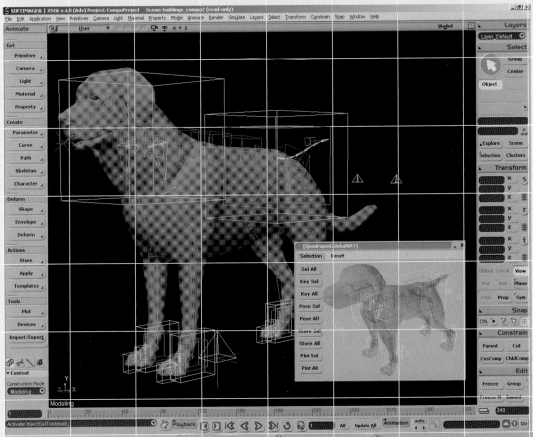

Top: **Maya from Alias.** Used in games such as *Gran Turismo 3*.

Bottom: **Softimage|XSI from Avid.** Used in games such as *Half-Life 2*.

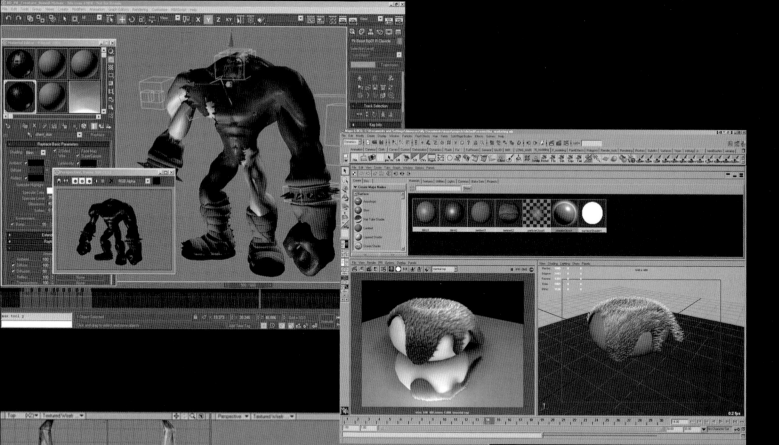

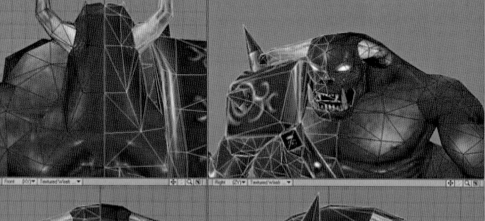

Above left: **3D Studio Max from Discreet. Used in games such as** *Call of Duty.*

Above: **Maya from Alias. Used in games such as** *Rallisport Challenge.*

Left: **LightWave 3D from NewTek. Used in games such as** *Doom 3.*

3D STUDIO MAX

The most widely known of the packages discussed here, 3D Studio MAX's status as the industry standard may now be in dispute, but it's still a safe bet for those wishing to get involved in three-dimensional construction. MAX's strength is not in animation, but in the construction of individual elements, objects, and scenes. It also has a very powerful internal lighting engine, of limited use for creating in-game items since videogame engines provide their own lighting, but critical for producing lifelike and compelling cut-scenes.

Notable games that use 3D Studio MAX: Konami's *Metal Gear Solid 2*, Rockstar's *Grand Theft Auto*

MAYA

Maya's biggest strength is its complexity, allowing experienced users to tailor it to their exact requirements. Of course, that's also its weakness, and newcomers to 3D art will doubtless find it intimidating. Maya's popularity in the movie and television industry initially brought it to the attention of videogame developers, but they've stayed with it because of its versatility. A powerful scripting language, excellent animation capabilities and dynamic simulation of all kinds of materials mean many consider Maya to be 3D design's future.

Notable games that use Maya: Polyphony Digital's *Gran Turismo 3*, Naughty Dog's *Jak and Daxter*

LIGHTWAVE 3D

If Maya's appeal is in having a wealth of options, then NewTek's LightWave 3D chooses simplicity to court its customers. Evolving from the Amiga-based Video Toaster that proved popular for low-budget CGI in the early-to-mid nineties, LightWave 3D's brutal animation system is compensated for by the speed at which it lets users create scenes. In other words it's simple but effective, with a deceptively large toolset, and it's increasingly popular with smaller companies that are producing games within short time frames.

Notable games that use LightWave 3D: Croteam's *Serious Sam*, Ion Storm's *Deus Ex*

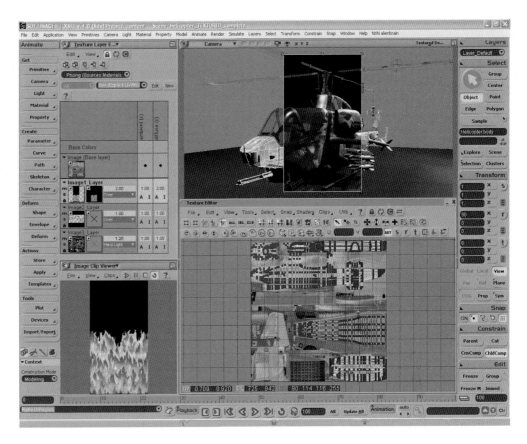

Above: Softimage|XSI from Avid. Used in games such as *Prince of Persia: The Sands of Time*.

SOFTIMAGE|XSI

Softimage's success in the movie and TV community has been helped by the fact that its parent company, Avid, produce a suite of popular editing packages. As you might expect, its strength is in movement, so its chief rival is Maya—and the recently adopted XSI format is helping it regain market share from its competitor. The software also now possesses direct support for Xbox and PlayStation 2 development, making it a popular choice among videogame developers looking for a minimum of compatibility headaches.

Notable games that use Softimage|XSI: Valve's *Half-Life 2*, Square Enix's *Drag-on Dragoon*.

PHOTOSHOP

Adobe Photoshop's all-encompassing fame as a photo-editing tool ensures even newcomers to the profession will have heard of it. An elegant, powerful software package that allows manipulation of two-dimensional images, Photoshop's chief employment in videogame design is in creating and editing textures to skin 3D objects with. Many an artist has spent hours in Photoshop coming up with that perfect concrete texture; it might not sound like much fun, but it needs doing, and Photoshop makes it as painless as possible.

Notable games that use Photoshop: Just about all of them

chapter 04. art and artists

DIFFERENT ARTISTIC STYLES

Below: *Baldur's Gate II*, from Bioware, 2000

Bottom: *Rez* from Sega, 2001

Opposite, top: *The Getaway 2* from SCEE, 2004

Opposite, middle: *Timesplitters 2* from Eidos, 2003

Opposite, bottom: *XIII* from Ubisoft, 2003

FANTASTICAL

Videogames have been about dungeons and dragons since the beginning, but it's only recently that their graphical engines have been able to approximate the fabulous artwork that used to adorn the boxes of their pen and paper namesake. A fantasy setting gives artists a chance to create their own mythos, carving imaginary beasts from raw lumps of 3D space and their own feverish imaginations. Unfortunately, the genre's popularity means that creating something orcish-yet-innovative is difficult; dreaming up new nightmares for players isn't as easy as you might think.

ABSTRACTION

Games which aren't tied to standard Earth rules let their artists' imaginations run free. *Rez* is a superb example of constrained abstraction. Faced with the opportunity to create five different levels representing the internals of a computer, the designers take electronic, organic, and mythological themes and weave them together with a sophistication that matches the game's synesthetic background. Artists plunging into abstraction's deep space must work within their own guidelines to create something that is still internally consistent; a complete free rein would create a visual mess.

PHOTOREALISM

While videogames have striven to achieve photorealism for some time, they are still some distance from achieving it, and its pursuit is something of a double-edged sword. Games like *The Getaway 2* make it their focus, and push consumers closer to virtual reality than ever before. The mainstream audience crave the opportunity to explore new, real spaces, and it becomes a selling point. But if your visuals tell the user that what they see on screen is meant to be real, then they are far more likely to spot the things that aren't—the points where the technology comes up short, and creates a gap between the on-screen action and common sense that your imagination isn't primed to fill.

CARICATURING

The solution, as demonstrated in *Timesplitters 2*, is an approximation of reality. The game has plenty of human characters, but they're all rendered in an exaggerated style that intuitively tells players that they're not in a space that follows humankind's visual rules, and allows the game designer to render a coherent world well within the capabilities of the system. The main problem is getting the style right; while few people have a problem with the way the real world looks, an artistic interpretation is much less universal.

CEL-SHADING

Somewhat out of fashion now, cel-shading is a visual style which "flattens" groups of colors to produce the look of a cartoon. While in-game objects must be designed with it in mind, the process of cel-shading a game can be as simple as changing a small piece of code in the game's rendering engine. Bright, simplistic and fun, the look was made popular by Sega's *Jet Set Radio* at the turn of the century, but has recently been championed by Ubisoft's firstperson shooter, *XIII*.

Q&A

SAM COATES, LEAD ARTIST, TEAM SOHO, SCEE

Team Soho's *The Getaway* was one of videogaming's most ambitious undertakings; it mapped out central London, and set a free-roaming crime thriller within its now-digital confines. The scope of *The Getaway 2* is even wider, the team employing videogaming's latest artistic techniques to make its universe as realistic as possible.

From the painstaking recreation of London street textures, through the videogame staples of 3D modeling and skinning, to advanced motion capture, art on *The Getaway 2* comes in a variety of guises. Helping stitch them all together is Sam Coates, lead artist at SCEE's Team Soho.

What's the most satisfying thing about your job?
Obviously watching things come together at the end of a project is creatively satisfying, the point where all the preparation and uphill slog comes to fruition and you can put in the personal touches and have fun polishing the game. But for me the really satisfying thing is meeting people who are playing your game and enjoying it, especially when they don't know you, who you are, or that you made it. Best of all is being at a party or even on a bus or train and overhearing people talking about the game you've made. Nothing beats hearing a total stranger talk about how much fun they're having. It makes it all worthwhile.

What's the biggest challenge facing videogame artists?
As well as learning a whole heap of techniques which have only previously been used in high-end rendering and postproduction, the three main challenges as I see them are:

Creating truly interactive worlds: at the moment the big thing is deepening the experience, allowing players to interact with many more objects and the world itself in new and interesting ways. Artists are having to learn to build with this in mind. We've come a long way with building static worlds that are visually rich, back up the action, and make it dramatic and exciting to play, worlds which are composed and lit to look stunningly beautiful. The trick is going to be to keep all of these qualities and push our worlds to be even better, while at the same time letting people interact more. Once everything has the potential to move, shift, and change, then keeping creative control is a new challenge.

Satisfying huge expectation and appetites: a significant part of the games market wants, and now expects, each generation of games to be a larger and more complex gaming experience than the previous generations. Giving them this without production times spiraling out of control is going to be a challenge. To make things even more complicated, at the same time as delivering larger-scaled productions we're also pushing to increase quality and make graphics which are closer and closer to the CG shots that people see in the movies.

Animation and AI cross-over: at the moment, games characters are rather lifeless and wooden. In the future I expect to see game developers spend much more time on animation systems that put much more characterization into the game animation itself rather than cut-sequences. At the moment it's very early days but we are just beginning to see this happen in a few titles and starting to pay off. The really interesting thing will be to see how animation tools have to change to keep up, I can see the game animator's role changing significantly with an entirely new set of tools to allow them to "direct" virtual actors and define their personalities and responses made up from much more complex blends of animation data.

All images: *The Getaway: Black Monday* by SCEE.

Is there anything you've learned while you've been in the job that you wish you knew from the start?

Well there are loads of different things but if I had my time again and could do one thing differently, I wish I'd studied production design after completing my first degree. It's taken me a long time to really find my feet and learn the additional skills and sympathies needed to translate my 3D skills and really make something dramatic and entertaining.

What's the best way of getting into a position as an artist or animator in the games industry? What qualifications / experience do you look for in an artist?

At the risk of sounding like a parent, get a good degree.

We take people from many different backgrounds, illustration, fine art, product design, sculpture, architecture, traditional animation, etc. There are also a lot of relatively new undergraduate courses that teach computer modeling and animation in general and some even have game-specific modules or optional components.

The time you spend at university is relatively short and, in my opinion, you should spend it learning the really core art and design skills behind what you do, observation, color theory, perception, composition, etc. The temptation is always to turn to computers too soon and learn software to get yourself your first job. Although this can work in the short term, you lose out on the foundations and have to relearn these skills on the job when the pressures of work mean you really don't have the time. The danger here is that if you don't have a solid general art education to fall back on, you essentially become a technician and constantly have to chase new versions of software to remain valuable to an employer. If you have a deeper skill set to draw on then you're much more likely to be able to contribute to the design process and be involved in the creative and decision-making side of things.

With this very much in mind, I think the best advice is not to get too specific too early on in your education. I would suggest either doing a first degree in a transferable arts or design discipline, then a more vocational or industry-related masters, or at the very least focus on courses that will give you good all-round design and art foundations rather than just access to computers and tutors who are good with software. Try to choose a course with links to a larger art and design faculty, preferably one that teaches animation and film as well, somewhere where you can study and socialize with people from other complementary areas and take modules in those areas yourself.

If at all possible, try and get some work experience while you study, preferably at a games company, if you're lucky enough to find one that will take you. Failing that any graphics or design agency experience will help, as would time at a film or television production company although places here are even more difficult to come by.

All images: *The Getaway: Black Monday* by SCEE.

03.05

BRITNEY
Britney Spears released her own videogame *Britney's Dance Beat* (above), which attempted to piggyback the popularity of the *Dancing Stage* games. While it was a glossy, stylized affair, featuring Britney's most popular songs of the time, it was utterly misjudged, offering a tepid version of a complicated genre. The choreography was lame—surprising, considering the on-stage exertions of Ms Spears—and the game short-lived.

PART 03. PRODUCTION
CHAPTER FIVE

AUDIO DEVELOPMENT

It's an oft-repeated phrase: "Games are following in the footsteps of movies." The comparison is regurgitated so frequently, it's rarely questioned. Yet while the wider issues are open to some debate, the early history of movies shares some remarkable similarities with the early history of videogames.

Consider the first examples of moving footage: blocky, grainy, and black and white. Ditto computer games. Movies were originally silent; the same was true of games (indeed, the computing equivalent of an organ player at the front of the theater was a C90 cassette on a nearby Hi-Fi, playing early 1980s pop tunes). And as audio standards improved in films, so the wider entertainment industries began embracing the medium. We're at a similar stage now where EA games boast more licensed music tracks than most compilation albums.

It wasn't like this in the early days, when maverick musicians were offered tiny sections of memory for audio tracks and sound effects. Simple, mono sound effects operating within a few hundred bytes were the audio capabilities of the first wave of dedicated consoles. As a result, most games only boasted a couple of grunts by way of a soundtrack.

Back then, game audio was a luxury few could afford because the system RAM was so low. Specific tools were few and far between. Coders developed their own routines, which usually involved programming individual notes into a hex editor. It was time-consuming and laborious—but as the challenges were so great, those early musicians pushed each system to its limits, and enjoyed doing so.

It wasn't until 1983 that Matthew Smith broke new ground in so many ways with *Manic Miner*. One of the most important advances was its first use of in-game music—a suitably awful rendition of *In the Hall of the Mountain King* from Edvard Grieg's incidental music to Henrik Ibsen's play, *Peer Gynt*. For the time, it was an impressive achievement, integrating the audio and sound effects on the one mono track.

Rapidly, each new hardware platform began to allow further progression. Three-channel sound appeared on the VIC 20 in 1981. Home computers of the early- to mid-80s even began offering end-user sound programs—the C64, for example, boasted a peripheral that fitted over its standard keyboard to offer a very simple synthesizer.

The most famous musicians of the era were Rob Hubbard, Martin Galway, and Richard Joseph—and the C64 in particular, with its complicated, digitally controlled SID chip, really drove in-game soundtracks. To this day, these original tunes are rerecorded and remixed, with many available on retro music CDs.

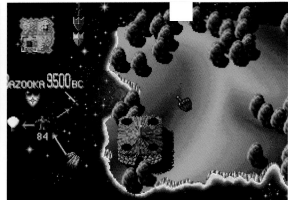

EA

Electronic Arts has invested an extraordinary amount of time and money in its in-game audio. Standardized across a delivery format called "EA Trax," the firm works with up-and-coming and established brands to provide the in-game soundtrack to the majority of its sports titles such as *NBA Live 2004* (above). Artists such as Franz Ferdinand, Robbie Williams, and Queens of the Stone Age have all worked with the publisher to include their own songs in EA titles. It's predicted that games are becoming a more powerful audio delivery tool than radio for a certain demographic. The evolution of the service will be to buy the tracks you're listening to.

NOMAD SOUL

French developer Quantic Dream embarked on an interesting collaboration with David Bowie for its *Nomad Soul* (1999). Bowie, along with Reeves Gabrels, wrote the entire soundtrack exclusively for the game, consisting of eight songs: *Thursday's Child, Something in the Air, Survive, Seven, We All Go Through, The Pretty Things Are Going To Hell, Omikron (New Angels of Promise)*, and *The Dreamers*, seven of which appeared later on David Bowie's album, *Hours*. He also featured in the game itself (below) along with his wife, Iman.

MEGA LO MANIA

Mega Lo Mania (1991, above) is widely considered to be the first game that employed professional voice actors. The game (above) hailed from much-loved UK developer Sensible Software, who liked to fool around. The original recordings for the *Mega Lo Mania* game had one of the main characters swearing. This was trimmed for the game to just say, "No way!" although the original audio files were still stored on the disks.

TALKIES

The advent of the CD (now DVD) as the delivery format of choice allowed developers and audio technicians to experiment with professional voice-acting. This was a radical sea change, yet one which caused unexpected outcry. Games such as *Day of the Tentacle* (above) were often released in two versions: one subtitled and one with spoken audio, which ran the danger of infuriating passionate gamers by featuring voices different from those they had imagined.

The 16-bit machines offered musicians even further options. Sampling—although it had been possible in a very limited capacity beforehand—became a practical way of further enhancing soundtracks. And things improved even further in the late 80s when Sega's Mega Drive offered FM synthesis. It was also around this time that the first PC soundcards were released. Prior to this, developers had to rely on the PC's internal Texas Instrument sound chip—capable of only the most basic of sounds. And the SNES boasted sophisticated audio power for the time— eight independent channels and advanced sample manipulation.

The real breakthrough in music soundtracks, as with so many game innovations, came with the PlayStation, which combined a modest amount of audio RAM—512K—with serious offline storage. Musicians could opt to load the entire soundtrack and sound effects in at the start, or stream from CD as needed. This former method resulted in an often retro quality: *Final Fantasy VII*, for example, sounded almost SNES-like as its audio was retained in RAM.

These days, audio directors have ever-increasing specifications to experiment with. The PlayStation 2 offers 48 channels of sound, across audio RAM of 2MB. PlayStation 3 will amplify this further. The challenge nowadays is what to do with it all….

AUDIO TOOLS AND TECHNICAL CHALLENGES

The tools used to compose, record, edit, and implement videogame music vary from team to team. Many audio technicians who've grown up with the industry are loyal to one particular package. Like learning a new operating system, sometimes the documented performance benefits are outweighed by the inconvenience of feeling your way around a new software package, particularly in a discipline that embraces so much experimentation.

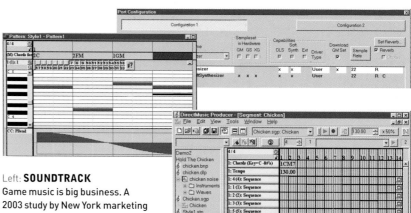

Left: **SOUNDTRACK**
Game music is big business. A 2003 study by New York marketing firm ElectricArtists found that 40 percent of games players purchased the CD of a band they'd heard in a videogame. Nine out of 10 respondents in the survey of 1,000 hard-core gamers said they remembered a game's music after they stopped playing it. Good news for Good Charlotte, who appeared most recently in *NFL Street*.

Above: **DIRECT MUSIC**
Released as part of the DirectX 7 SDK, DirectMusic—the API—and DirectMusic Producer are Microsoft tools designed to plug composers into the heart of its operating systems. Applications that use the DirectMusic application programming interface are not restricted to playing content from DirectMusic Producer. They can play wave and MIDI files, and can construct music and sound effects by playing individual notes on available DLS instruments. However, the full power of DirectMusic can be unleashed with files authored in DirectMusic Producer.

The truth is, there's no one package endorsed by all. RenderWare's dominance of the independent development sector makes it an obvious choice for those already using other elements of the package. Subsequently, using RenderWare Audio is often a convenient decision—and its diverse feature list, small memory footprint, and portability makes up for the power of an independent suite of software.

DirectMusic, GameCoda, Nuendo, and SoundForge are other popular choices out of a confusing array of competing applications. Aspiring game audio engineers will often learn a tool from a mentor and stick with that for many years. Typically, the features offered by the major packages are present in many others—so portability from platform to platform does need to be considered. Regardless of how competent an operator of various applications an individual can be, all of it is worthless if that program does not integrate effectively with the game engine. For that reason, many large developers working on bespoke engine technology will also create their own music drivers.

The best game audio hails from teams or individuals in continual touch with the design and development team. Long gone are the days where a musician would be presented with a brief which listed sections of music and required sound effects and told simply to get on with it.

Adaptive or interactive soundtracks offer the greatest scope for creativity. And a modern game can require hundreds of individual sound effects—excluding any recording dialog. It's for this reason that audio requirements need to be drawn up at the design document stage. As well as presenting a framework for the overall structure and volume of sound required, it'll also offer a hint of how realistic any audio aspirations are.

It's important to consider which sections of the game actually require music. Like enthusiastic kids coloring with crayons, it's often possible to cram too much into a finite space, ruining the overall effect. Music pacing is a mechanic gamers understand; when the score goes quiet, they know they're in trouble.

Movie musicians score over rough cuts. While this is rarely possible in games—test levels often bear scant relation in all but the most basic mechanics to finished code—it's vital to see the game in production throughout. Integral teams have

Right: NUENDO

Aimed at the audio for film, video, and interactive media markets, the Nuendo Media Production System is a modular system based on an audio software application for the Macintosh and Windows 98/NT/2000 platforms, which includes several hardware accessories. Nuendo features up to 200 tracks of 24 bit/96 kHz digital audio, advanced-featured surround mixing, a Video-Track, and MIDI-Tracks, along with the most comprehensive functions for digital audio available.

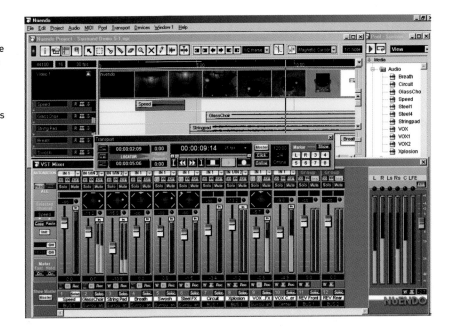

Below: FABLE

Movie composer Danny Elfman recently composed the main theme for Lionhead's *Fable*. It was an extravagance, for sure, and of questionable contribution to the game's overall success. But that's not the point—not only will Elfman's involvement encourage other high-profile composers to tackle the medium, but Lionhead's attitude to audio is encouraging for interactive musicians who must often fight to get a larger share of the total budget.

Below: SOUNDFORGE

Soundforge is the industry standard for editing sound files and has long had excellent support for MP3. It's a meaty program with an intuitive interface and superior speed—vital when processing modern soundtracks. It can batch-process audio files and can also accept video files. Loop creation and spectral analysis capabilities complete the picture along with the capability to rip from and write tracks to a CD.

this advantage over external musicians, but even storyboards and movie files when available can provide inspiration on the central themes, if not the timing.

Frequently, traditional rules need to be ripped up. Composition classes often emphasize the importance of repetition—and videogame music may have historically been famous for tunes based around a single central theme—but tastes have changed. Modern gamers expect diversity. A 30-hour game needs more than 30 minutes of music.

Don't be afraid to experiment. Sound can often hail from unusual sources. Specific sound effect libraries can prove expensive, while home-grown audio can be used in unusual ways—standard animal noises reprocessed in imaginative ways, for example, can provide effective monster noises.

This type of cost-conscious attitude is often vital. Research has shown that videogame players can rate the audio track forming as much as 30 percent of their overall enjoyment of a given game. However, typically, funds are all too often allocated to other areas over and above sound—with often less than five percent of the total development budget under the control of the audio director.

But don't let all this discourage you. Game audio is being increasingly recognized—both by the industry itself and those outside of it. BAFTA (the British Academy of Film and Television Arts), for example, acknowledges and honors the very best in-game audio. There is a trend for top talent such as Danny Elfman—alongside contemporary pop musicians—to be eager for their work to be featured in games. It was recently suggested that modern gamers hear more audio through computer and videogames than anywhere else. Maybe the Buggles were right after all: Videogames killed the radio stars.

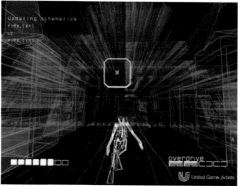
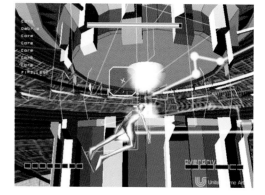

Above, left to right: **Three images from** *Rez*, developed and published by Sega.

Below: *FIFA 2005*, published by EA.

REZ

A game that has to be heard as well as seen, *Rez* divided the gaming community with its innovative use of visuals and audio—but to those in the know, it's regarded as one of the most important games of the current era. Hailing from Sega's United Game Artists stable, who had previously developed the insanely catchy and stylish *Space Channel 5*, it's an audio-visual tour de force. Players assume the role of a hacker sent into a computer to eliminate a virus. So far, so *Tron*. But *Rez* excels through the simplicity of the game, the beautiful design, and the interactive audio.

Each level begins with a simple techno beat. Enemies appear on screen and can be shot individually, or grouped together in a high-scoring chain. Gameplay-wise, it's as on the rails as you get—but the real interaction comes from the TV's speakers. Every time an enemy is targeted, it emits a beat—be that a synth, a rim-shot, or any other type of electro pulse. As they're destroyed, they also emit a sound—not an explosion as such, but yet more beats. Everything is timed to perfection. Rather than producing a rambling, jumbled mess, the techno soundtrack works brilliantly, even appealing to those who despise the music-game genre.

As the level design and enemy frequency increase in intensity, so does the underlying beat. Players discover themselves tapping their feet along with their fingers, as the hypnotic fusion of simple vector graphics, metamorphosing upgrades and incessant, pulsating audio combine to create a unique gaming experience.

Rez can be completed within an hour. But that's not the point. Most who fall for its seductive beauty find themselves treating it more like an album than a game—simply skipping back to the start and listening to it all over again.

FIFA SERIES

On the pitch, the *Pro Evolution Soccer* series beats the *FIFA International Football* series about a million-nil. But the latter's enduring populist appeal is undoubtedly down to EA's trademark polish, and this is nowhere more evident than in the sophisticated commentary technology.

The 2004 incarnation of the series is reputed to have used over 20,000 separate lines of commentary, split between the resident pundits. As a feat of logistics it's impressive enough, but the skilful weaving of these disjointed lines into coherent and sensible observation is what really astounds.

Coding routines to recognize on-screen player actions and pull voice from a bank of sounds is a challenge. Konami's *Pro Evolution* series fails miserably, and is nothing more sophisticated than streaming "He shoots!" (or similar) whenever the shoot button is pressed. When players are in the box, this is obviously relevant. But when the button is hit accidentally from inside the player's half, it's as amateurish as it is inappropriate.

EA, however, has implemented a sophisticated system that analyzes context as well as button presses and joystick waggles—with almost total success. The banter between the two men on the microphone appears almost natural—certainly as lifelike as we can expect from an audio system stringing random lines of text together. Little touches, such as player names recorded in various levels of excitement and the illusion of memory, as commentators recall earlier misses, complete the illusion of spontaneity. And add to this the authentic crowd noises—complete with celebratory cheers and derisory boos—and it's the total package.

MONTY ON THE RUN

When Commodore 64 magazine *Zzap! 64* awarded *Monty on the Run's* music 98 percent, it was more a commentary on the state of in-game audio than the quality of that particular soundtrack—amazing as it was for the time. It was, however, an indication of the shape of things to come, as its composer, Rob Hubbard, went on to dominate the airwaves for a generation of games. While Rob's innovative methods for squeezing the utmost from simple hardware aren't relevant for today's powerful home consoles, they do offer thoughts for writing contemporary music for limited specifications, such as the emerging mobile platforms, for example.

Back in the day when simple sound chips offered little scope for high-quality audio, Rob crammed so much life into the three-channel audio that it compensated for the game's derivative platform approach—possibly the first example of music genuinely enhancing the overall experience.

Rob built his own music utility, which was able to take hi-fi samples and compress and arrange them into code suitable for the 64's SID chip. For *Monty on the Run*, he managed to squeeze in pleasing violin samples and a guitar solo; literally unheard-of in those days. While these restrictions don't apply to today's audio technicians, the spirit of experimentation lives on.

Below: *Monty on the Run*, published by Gremlin.

Above: *GTA: Vice City*, developed by Rockstar Games and published by Take 2 Interactive in 2002.

A prolific composer, Rob was responsible for more than 75 Commodore 64 games between 1985 and 1989, producing classics such as *Sanxion*, *Zoids*, and *International Karate+*. His distinctive style—which he applied brilliantly to diverse genres, both gaming and musical—proved so popular, that his credits on a game could boost sales.

Rob still composes, but mainly for his own pleasure. In 1989 he joined Electronic Arts, providing soundtracks for its turn of the decade titles. He remains there to this day under the guise of audio technical director.

GTA: VICE CITY

Yet another example of the GTA series as trail-blazer. The in-car radio has been used throughout the series, but it really came into its own in *Vice City*, a game which showed the industry how to cooperate effectively with the music business.

As *Vice City* is based in the '80s—the decade much of its audience grew up in—the soundtrack is comprised almost entirely of original '80s music. Of course, the developer was helped by the enormous success of *GTA:III*, which dominated the charts the year prior to *Vice City*'s release. Its sales obviously convinced the record labels of the benefit of widespread in-game distribution, rather than simply demanding significant and restrictive licensing fees.

The soundtrack took eight months to assemble—a huge time to allocate to audio. The decision to pursue such a wide range of music was dictated by the game's free-roaming style of gameplay. *GTA III* boasted a soundtrack of around three and a half hours, which is lengthy in anyone's book—but consider the fact that players could enjoy upward of 100 hours roaming Liberty City and one can appreciate how its open-ended structure could have been compromised by repetitive audio.

Vice City's soundtrack spanned seven CDs when it was released separately, each crammed with a distinctive style that reflected the playlists of the individual music radio stations. Users were given the option to change radio stations—though not individual tracks—at will, the idea being to create an audio canvas that would reflect the type of action the player was involved in. Players soon decided upon favorite stations for particular pursuits, be they cruising along the beach, tearing through streets on high-speed pursuits, or simply causing random havoc. Sure, it's interactive audio in the most basic sense, but the way it's done is an absolute triumph.

Q&A

RICHARD JOSEPH, AUDIO DIRECTOR, ELIXIR STUDIOS

Richard Joseph started out in the games industry in 1986, working with publisher Palace Software. Since then, he's worked variously for The Bitmap Brothers, Millennium, and in a freelance capacity before joining Elixir Studios where he occupies the position of audio director.

Over the course of his career, Richard has composed and implemented soundtracks for over 100 games, including such seminal classics as *The Chaos Engine, Speedball 2, Gods, James Pond, Mega Lo Mania*, and *Sensible Soccer*. His company Audio Interactive produced the soundtrack to *Theme Park World*, which won a BAFTA award. Most recently, Richard and the team at Elixir have completed the score to *Republic: The Revolution* and *Evil Genius*, which was also nominated for a BAFTA.

How did you get involved in writing music for computer and videogames?

Just prior to joining the industry, I bought a Sinclair Spectrum. It absolutely fascinated me. I was keen on music technology anyway—always experimenting with synthesizers, tape recorders, things like that. This was before MIDI came out; we were playing around with various early computer-based keyboards like Emulators and Fairlights, though they were very expensive. It was an interesting time. The technology was very basic. Yamaha brought out a thing called the CX5M, which I've still got. That was relatively cheap thing—something like $800 or so. It was a dedicated music computer, with eight mono-channels using FM synthesis.

I'd been recently commissioned to write 100 tunes for children's story tapes. I spent most of the early time doing those and experimenting with this new technology. Then, one day, I picked up a copy of *Melody Maker* and in it was an advertisement for a games musician. That kind of thing was unheard-of in

those days—there must have been only five people or so in the country doing it. So I saw this advert and thought: "Right, I've got 100 tunes; I'll find the best 10 and take those to them."

I got the job and dumped everything else I was doing before, which was the usual musician stuff of trying to get into TV, radio, adverts, film…that world, as such.

How did things differ back then?

Back then, I'd use something like 3K to do a whole soundtrack, then the programmer Richard Leinfellner would come on the phone and say "snip, snip, snip," and I'd need to get it into 2K. And that was for audio and sound effects.

We were always very ambitious at Palace. Take *Barbarian*, for example. Steve Brown, the designer, wanted the soundtrack to sound like a *Conan* movie. What they wanted me to do was make the Commodore 64 sound like an orchestra, which, of course, was impossible. However, you could use various devices to get the feel across, to emulate the sound of an orchestra—and that's what I tried to do.

Back then I very much had to prove myself—I was competing against someone like Rob Hubbard, who was a genius. So every single thing I did I'd labor over. Take *Stifflip and Co*, for instance. With that, I tried to compose a very traditional English-sounding audio track. It wasn't the sort of thing you'd hear at the time.

You were among the early pioneers of interactive music, particularly with *The Chaos Engine*. How did that come about, and what did you learn about creating interactive pieces of music?

We realized when we were creating the game that it was perfectly suited to small sections of music. The game had many small areas that needed to be completed in sequence, and each of those reached a climax. So we thought it'd be nice to have different music for each section.

During the game's development, I'd spent a serious amount of time listening to early Prodigy. Analyzing it, I'd

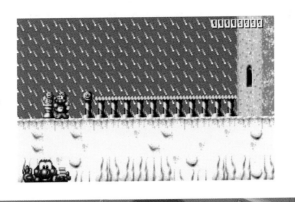

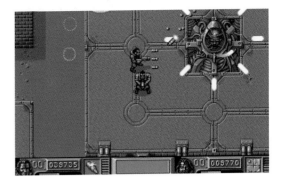

Far right: *The Chaos Engine*, developed by The Bitmap Brothers.

Right: *James Pond 2*, developed and published by EA.

Below: *Evil Genius*, developed by Elixir Studios.

figured out it worked in simple one-bar phrases. That was all they needed for each section: simple one-bar motifs.

I felt it was possible to pull that down even further, into two beats—that is, a soundtrack that could change every two beats. It really suited *The Chaos Engine* to have music like that, so you could go from one section to another and within just two beats the whole sound had changed.

We also made it so that if you returned to an area you'd previous completed—that is, collected everything you needed to, and shot every enemy—the game would move to a slower version of the original music which said aurally: "Hey, I've done this bit." We pieced together a load of different ideas and it just gelled.

But what we learned was that this wasn't an interactive soundtrack in the way many people think of it. I firmly believe

that a truly interactive soundtrack—one that puts layer upon layer—is not practical. It doesn't work.

I've heard soundtracks where they attempt to do this. You'll be walking along and all of a sudden, a hi-hat will come in or something. You can't do this with music. If you take bits out or add bits in, it's not the same. Music is the sum total of what you're hearing. It's built specifically to be that piece of music.

Of course, tastes will change. I believe in a generation's time the way we listen to music will be radically different—and this kind of layered music will become more acceptable. You'll be able to have contrasting melodies—say, one "good" piece of music over a "bad" piece—played simultaneously. It'll be new music that we've never heard before. People will be able to work interactively with it because they'll have grown up with it. It'll sound horrible to us, of course, but those growing up with it will find it perfectly acceptable.

Does it pay to use off-the-shelf tools or your own proprietary technology?

I tend to favor our own technology. My experience of modern sound tools is not great. I got hold of DirectMusic, installed it, started working on it, and dumped it virtually straight away. I felt it was a program that had been put together by people that weren't writing music for games, or to entertain other people. It was like an academic exercise more than anything else. I know some people who have attempted to make careers using it, but I firmly believe they're barking up the wrong tree.

I will work with postproduction stuff like *Nuendo* and *Soundforge*. But mainly we work with our own proprietary technology. Our programmer Andy Mucho has written some amazing drivers that'll power the audio. We've just worked on two realtime strategy games. I call them four-dimensional games, because you've got your width, height, and depth—but you've also got time. It's not like a film, which is entirely linear—something could literally go on forever. And things requiring audio cues can happen anywhere at any time.

What we've had to do is build software that will cope with this. If you've got a thousand things going on in front of you, you've got to be able to make sure that only the most relevant sounds are heard at any given time. You don't want people to go and switch it off.

Andy's an amazing programmer. With *Evil Genius*, it was the first time I've seen a magazine comment specifically on the audio technology. And that's immensely rewarding.

What are the things to bear in mind when recording dialog?
You've got to be careful of actors hamming it up just because they're doing a game. Consider that you might hear a phrase a dozen times—the skill comes in making sure that the delivery of it is something that you hardly notice.

A game is developed over a long period of time. You have to keep going back and changing dialog. So it's really important to make sure all your settings are the same every time you go back into the studio, otherwise you'll get a completely different tone. Another important thing to remember is to ensure that key voices are performed by people who know what they're doing.

Can a good soundtrack really make a bad game better? Can a bad soundtrack really detract from a good game?
Yes, to both questions—although it's made more difficult because music's always a matter of taste. For *Republic*, everyone loved the soundtrack—we got a BAFTA nomination for it, and it was fantastic. But then I went up on a forum and saw a post that said: "I think the music sucks." What I realized was that this person hates orchestral music. For him, the music didn't work and it ruined the game.

Below: *Sensible Soccer*, developed by Sensible Software.

Bottom: *Theme Park World*, developed by Bullfrog, with a BAFTA-winning soundtrack.

Below left: *Republic: The Revolution*, developed by Elixir Studios, with a BAFTA-nominated soundtrack.

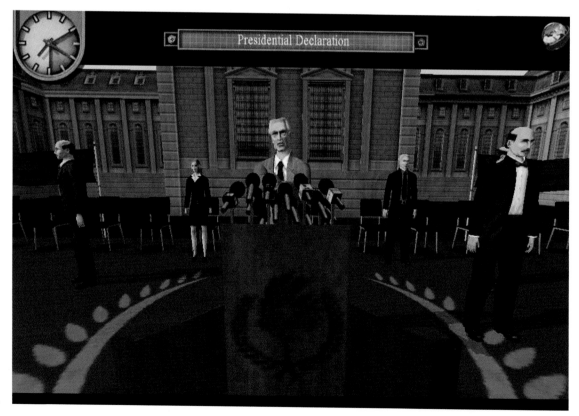

Take *Doom 3*, for example. You play it and you pick up on all the sound in the background. All the rooms have a pitch or a sound to them. It's like "Music Concrete" (experimental music using tapes and electronics from the 50s and 60s); it's music that isn't music. And it works. So well, in fact, that I think the developers actually ended up replacing the original music. Which appears to have been a great move. It's making a lot of others doing game audio think innovatively about the way they create their own soundtracks.

It takes a bold decision to do something as different as this. With *Gods*, we decided to have no music at all in the game, because we really wanted to create a "You're there" atmosphere. You don't have music in real life. And in *The Chaos Engine*, we decided to have no bullet sounds—again, something not considered the norm.

But that's what I'm about; experimenting with weird ideas. One of my favorite soundtracks is *Mercenary* on the C64, which has no music and virtually no sound. But it's so atmospheric. It's perfect.

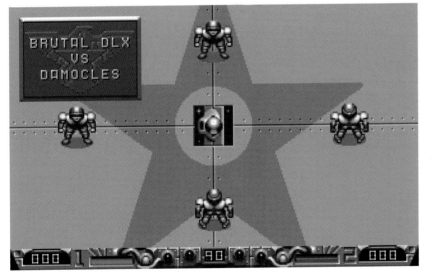

Above: *Speedball 2*, developed by The Bitmap Brothers.

Can any traditional musician write game soundtracks?
It's difficult. Movies and TV are linear experiences. Each moment is timed to perfection. You'll tug at the heart strings of someone and then maybe throw something else straight at them. But all the time, the music is timed perfectly to the flow of the film. But with games, the player is directing it.

Take something like a thirdperson game. You can have a bit of music that represents going to the next puzzle, which can be a linear piece. But then when the player reaches this puzzle, hours could be spent trying to solve it and immediately the linearity drops away.

People often get stuck over this idea of interactive music. But it's quite simple to produce a never-ending piece that reflects the state of the game and still remains musically "correct." We do this by creating a pool of musical phrases, which we splice together at random. If you have enough of these you can create the illusion of a never-ending piece. In simple terms, all you then need are three states—neutral, good, and bad. It's then just a case of swapping between these three pools depending on how well you're doing in the game.

Is the tendency to create your own sound effects, or buy them off the shelf?
We do both. I'll try wherever possible to go out and do location recordings. At the beginning of the year, for example, I went to France to record a load of frogs in the forest. If you can do it yourself, it's best to get it that way. You've a much better idea of the material you're after.

Sound-effect libraries exist on the Internet. You can get hundreds of thousands of effects and samples. The BBC Sound Library's up there for instance. So if I'm after a particularly specialized sound, I'll look there first. You have to be careful, though. There was a tale recently of someone paid to go to Hollywood and get effects from a top postproduction house. And the results were rubbish.

You've got to be creative, though. Look at *Star Wars Episode One*. For the Pod Racer sound effects, they actually used a lion's growl as part of the engine sounds. You wouldn't realize this, of course, but it adds an intensity to the effect. A lot of this creativity is rubbing off on games—people from film schools are bringing these techniques. The most important thing to do is to make sure that if a player hears something hundreds of times, they are never bored of it.

03.06

PART 03. PRODUCTION
CHAPTER SIX

VIDEOGAME NARRATIVE

It could be argued that all games tell stories. And to a point, it's true. *Space Invaders* boasts a basic plot, and one on which Devlin and Emmerich would happily base a $71 million movie.

A tenuous link between games and movies, sure—but there's a more concrete relationship between the two. The explosion of the medium into the public consciousness has resulted in a strange trading of blows between the movies and videogames. However, that's not stopped Hollywood professionals from aiming to work at least briefly in the games industry. Spielberg, the Wachowski Brothers,

From an early age, we need to be told stories. Whether it's parents educating children with simple tales featuring colorful characters, or playground battles and heroic rescues—if we're not being told tales, we're inventing them for our own distraction.

In the earliest days, computer and videogame developers reserved narrative effort for the adventure or role-playing genres. Primitive text-based adventures lacked the sophistication of even the most basic of stories, creating a world restricted to simple location descriptions. Nonetheless, anecdotes abound of grown-up gamers recalling extraordinary vistas and panoramas illustrated by the computer—only for them to realize that they originated from simple text-based games. Their imaginations had colored in complex backgrounds to the words.

DRAGONS AND PRINCESSES

This lack of narrative endeavor in the early computer and videogames can be easily explained—quite simply, there was barely enough processing power to move the characters, let alone illustrate their adventures. Sure, princesses were saved and dragons slain, but that, literally, was the start and end of the story.

and George Lucas have all tried their hands at making games. And the main roles they occupy are in direction and scriptwriting, two of the most important narrative skills.

While the arrival of movie talent has met with varied success, there can be no doubt that standards in game narrative are improving. And this is necessary for the medium to be taken seriously. Often, videogame stories are rubbished as clichéd and derivative. The industry itself seems to dismiss the importance of plot, choosing instead to emphasize in the box-blurb the number of levels and weapons.

THE QUEST

The adventure genre still leads the way in videogame narrative—though that has diversified over recent years to include more action-orientated titles. *Deus Ex, Tomb Raider, Broken Sword, Final Fantasy,* and *Metal Gear Solid* are all very different games, but the central quest theme is constant in all.

The rare exceptions prove narrative is an area worth exploring. Good stories appeal to both male and female players—and when many games struggle to recoup their initial investment, it's important to ensure their target market is as wide as it can be.

```
* ADAMS ADVENTURE * (VERSION 1.0/416)
(C) ADVENTURE BOX 3435 LONGWOOD FL 32750

   THIS PROGRAM WILL ALLOW YOU TO HAVE AN
ADVENTURE WITHOUT EVER LEAVING YOUR
ARMCHAIR! YOU WILL  FIND YOURSELF IN A
STRANGE NEW WORLD  YOU'LL BE ABLE TO
EXAMINE, TAKE AND OTHERWISE MANIPULATE
THE OBJECTS YOU FIND THERE  YOU WILL
ALSO BE ABLE TO TRAVEL FROM LOCATION TO
LOCATION.

   I'LL BE YOUR PUPPET IN THIS ADVENTURE.
YOU COMMAND ME WITH 2 WORD ENGLISH
SENTENCES  I DO HAVE OVER A 120 WORD
VOCABULARY SO IF A WORD DOESN'T WORK
TRY ANOTHER!

   SOME COMMANDS I KNOW: HELP, SAVE GAME,
QUIT, SCORE, TAKE INVENTORY.

   THE AUTHOR HAS WORKED OVER A YEAR ON
THIS PROGRAM SO PLEASE DON'T COPY OR
ACCEPT A PIRATED COPY! NOW HIT RETURN!
```

```
You are in a small clearing half
    hidden amongst the trees.
```

ADVENTURELAND

The first of the Scott Adams text adventures, *Adventureland* (1978) used simple two-word commands throughout the game (top). Scott Adams' series is one of the most fondly remembered of the early adventure genre, although his reputation began to wane as he tackled licensed properties toward the mid- to late 80s.

CITY OF HEROES

It can work both ways. Some games prove so popular, they are turned into books—an endorsement of the narrative if ever there was one. The most recent example of games being licensed into a series of books is NCSoft's *City of Heroes* (top right). The books are scheduled to appear in 2005. The game features 20 different ongoing story arcs as villain groups menace Paragon City and react to player victories and defeats.

THE HOBBIT

The Hobbit (1982), obviously licensed from J.R.R. Tolkien's *Lord of the Rings* prequel, was a fairly straightforward interpretation of the tale. The game was first developed for the Apple TRS-80, and reissued on the Spectrum to take advantage of its superior graphics (above). The original Spectrum version was called 1.1 to make it appear enhanced. A version 1.2 was subsequently rereleased with several bugs fixed.

TOMB RAIDER

Most games tell stories using linear sequences or cut-scenes to top and tail the sections under the control of the player. Although cinematic techniques have improved over time, it's remained this way since the industry experimented with interactive fiction. Bold attempts have been made to try to break free from this rigid format—but as games such as *Tomb Raider* (above right) have proved, it can work very well .

LUDOLOGISTS VS. NARRATOLOGISTS

There are those who claim that computer and videogames should be about the experience of playing rather than the pursuit of narrative. The opposition argue that games should reward players not just in the form of subsequent levels and challenges or an end-of-level ditty, but something more meaningful.

    These two camps are divided, respectively, into Ludologists and Narratologists. And an example of their differences is illustrated by imagining their views on *Tetris* (1985) and *Myst* (1995). It is widely agreed that *Tetris* is one of the greatest games ever created. Narratologists would question its worth as there is no intentional storyline.

    On the other hand, *Myst*—which typical gamers despise due to its utter linearity (not to mention obscure design)—would be claimed by Narratologists to be of significantly more merit, due to its imaginative dreamworld and intellectual challenge.

    The truth, as ever, is somewhere in-between. Games should play well, above all else. But if they can tell stories, too, then so much the better.

NARRATIVE PROCESS Boy lives happily with his uncle and aunt. Then they are murdered. In pursuit of retribution, boy becomes powerful Jedi, hangs out with scum and villainy, nearly makes out with his sister and ends up with 50 percent fewer hands in the sequel. The end.

Had George Lucas not spent a significant amount of time drafting the structure to the *Star Wars* universe, there's no doubt that the movies would not have enjoyed such enduring appeal. And the same goes for games. If you're serious about creating a narrative that will engage, then the structure needs to extend far beyond the actual start and end of the story.

There are three vital documents necessary in developing a strong in-game narrative. The first is the story, told from start to finish. This, typically, will be under 20 pages long, and will detail the events specific to the game. Locations, actions, "inciting incidents"—all need to be scribbled down in chronological order. After revisions—and there's no limit on these—you should have a plot that is interesting, exciting, and features the correct pacing necessary to hold your audience's attention for the duration of the game.

THREE-ACT STRUCTURE

Games should adhere to a structure—for many, the three-act structure is suitable. Don't be discouraged or frustrated by the word "structure"—it's something that works for a reason. This structure includes elements such as the "inciting incident," which is an event or action that radically changes the balance of the protagonist. In a movie, the inciting incident needs to happen within the first quarter, but in a game many argue that it must come much sooner—ideally in the introduction.

If the inciting incident doesn't happen immediately, the game needn't be pedestrian up until this point. *Prince of Persia: The Sands of Time*—a game with a wonderful narrative, and perhaps the most perfect ending ever featured in a videogame—kicked off with a dramatic set-piece, but it wasn't until those sands of time were unleashed and the wider picture revealed that the game truly began.

The inciting incident will set up what many call the "obligatory scene." That's where the main character is going to resolve the tale—be that through conflict (that is, defeating those who sought to harm him) or restoration (putting things

Below: *Prince of Persia's* success was obviously not just down to its narrative. However, those who completed the game were treated to a textbook example of how to weave a decent story into an even more decent game. Perfectly paced, the game kicks off with a dramatic opening that doubles as a tutorial. Then, at the end of the first act—roughly an eighth of the way in—the central quest is revealed. *Prince of Persia* uses the classic double-act mechanic, advancing the plot as dialog is exchanged both in-game and through brief cut-scenes. It also cleverly integrates brief glimpses into the future, both to offer hints at obstacles yet to be overcome, and also to sow the seed of events yet to happen. The ending—far from being the disappointment of the majority of titles—is satisfying and surprising, and offers a strong reason to play through once again.

Left: Of course, the horror setting helped. But beneath *Resident Evil's* gory façade was a structure that would allow developer Capcom to extend the game into a hugely successful series encompassing many different genres beyond the straight action adventure. Generic and clichéd in places and with the occasional telegraphed revelation, the game nonetheless retains player interest far beyond the climatic ending—and its followups have generally enhanced the original story.

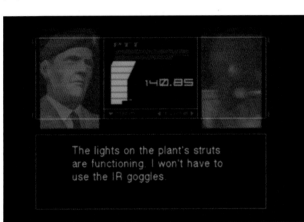

ay she decided to take piano lessons...The piano teacher was a young and handsome man.

Left: A genre in which it's difficult not to leave the player satisfied is the classic murder mystery. With 1991's *Cruise For A Corpse*, Delphine advanced the plot not so much by solving common object-based puzzles, but by talking to the right people about the right subjects at the right time, thus collecting clues. The game's clock advances in ten-minute intervals whenever an interesting clue is discovered, allowing the developers to integrate a crude timetable of where the assorted characters would be next. This is a clever narrative tool, abusing realtime principles in favor of allowing the player to progress at his own pace.

Left: A bold attempt at weaving a new interactive narrative into an existing world was Gathering of Developers' three-part *Blair Witch* series of games. All published in 2000—a feat of logistics only possible by offloading the license to three development teams—they attempted to expand on the myth in the original movie. Despite some continuity errors between the three titles, it was an interesting experiment—although the movie sequel released the same year and the overall quality of the trio diminished the reputation of the franchise. Each game was set in a different historical period, offering the writers a blank canvas upon which to interpret the film's folklore. Subsequent titles such as *Enter The Matrix* and *Knights of the Old Republic* followed this lead, with varying levels of success.

PASSIVE? OR INTERACTIVE?

There are two main methods of advancing the plot—through passive cut-scenes or as a natural part of the gameplay. Both have their benefits. Cut-scenes offer the director more creative freedom; by snatching control of the players, there is no need to worry about them doing things that might break the flow of these pivotal moments.

There has been a tendency over recent years to make these cut-scenes much more elaborate, with some of them running into tens of minutes. If this is your preference, go make a movie. While there is no doubt that gamers often admire lavish cut-scenes, they are ultimately frustrated by spending significant amounts of time not operating the joypad.

Exposition can be handled more smartly and seamlessly in-game, through dialog or commentary. Text needs to be punchy and to the point, though there is room occasionally for the odd flowery moment if it cements a personality trait rather than specifically telling the story.

Ultimately there is neither a right way nor a wrong way—and, ideally, a game should utilize a mixture of passive and active exposition. However, if exposition is handled clumsily, you run the risk of boring the player with noninteractive sections. Be warned.

The lights on the plant's struts are functioning. I won't have to use the IR goggles.

back to how they were). It's called "obligatory" for a reason—the audience expects it, and will be left naturally disappointed if the ultimate conclusion doesn't meet that expectation.

The end of every "act" should build to a peak, ensuring the pacing rises and falls. These peaks should build toward the end of every act and drop off at the beginning of the next section. It goes without saying that the end of Act 3 should boast the largest climax of them all.

Once you're happy with your plot, it's important to draw a detailed timeline of what every character featured in the game is doing and where that character is at any one time. Often this information won't be used directly—but the audience can sense whether you, as a storyteller, really know your world. If you don't, they quickly stop believing. It will also provide you with natural references to integrate into the script.

Finally, it's useful to have a background document that details every character's history, along with a summary of the overarching plot. This will provide a rich source of additional information that can be introduced into the script where appropriate, and provide the writers with the background that they need to get the characters' dialog and voices right.

NARRATIVE CASE STUDIES

Integrating narrative into interactive entertainment is a difficult skill. While there are many examples of competent storytelling within the art of videogames, the following four examples have been highlighted because they illustrate individual facets—both from a "how to" as well as a "how not to" perspective.

METAL GEAR SOLID 2 (2002)

Following the global success of *Metal Gear Solid* on the PlayStation in 1998, Hideo Kojima set out to better the original in every way. With the benefit of a new, more powerful platform in the PlayStation 2, many argue that he lost sight of what made the original so revered. Weighty cut-scenes—some demanding close to 30 minutes of viewing—and labored text-based conversations using the in-game communication device, tested players' patience, and the resulting game divided opinion among the gaming fraternity.

The question of gaming and identity was extrapolated throughout PlayStation 2. Cleverly, Kojima surprised fans by switching characters one third of the way in. Instead of playing the cold, hard central character Solid Snake, MGS2 forced gamers to assume the role of almost his direct opposite—the blonde, sensitive Raiden. And while many felt cheated that they weren't once again able to play videogaming's equivalent of Rambo, it afforded a perspective of Snake that would not have been possible. You could appreciate the character more by not controlling him.

However, nothing could forgive the messy, rambling plot. Arbitrary twists and turns confused all who played it, resulting in an ending as unsatisfactory as it was convoluted. The attack of September 11, 2001, on the World Trade Center resulted in the development team dropping a climactic cut-scene showing the Metal Gear Ray's destructive route through New York. The game simply cut from one location to another. Players were so confused by this point in the game, they simply shrugged it off. An essay in how not to do it—despite being a valiant effort.

Above right: ***Metal Gear Solid 2**,*
developed by **Konami.**

Right: The ***Broken Sword** series,*
developed by **Revolution.**

THE BROKEN SWORD SERIES (1992-2003)

Revolution founder Charles Cecil has been an exponent of videogame narrative for the duration of his time in the industry, and his tireless campaigning for gaming to adopt the grammar of movies has inspired a young generation of game designers. The *Broken Sword* series is his most famous creation, and is widely regarded as one of the greatest examples of videogame narrative.

This success is due to two main factors. In the trilogy to date, the narrative has drawn on real-life mysteries and legends—the Knights Templar in the first, the Mayan Prophecies in the second, and the Voynich Manuscript in the third. This has not only provided the series with a solid backdrop, but also piqued the interest of many who have played the games. Many *Broken Sword 1* players, for example,

subsequently went on to find out more about the Knights Templars and the Holy Grail.

More obviously, much of *Broken Sword*'s success can be attributed to the will-they-won't-they? relationship of its central duo. George Stobbard and Nicole Collard's continual fighting is typical of many male/female pairings, but it's rare to see such interest handled so eloquently in a videogame.

Of course, the game's style helped enormously. But rather than rely on long cut-scenes to advance the plot, Cecil keeps the action in-game and dialog-driven. Even in the third game's attempt to drive drama through video sequences, players needed to remain alert, as life-or-death decisions were usually not far away. While these "action sequences" were not entirely successful, they do provide alternative thinking for those wishing to avoid lengthy cut-scenes.

PLANESCAPE TORMENT

Planescape Torment was based around an interesting concept. A traditional role-playing game set in the *Advanced Dungeons & Dragons* world—with its familiar rules and structure—it ran the danger of disappearing among a sea of similar titles. But what made the game stand out was the quality of the plot and the strength of its dialog—two things rare in the world of videogames.

Assuming the role of a character who cannot die, *Planescape's* world is structured but nonlinear. Players opt to progress as they see fit, treating NPCs with contempt, admiration, or something in between. This could have resulted in a jumbled mess of conversational anomalies, but the sophisticated storytelling engine permitted the developers a huge degree of freedom—freedom that is handed over to players as they journey through *Torment's* world, forging friendships, alliances, and creating grievances as they see fit.

The player's moral alignment and affiliation with different factions are impressively flexible and have a significant impact on the course of the game. Characters can switch character class allegiances on whims—unusual for a genre that typically restricts such decisions. The immortal premise actually works for the game, rather than against it. What's more, the lead character's immortality means that players rarely abuse the Save or Load system, maintaining the solidity of the game world.

Planescape marked a bold step in videogame narrative, and one which was not entirely commercially successful. A shame, as its brave attempt to introduce intelligent role-playing should have been rewarded with much more than a swift appearance in the bargain bin.

Left: *Deus Ex*, developed by Ion Storm.

Right: *Planescape Torment*, developed by Black Isle.

DEUS EX

Warren Spector has almost single-handedly taken it upon himself to pioneer the nonlinear action adventure, with *Deus Ex* proving to be his most successful attempt to date. While the standard plot—shady government agency, viruses, terrorism, and so on—could have proved derivative initially, it was the storytelling skill and implied freedom that really captured the imagination. Most impressively, he did this in a firstperson game—typically the most linear of all genres.

Of course, no computer or videogame could ever be truly nonlinear. But Spector and his team structured the game's back-end to offer the illusion of freedom, advancing the same story through many different mechanics. Players with a penchant for gunplay could find NPCs reacting to them differently later on, aware of their hardball reputation. Brilliantly, the game's expansive back-story is never fed down the throats of its players. A wealth of background information can be found in various documents and computer terminals—as well as from in-game characters. Kojima would have forced players to read every single character. Spector has enough confidence in both his players' intelligence and his own storytelling ability to permit a greater degree of freedom.

Cut-scenes are rarely intrusive—a necessity, thanks to the game's perspective. Switching from firstperson to thirdperson would detach players from the in-game world, shattering the feeling of existing within a realistic environment. Indeed, it's the consistency of the story and the aplomb with which multiple solutions were designed and implemented for almost every section that enabled players to become so immersed in a rich, atmospheric tale.

Q&A

CHARLES CECIL, REVOLUTION SOFTWARE

Charles Cecil began writing games in 1981. Since its inception, his company, Revolution Software, has pioneered the use of traditional storytelling techniques in interactive entertainment, most successfully with the *Broken Sword* series of adventures, which built on the narrative success of such titles as *Lure of the Temptress* and *Beneath a Steel Sky.*

What do you think of the standard of storytelling in games?
The quality of storytelling in videogames is generally quite poor. That's not because the people who tell the stories in the games lack talent, but because the narrative in an interactive environment has an additional dimension over linear narrative. The opportunities and constraints of this extra dimension need to be understood both creatively and conceptually.

The wrong solution is simply to force a linear story into a game through cut-scenes rather than through integrating the story into the gameplay. That's where many games go wrong—not least because the end-result usually involves lengthy exposition scenes, which, frankly, quickly bore the player.

The development of a grammar for interactive storytelling is vital in order to move the art-form forward. There are two schools of thought. I follow the line of: look at the way films work, understand their grammar, and then work out how to apply that to games. The other school says: forget about other media, interactive entertainment has nothing to do with linear movies. We're our own medium, so let's invent our own rules as we discover them.

The reason that I think they are wrong is simple. If you look at great artists in any field, they only tend to break the rules after they have mastered them. Picasso, for example, was a brilliant classical painter, but only after he mastered his craft did he go on to experiment. Without his mastery of the rules of his art, his improvisation would have been meaningless.

What are the essential ingredients of a good narrative?
You have to tell a great story and present it within a structure that is logical and makes sense. Jean-Luc Godard summed it up well when he said that a story has to have a beginning, a middle, and an end—but not necessarily in that order. And that's the heart of it. You have to present a story with a structure—the design of the structure is up to you.

What, ideally, should come first: the plot, or the gameplay mechanic?
It really depends on the game. There is no doubt that plot must support gameplay—gameplay is king. But if the plot and the gameplay are genuinely intertwined then they will need to be designed in parallel. Ideally elements of the plot would develop systemically—so the author designs the rules for the plot which the player then creates! To an extent this happened in *Grand Theft Auto III*—with an overarching linear plot running in parallel with player-created systemic subplots. This is one of the reasons why the game was so well received. In doing this, we got a glimpse of the future of storytelling in the interactive medium.

But isn't GTA's narrative actually fairly basic? It's a series of missions interspersed with cut-scenes...
Clearly, in *GTA*, you had the overall linear narrative, but within it you had player-created systemic substories. That's what makes the game so appealing; the freedom of the systemic, within the structure of the linear. That's why it worked.

Top: *Broken Sword II: The Smoking Mirror*, by Revolution Software.

Above: *Gold and Glory: The Road to El Dorado*, by Revolution Software.

I would argue that its staccato storytelling is part of the game's strength. The player can play the game at their own pace, and the pace rises and falls with a great rhythm throughout each mission. By way of example, I remember a particularly good mission in which you have to hijack a van. Finding it and tailing it is fairly low-key, but then you ram it and it accelerates to escape, then you hear sirens, then the police cars arrive and while you continue ramming the van, they are ramming you. All hell has broken loose. And then you steal the load, outrun the cops, and normality returns.

So the pace really varies, like it does in any good narrative. But it varies under the player's direction, and that's part of the brilliance.

Is there anything specifically that we can learn from the structure of movies?

Absolutely. There are several great books on this subject— I would recommend *Story* by Robert McKee, or David Freeman's book *Creating Emotion in Games*, which specifically takes film techniques and applies them to games. I have attended several excellent lectures by Robert McKee and he concentrates on structure and how to create an emotional and engaging story. One element that is of relevance is what he calls the "expectation gap"—the difference between what the protagonist, and therefore the audience, expects and what then happens. The expectation gap creates interest and emotion—and therefore drama. If a game does not create expectation gaps then it feels flat. A criticism of *GTA3* is that there were few expectation gaps—what you expected to happen generally did happen. Had they addressed this, the game would have been even better.

However we are still pioneering this exciting new art-form. Games are in their infancy, which puts us in the great position of being able to make mistakes, provided they are not too serious and we continue to innovate.

You've been developing narrative-led video games since the early 1980s. What are the most important things you've learned about conveying the background story?

In an adventure there is a lot of story to tell. A golden rule is to hide the exposition. We do this by integrating the story and the gameplay—which means that our linear cut-scenes need only be relatively short. We also realized very early on that if you have two protagonists, then those characters can exchange dialog that can be witty, fun, and also convey exposition. So when George and Nico—the main characters of the *Broken Sword* series—exchange quips, we're actually furthering the story in a subtle way.

You can hide exposition in several ways. One effective way is to integrate the narrative with the gameplay itself—so

Above: *Broken Sword: The Sleeping Dragon.*

Opposite page, top to bottom:
Lure of the Temptress
In Cold Blood
Who Wants To Be A Millionaire?,
all by Revolution Software.

What we could do in our first game *Lure of the Temptress* is not that much different from what we can do now. We designed the game so that the player could go and talk to a huge number of characters about what was relevant at that point, but as the game advanced, their dialog was replaced to reflect new situations. And that was quite interesting because it meant you could go back and talk to people, and they would say completely new things based upon the fact that the world had moved on.

The other thing that people really liked was that we had characters who'd walk around doing their own thing—a system that we called Virtual Theater. I've always regretted the fact that we didn't really exploit Virtual Theater in later games. But the way that characters had freedom to do what they wanted to conflicted with the adventure idea of a multi-linear narrative in a nonlinear environment. I've always been aware that Virtual Theater was a glimpse of what was possible. Our future adventure games will definitely revisit this idea of characters having their own independent lives.

as the player advances through puzzles, the story is gradually revealed.

The other way is, instead of having a few great chunks of exposition, you actually break it up into lots of little sequences. So you're continuing to entertain the player, hopefully making them laugh, hopefully making them gasp, but at each point the story is being drip-fed, so we don't need the extraordinary lengthy cut-scenes that have become prevalent in many Japanese games. I used to assume that Japanese gamers liked lengthy cut-scenes—but recently a Japanese journalist complimented me on writing games that hid their exposition!

Have you been able to exploit the technology at your disposal better as processing power has improved?
Absolutely in terms of graphics, physics, AI, etc. In terms of narrative, I think that our creativity has limited our progress rather than a lack of processing power. Technology is way ahead of what we've needed, and we're still catching up with it.

The *Broken Sword* series has always been applauded for its narrative. What do you think is it about the game that appeals?
One key element is that we feature authentic ancient artifacts and draw on historical references that allow us to blur the boundary between fact and fiction. For our first *Broken Sword* game, *Broken Sword—Shadow of the Templars* (1996), the Knights Templar provided a wonderfully rich subject—there was a historical conspiracy, chivalry of the knights (tempered with barbarity), a fabulous treasure that was lost and never found, and the Order really could exist in some form of secret society today. All of these things combined and culminated in a very exciting way.

It is interesting to note that Hollywood is making a plethora of films that feature the subject matters that have previously been covered by the *Broken Sword* games. In November 2004 the movie *National Treasure* was released, in which the protagonist (Nicolas Cage) finds himself in a race to find a long-lost treasure taken from Europe to America by Templars. In 2005 the Ron Howard directed movie *The Da Vinci Code* (based on the novel by Dan Brown) will feature a French female and American male protagonists in a race to find a Templar secret (sounds familiar?) that threatens to rock the Catholic Church. The subjects covered by *Broken Sword* games have a habit of foreshadowing the zeitgeist—which is why, I believe, they feel fresh and cutting-edge.

The influx of talent from external industries has met with mixed results. What are the important things to remember when dealing with skills from traditional scriptwriting and filmmaking?

It is absolutely vital that the vision-holder—or the auteur (if you want to be pretentious)—needs to keep control of and drive the vision. And that vision-holder must understand and maximize the gameplay experience. Provided the script-writer, the artists, the directors, the cinematographers, and the orchestrators work under the direction of the person driving the vision, then they can be enormously valuable. If they take over and say "Well, actually, we can do better than you," then you have a disaster on your hands. So the key is having one person who drives the vision, but controls and uses the people around as part of a valuable creative team.

Back in the early 1990s bosses at publishing companies decided that people didn't want to play games, but instead wanted to watch "interactive movies." And to make them, control of the vision was passed from game designers, who understand the interactive experience, to filmmakers who don't. The result was an unmitigated disaster, which is a shame because the idea of creating a game that is as emotionally compelling as a great movie is a worthy goal.

How do you base a game around an existing narrative—for example, a film or book license?

The easiest way of adapting a license, of course, is to write a side-scrolling jumping game or a firstperson shooter, but that's missing the point!

How to write a narrative-driven game based on an existing story is far from obvious. A few years ago we were approached to write an adventure game based around Dreamwork's animated movie *Gold and Glory—Road to El Dorado*. I was pleased with the solution that we found.

The movie featured two happy-go-lucky chancers who set off in search of gold and adventure. Building on the characters, one of the fun elements of the movie, I decided to set the game after the movie ended and have the two protagonists stranded on a raft, telling their versions of the story to a girl they wanted to impress. In retelling their highly exaggerated versions of the story, we were able to imply that part of their versions were true and part were fiction—hence, able to work in original events that stuck to the vision of the film. It was fun because we could tell the same story, but in a different way.

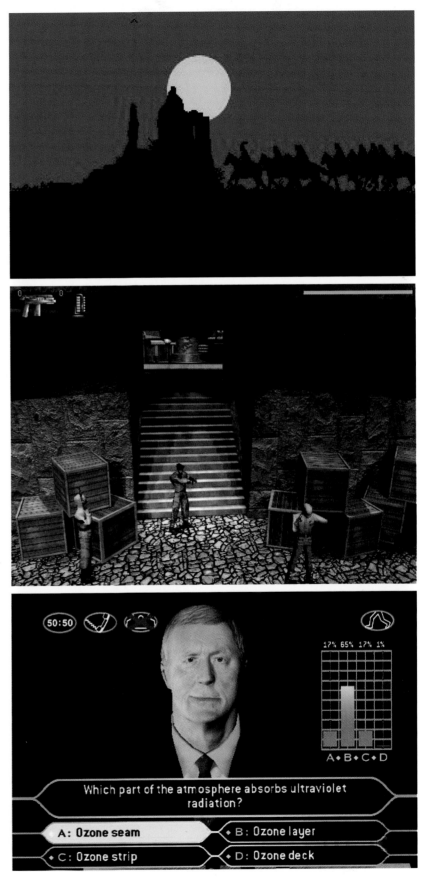

Halo: Combat Evolved, developed by Bungie and published by Microsoft.

PART 03. PRODUCTION

CHAPTER SEVEN

TESTING

Testing is perhaps the most unfairly maligned part of the development process. Although Quality Assurance (QA) departments are intimately involved throughout development, the position of tester is frequently considered to be just an entry-level position, or a stepping stone to a position of greater responsibility. Consequently, testers, and the testing process, are all too frequently looked down upon by other elements of the development team, and blamed for their apparent lack of rigor by customers who encounter a bug or glitch in a released title.

VALUABLE FEEDBACK

But the dogged foot soldiers that are found in QA departments are crucially important to the development effort: they provide valuable feedback from a position that isn't so close to the process that they're blinded by it; they ensure that a game's functionality isn't compromised by bugs and glitches; and by helping games pass the approval processes laid down by manufacturers, and meet the strictures of content rating systems, they can ultimately save publishers and developers money. In order to fulfill this valuable role, testers work fiendishly hard, playing games to excess with the unnatural (and frequently not very enjoyable) intention of breaking them. And yet in worst-case scenarios their feedback is ignored but they're still blamed for any bugs in the final game.

QA resources are typically provided by both the developer and the publisher, with the average team consisting of around ten testers at a developer, supporting a publishing QA department of around 200 people, whose efforts are divided across various projects at any one time. While early testing is typically directed toward more design-related issues, such as nuances of control and interface, by the end of production, this will generally have given way to more technically weighted feedback, with the majority of effort devoted to identifying and prioritizing bugs and glitches, and recording them using bug-tracking tools. The final element of the QA process also comes toward the end of production, when testers make sure that the game meets the guidelines laid down by the manufacturers for their hardware approval.

192/250

Your base is under attack!

Above: *Jak and Daxter*,
developed by Naughty Dog.
Left: *Ratchet & Clank*,
developed by Insomniac Games.

QUALITATIVE TESTING

The initial stages of QA involvement can occur very early during development, providing scope for testing departments to provide useful feedback regarding design. While the rest of the team is producing early milestone builds, or, even earlier, technical prototypes and/or vertical-slice demos, testers will diligently and exhaustively play through these sections of the game. They will then provide comments about such issues as interface and control by liaising with the producer, who communicates this feedback to the rest of the team where necessary. It's rare, though, for QA departments to continue to have significant input into major design issues after a game is feature-locked (*see over*).

Nevertheless, forms of qualitative testing can continue: although it's not widely considered to be an essential component of production, focus group testing can provide valuable information that's beyond the scope of the typical QA team. And although creative firebrands might balk at the prospect of subjecting their grand designs to the critical faculties of the unwashed masses, posing the right questions of focus groups can give designers a lot to think about and learn from.

During a talk at GDC Europe in 2002, Bill Fulton, the founder of the Microsoft Games User-Testing Group, outlined various improvements that were made to the company's titles in the wake of focused consumer research. Most notably, the group discovered, after experimentation, that the preference of players for inverted or uninverted pitch controls in firstperson shooting games is a deeply ingrained one that's not easy for players to relearn, and very few people were equally at home with either control method. Consequently the option to invert the pitch control was integrated into the opening cutscenes in *Halo: Combat Evolved*, a game that benefits enormously from an almost sublime attention to detail.

Other games to benefit from focus testing include *Ratchet & Clank,* and *Jak and Daxter,* both developed under the auspices of the Cerny Method (*see page 51*). But there are drawbacks to focus testing if the wrong questions are asked, and the process has to be closely monitored to make sure that participants don't try to second-guess the basis of any questions, giving the answers that they think they are expected to give.

TECHNICAL TESTING The real substance of a QA team's efforts don't start until after the development team has locked down the set of features that will be going into the final game. It's at this point that the testing process shifts to the real meat and drink of any QA team: bug hunting.

CLASSIFYING BUGS

QA departments generally divide bugs across four categories, indicating their severity and the priority with which they need to be fixed:

A-CLASS BUGS

These include bugs that cause the game to crash or lock up, or that would cause the game to fail to receive console manufacturer approval. Also, bugs that cause installation to fail, or features that don't function.

B-CLASS BUGS

Although these are also undesirable, they're more likely to feature in a released game if deadlines are pressing. They include major graphical glitches, such as scenery pop-up and frame-rate issues as well as front-end mistakes and localization errors.

C-CLASS BUGS

These frequently fall by the wayside unless they can be quickly and easily solved, and consist of minor slipups such as spelling errors and minor graphical or audio glitches.

D-CLASS BUGS
(ALSO KNOWN AS WISH CLASS BUGS)

Typically these are actually suggestions rather than bugs, including items such as an unintuitive front-end, or an unappealing color scheme and so on.

The fundamental task of the tester is to root out bugs that range from minor art glitches to wholesale crash bugs, making sure that these are effectively communicated to the programming team who then need to remedy them. It goes without saying that none of these ought to appear in the finished product; but with the funding for development frequently incumbent upon developers meeting milestone requirements, testers need to be engaged in the pursuit of glitch-free perfection as early as possible.

Thus testers are required to meticulously play through unfinished early builds of the game code, frequently for a stamina-sapping length of time. Some testers will need to draw up a table or checklist to assist them to methodically test every permutation of gameplay variables. This could, for example, be as simple as testing every possible combination of character model and weapon in an arena combat game, or the more complicated task of going through every possible conversation with every different character in a complicated RPG. Others will need to test the game's compatibility with every different variation of hardware (which, of course, requires much less work for console versions of games), while others still will need to simply play through the game.

The need to track the fate of any bugs that are discovered requires specialized tools for logging and prioritizing them. Testers will typically use video recordings of game sequences, or screenshots to demonstrate the nature of the bug or glitch, so any tool needs to be able to attach such associated media files with the bug entry. Once the tools are in place, the testers are then free to do their work: any glitches are entered into the logging tool; the game's producer will then assign that bug a priority depending on how pressing the need is for it to be fixed, and allocate programming resources; finally, the fixed code will be reassigned to the testers, for the cycle to start again.

HARDWARE APPROVAL

Perhaps the most important facet of QA is ensuring that the finished game meets the approval procedures of the console manufacturers. Although this step isn't necessary at all for PC games, most games these days are developed for one or more console (currently PlayStation 2, Xbox, and GameCube). Each hardware manufacturer has its own set of hoops that developers and publishers need to jump through before they will allow a game to grace their hardware, such as Sony's Technical Requirements Checklist (or TRC). Indeed some manufacturers even use automated tools to test the console approval compliance status of games.

These guidelines and restrictions ensure that each console is home to no objectionable content, and that the consumer's experience with such things

Opposite, above and below: **Atari** scored a couple of own goals with *Driv3r* and *Enter the Matrix*. Both titles were bugged and glitchy, perhaps because they were rushed out to meet deadlines imposed by the commitments of financial reporting. *Driv3r* featured flying cars performing doughnuts in the sky, and missions that would complete at random, and although *Enter the Matrix* couldn't quite match showstoppers such as these, it was nevertheless very rough around the edges.

Obtaining hardware approval isn't just about technical glitches and bugs. Both *Broken Sword III: The Sleeping Dragon* (above) and *Metal Slug 3* (right) were refused approval by Sony for the U.S. market because they were considered too old-fashioned for the brand.

as memory card interfaces are consistent and trouble-free. While most manufacturers provide training seminars for QA teams to attend in order to make sure that developers and publishers are au fait with the precise nature of these requirements, there's no substitute for experience. Indeed since the console approval process can last up to two weeks, and typically takes more than one submission, failing to meet approval guidelines can prove to be very costly to publishers who have to revise marketing and distribution schedules. Allied to the fact that it's not uncommon for a game to fail on a single bug, the process demands the utmost attention to detail.

NOTORIOUS BUGS It should come as no surprise to find that the occasional bug can rear its ugly head in games released to retail. Equally, it's hardly shocking to find that glitches are more common in the sorts of big, expansive, emergent videogames that are more difficult to test. But this does present the irony that many of the most bug-ridden games are also the best available.

SOME GAMES THAT CONTAINED BUGS

KNIGHTS OF THE OLD REPUBLIC
LucasArts (2002)
Although it's possible to play through BioWare's magnificent *Star Wars* RPG without encountering a single glitch, the range of bugs discovered within *Knights of the Old Republic* (below) is enough to make even a Wookiee flinch. Indeed, in one of the game's more memorable malfunctions, the lead character's entire party of allies would slowly be transformed into Wookiees. Other anomalies included the appearance of a "Galaxy Droid" who could escort the party to any planet in the game, and floating and invisible characters. Again, however, the number of bugs is directly related to the sheer range and variety of interactions that the game world affords the player.

GRAND THEFT AUTO III
Rockstar Games (2001)
A game that allowed players to explore an entire city across three islands, which gave players the freedom to interact with this world in an apparently endless variety of ways, was inevitably going to feature the occasional glitch. Nevertheless, the extent and variety of the glitches found in *GTA III* were exceeded in scope only by the ambition of the game itself. From randomly missing traffic, to typical "falling through scenery" bugs, the game had them all. There were also some neat glitches that actually added to its appeal, such as being able to get to the third island early (by exploding a car near a roadblock), and being able to play with your character dressed in a prison uniform.

SUPER MARIO SUNSHINE
Nintendo (2002)
Given Nintendo's reputation for staunch quality control, and the solidity and bug-free nature of its predecessor, it was disappointing to learn that *Super Mario Sunshine* (left) was afflicted with bugs and glitches aplenty. Now, by any ordinary yardstick, many of these were truly inconsequential—Mario appearing to walk on air, or sink into the ground in certain instances, for example. But Nintendo had historically set its standards so high that they became painfully apparent. This was compounded by more serious errors (such as falling through the bottom of the galleon in Pinna Park, which was probably the most oft-cited niggle of Nintendo's disappointed fan following).

LIFE

AND SOME THAT DIDN'T

**ETERNAL DARKNESS:
SANITY'S REQUIEM**

Nintendo (2002)

The crash bug is truly the bane of the developer's (and tester's) existence. Pity the gamer then, who, for no apparent reason, is forced to witness their game resetting itself. Unless they're playing the magnificent *Eternal Darkness*, which uses simulated technical flaws and glitches to evoke a deeply unsettling atmosphere as your character's sanity gradually dissipates. Thus, during key sequences depicting the gradual onset of psychosis, the player's TV appears to change video modes; items appear to go missing from the inventory; the game

will apparently reset; and, most unsettling of all, the game appears to delete your Save Game after ending a game session.

**METAL GEAR SOLID 2:
SONS OF LIBERTY**

Konami (2001)

In a similar vein, toward the end of Hideo Kojima's masterpiece, the depiction of the gradual disintegration of an AI entity is conveyed by simulating various types of glitchy behavior—most notably, by presenting the player with a "Fission Mailed" screen (so it's actually obvious to the astute gamer that it's not an authentic Mission Failed moment—although it's still pretty disconcerting).

ASAD HABIB, QA MANAGER, KUJU ENTERTAINMENT

Over a career spanning seven years, Asad Habib has tested games for the likes of Gremlin Interactive, Atari, and currently Kuju Entertainment. Over this time he has tested games on a variety of hardware platforms, ranging from the Sega Saturn to Sony's PlayStation 2, and even cell phone platforms.

What sort of skills do you need to make a good tester?

Being able to cope with repetitive tasks is a key part of being a tester. Some people might like the idea of playing games, but imagine being saddled with a game from a genre that you didn't like; you'd still have to test the game. Day in, day out, and not for days or weeks, but for months and months!

How important is testing and QA to the overall development process?

Very important! Just look at the lambasting the latest *Tomb Raider* title received in the specialist and mainstream press due to its bugs. A bug-ridden product can ruin the enjoyment of a game and undo months and months of hard work in development.

How is testing integrated into the rest of the development process? What points of contact and interaction are there, for example, between QA/test staff and the rest of the development team?

QA staff are always expected to provide good communication and be open with the development team, simply because they are the front line for the artists and programmers, so it is vital that any problems are communicated in the proper channels as early as possible. Test integration as early as possible is key, as this makes the whole test team feel a part of the development of the game and not a separate entity, as can sometimes be the case. For QA departments at large publishers it is sometimes even more isolated, working with developers that are located across the world, which presents a bigger challenge. The main points of contact would typically be a lead tester liaising directly with the producer at first.

How well is the testing process usually integrated into the overall development process, in your experience?

It varies wildly. Sometimes the testing process is, literally, a piece of paper with a list of bugs written on it. At the other end of the scale there are projects with 20 people working on 10,000 bugs using a third-party bug tracker. Obviously the more complex and bigger the game the greater the testing resources required.

Usually there are two sides to the Quality Assurance program. Development QA is literally the front line of the development team. The program starts very early during the project, and can range from providing input for a first pitch (if a demo is made, for instance) to the more common requirement of checking milestones before they are delivered to the publisher.

Left and below: *FireWarrior*.

Far left: *Advance Wars: Under Fire*; both developed by Kuju Entertainment.

Development QA consists of the early checking of prototypes. This involves such things as checking the frame rate, checking the controls, the art and overall look and feel, and sound as well as individual engine components (for example, the physics in a racing game or the character interaction in an RPG).

Publishing QA, on the other hand, tends to focus on the last three months of the development cycle and in particular the requirement to pass the game through the approval processes of third-party manufacturers such as Sony and Microsoft. This requires comprehensive test plans, and the coordination of each of the third-party manufacturers' standards and guidelines checks (TRC checks for Sony; TCR for Microsoft; and Lot checks for Nintendo). Typically at this stage the onus is on mass bug-finding: collision checks, falling through the world/map checks, crash bugs, licensing issues (very important), graphical glitches, control system bugs, front-end anomalies. Literally the whole gamut of bug testing.

What do testers actually do? What makes up their average day?
Find bugs! Typically a tester will come in, in the morning and load up his or her e-mail and bug-tracking software. Assuming a version is ready for him in the morning he will check against the list of marked fixes on the buglist, which the development team should have done. The first priority is then systematically going through the list to see which bugs are still in and which bugs have passed. Once this is done, any new bugs found along the way are also inputted.

Does the development industry place enough importance on the testing process and the people responsible for it?
In a short word, no, which is a shame. Tight budgets and timescales always cut into QA time on a product. But when QA departments input bugs, they also record suggestions for improvements that could be made. It would be an interesting exercise to compare this list to the problems that people complain about upon release. You might be surprised at the similarity. Companies that do invest time and people on QA usually reap the rewards in the shape of better review scores and so on.

How important is a quality-testing department to making sure that console approval and rating processes run smoothly?

This is the life and blood of publishing QA. Any department that regularly fails at console approval is soon an ex-QA department. Typically a game can expect to pass the second time around. Successful liaison with the console approval QA departments is key. Manufacturers now offer training seminars to communicate standards, and some have automated tools for testing their console approval compliance status.

Do you have any memorable or informative experiences, or examples of interesting glitches that got through?

One that stands out was for a soccer game that was due for release and submission. The producer came down and said he wanted me to test it before they sent it in the afternoon. Most of the testing had been done. When I got the game I wondered what would happen if I fouled a player off the pitch? Would the game be stupid enough to break? Surely not. So I positioned a man outside the boundary, selected another player and made him dive in. Immediately the ref gave a free kick. Outside the soccer field!

Or there's the time I was woken up at 2 a.m. to ferry a mastered game to Sony, only to receive another phone call at 4 a.m. saying a bug had been found so could I please return to pick up the new version. That was a long day.

How important is outsourcing to the localization process?

If a sufficiently big internal localization team is not built up then outsourcing localization is key for titles. There is a definite need for them simply because not all organizations are big enough for in-house localization. Good communication with the outsourcing team or teams at all stages of the localization process saves time later on. For example a simple task, such as cheats not being sent through early enough, might mean the localization testers spend a full day getting to the end of the game. when instead it could have been done in half an hour. Therefore checklists with all the important information needed by localization teams are not uncommon in QA departments.

What are the most common mistakes that developers make when working with QA departments?

Not giving enough time early on due to milestone commitments. All too often QA gets put on a back burner.

Among the games that Asad Habib has tested are:
From left to right: *Driver 2*, developed by Reflections Interactive; *FireWarrior*, *Advance Wars: Under Fire*, and *Reign of Fire*, all developed by Kuju Entertainment.

POSTPRODUCTION

04

ANIMAL CROSSING
The insistence that titles distributed in the European Union should cater to five different languages has been the bane of many a publisher. *Animal Crossing*, for example, was not released in the UK on GameCube for a couple years, despite being available in the English language thanks to an earlier Australian release. While a united continent can have many benefits, gamers are often unhappy with the protracted wait.

PART 04. POSTPRODUCTION
CHAPTER ONE

THE POST-PRODUCTION PHASE

With the game considered functionally complete, the postproduction phase begins in earnest. Postproduction is the final push through to full completion, with the aim of reaching a gold master—fully finished code which is suitable for mass duplication—as quickly and efficiently as possible, while testing the title thoroughly and addressing any bugs that arise. It's an immensely frustrating time.

The industry turns strangely Greek at this stage. An "alpha" version is the first time the game can be played from start to finish, with all features complete. It will be buggy in places—but that's the point. With these bugs documented and fixed, the game is reissued as a "beta" version; one that is almost complete. It may undergo several revisions at this stage, until it meets all appropriate approvals processes and can be considered finished.

The time needed for a title to move from alpha to final gold candidate varies considerably. A title intended for the PC platform, for example, has no official approvals process, so can go to market theoretically in any state—particularly given the ease nowadays of distributing patches to customers after release. Console titles, on the other hand, have an obligation to meet quality conditions set by the hardware manufacturers.

For console releases, the developer or publisher will have obtained concept approval early in the development process—however, if the final code is substandard, a detailed list of failings will be provided. Repeated resubmission is expensive, so the postproduction process must predict and address substandard sections of the code.

REGULATION BOARDS

Another body interested in approving content is the statutory regulation board, if it exists. In Europe, Pan European Game Information (PEGI) offers guidelines that dictate how a game should be restricted. This is a voluntary system, but is adhered to by every commercial games publisher. The British Board of Film Classification (BBFC) may need to issue a legally binding age restriction, in the case of violent or offensive content. The submission process here is longer and more expensive.

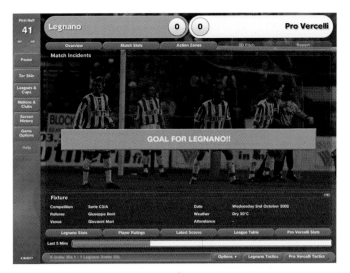

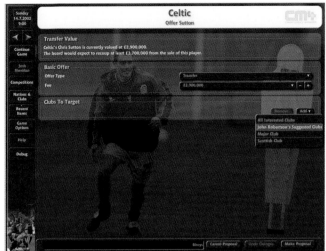

PATCHES

It's a difficult decision to know at what stage of postproduction to authorize the release, particularly when placed under pressure from a publisher to "ship now, patch later." Often, it's a business decision from both publisher and developer, but it's frequently the developer that takes the flak. Sports Interactive gave in to pressure from its publisher at the time in releasing the hugely anticipated *Championship Manager 4*. It issued an update patch that fixed a vast range of code complications across the entire game. The number and range of features addressed by the first patch was an embarrassing admission for the developer, and a PR offensive was required to placate the game's huge fanbase.

The game will have been tested at various stages throughout development, but once the title hits alpha, the testing resources are increased. The first pass will identify major bugs and gameplay issues. With these documented and addressed, the game is granted beta status—and is usually representative enough to be distributed to the specialist press for appraisal, provided any major flaws due to be addressed are highlighted.

Depending on the resources and timing available, attention will now be given to creating a playable demo. This is a crucial marketing tool—yet it is surprising how frequently these playable teasers fail to offer a representative taste of the final title. Official console magazines have guidelines that dictate how large these demos can be, and the maximum and minimum length of time consumers should be able to spend playing these trial versions. Developers should understand these restrictions and create demos that offer enough to whet players' appetites—and certainly not discourage them from buying the game.

THE RATINGS EXPLAINED

The Pan European Games Information (PEGI) age rating system is a pan-European age-rating system for interactive games. Designed to ensure that minors are not exposed to games that are unsuitable for their particular age group, the system is supported by the major console manufacturers, including PlayStation, Xbox, and Nintendo, as well as by publishers and developers of interactive games throughout Europe. The age-rating system has been developed by the Interactive Software Federation of Europe (ISFE) and has the enthusiastic support of the European Commission, who considers the new system to be a model of European harmonization in the field of protection of children.

Started in the early spring of 2003, PEGI replaces existing national age rating systems with a single system that is identical throughout most of Europe. The game rating appears on the front and back cover of interactive games, and retailers provide information on the new system.

The age-rating system comprises two separate but complementary elements. The first is an age rating, similar to some existing rating systems. The PEGI age bands are 3+, 7+, 12+, 16+, 18+. The second element of the new system is a number of game descriptors. These are icons, displayed on the back of the game box, that describe the type of content to be found in the game. Depending on the type of game, there may be up to six such descriptors. The intensity of the content is appropriate to the age rating of the game.

The combination of age rating and game descriptors allows parents and those purchasing games for children to ensure that the game they purchase is appropriate to the age of the intended player.

Many publishers deliberately aim for a higher rating, assuming it will result in an increase of sales. This is a slightly erroneous theory. Adult-rated games sold only seven percent of volume in the UK during 2003. Seventy percent of games released are classed as suitable for all.

Thoughts often turn to copy protection at this stage. Traditionally, technologies such as Macrovision's SafeDisc have been used to "wrap" the main code in a high-security package that deters casual copying. However, experienced hackers have been able to bypass any "wrapped" security reasonably quickly—and having stripped the core code of its protection, distribute the game easily via Internet newsgroups and peer-to-peer services.

A new solution has recently been pioneered, and this offers significant security enhancements that can delay the time between release and free distribution. By integrating dormant security calls deep within the code—procedures that can affect gameplay at key points specified in advance by the programmers—the "hack-free" period can be extended, resulting in increased income for both publisher and developer. Research has shown that a large percentage of those who would download an illegal copy become frustrated with its lack of appearance within a few weeks of release and purchase a legitimate copy.

NTSC TO PAL

In the old days, publishers bringing titles from the USA to Europe treated their consumers with something bordering on contempt. The early PlayStation titles were often blighted by large horizontal black borders as publishers sought to minimize the cost of properly converting titles from one video format to another. Players of PAL *Final Fantasy X* (above), for example, had to tolerate so-called "letterbox" displays. Thankfully, consumer reaction—and the increase in gray imports—forced a reappraisal of the situation, and games these days rarely suffer from hideous letterbox displays.

A European console release usually needs to cover five key languages: English, French, German, Italian, and Spanish, typically on one CD or DVD. While translation will have been ongoing throughout development, the postproduction phase is where it all comes together. Any regional differences—for example, lowering gore levels for the German market, or removing references deemed tasteless in other markets—will be implemented during this stage. Thinking about this process in advance and structuring code that can be easily stripped and replaced can save a whole heap of time during this period.

Additionally, the team may be required to convert the code to run on other television standards—from NTSC to PAL or vice versa. As well as different resolution, there's a difference in speed, which can impact on essential in-game timing. It's an important thing to consider throughout the development process—but there will invariably be some differences that affect the final code when it's translated from one format to another, and these will need to be addressed during preproduction.

With the gold candidate submitted, PC developers also turn their attention to developing the inevitable patches—small (in theory) pieces of code that address problems that for whatever reason make it into the final game. Usually, this is down to time pressures from publishers keen to publish within their fiscal quarters in order to hit their targets, and it's become a widely practiced way of distributing PC games. However, consumers obviously object to the inconvenience of

METAL SLUG

SNK is renowned for its output of high-quality, hardcore titles, which appeal to fans of more traditional action games. Its Metal Slug series—home conversions of arcade smashes—is probably its most popular range, with fans the world over. It is also an illustration of the format holder veto. While the games have been published to great success on PlayStation throughout the East and Europe, Sony Computer Entertainment America has restricted its publication for the format there, presumably considering its two-dimensional visuals as inappropriate on its console, which boasts significant three-dimensional processing power. SNK has begun experimenting with 3D titles that will address these concerns—and U.S. releases are scheduled.

seeking out and installing these patches, and negative feedback can be aimed toward developers who habitually push their luck. The situation is often so bad on PC that third-party applications such as *Game Shadow* can charge users a premium to track the distribution of relevant patches.

Console titles have traditionally been immune from the horrors of patching—thanks to the approvals process outlined earlier in this chapter, which, in theory, ensures all is present and correct prior to duplication. However, games that use online gaming services such as Xbox Live have recently begun using patches to address server issues, and, in extreme cases, tweaking the game to address flaws being exploited by its users. Given that the users of online gaming services must have broadband in order to connect, console patches are less intrusive. But it's possibly the start of a worrying trend.

The postproduction phase also marks the climax of marketing activity. Once the game has reached this stage, publishers can be reasonably confident of a firm release date, and confirm the marketing they have booked. PR activity ramps up to ensure the target audience is aware of the quality and the release date. Journalists will be given access to code in order to generate positive editorial; TV and print spots will be created and placed to hit the proposed release date offered by the duplication plant.

The industry has reached a stage where it is able to predict with reasonable accuracy the potential commercial demand for a sequel, and the end of the postproduction process may often see initial work begin on a potential follow-up. Ideas lopped from the final version of the original title often prove ideal starting points for the followup, though it's important not to start shouting about this immediately. The public does not like to feel short-changed or obliged to spend even more money on subsequent purchases—as we'll explain in our next book!

CARMAGEDDON

How legislation differs from territory to territory is best exemplified by Germany's attitude to violent computer games. Simply, it doesn't tolerate them—requiring any developer who wants an official release in the country to substantially alter their code. Consumers in the territory often feel cheated by the green blood (implemented to imply the enemy is robotic or zombified), but an easy way around this exists, as most famously illustrated by *Carmageddon*, which applied the tactic to many of its iterations. The PC version was simply patched (unofficially, of course) which neatly sidestepped the classification requirements of the boxed version. The result? Everyone who wanted an on-wheels gorefest simply applied a small EXE file, which returned everything to its bloody glory, just as the developer intended.

CASTLE WOLFENSTEIN
It's illegal for videogames to depict Nazi paraphernalia in Germany. Indeed the official website for *Return to Castle Wolfenstein* provides a warning for German users that this material is featured.

PART 04. POSTPRODUCTION

CHAPTER TWO

LOCALIZATION

Until relatively recently, it was possible for developers and publishers to focus their titles on a single market, such as the USA, Japan, or Europe. Increasingly these days, however, the need to sustain significant team sizes, Hollywood-style production values, licensed content, and big-budget marketing campaigns requires games to sell across multiple territories to recoup their costs. According to research agency DFC Intelligence, publishers need to sell around half a million copies of a game just to break even—which essentially means selling games on a worldwide basis.

For this reason, the localization process, which has historically been a simple matter of tacking on a few quick text translations to the end of the development process, has become an integral part of the development cycle, and so needs to be addressed from the outset. According to DFC, the U.S. videogame market was worth $10 billion in 2003, but according to European trade body ELSPA, the western European market was only $1.2 billion shy of this, and is growing more rapidly. Meanwhile the Japanese market, although declining in size, is still important at around $5 billion, and there are a number of other emerging markets, such as South Korea and eastern Europe.

Localizing videogames for these widely disparate markets is more than a simple question of translating words into different languages. It requires meeting the technical challenge of ensuring that games function across different TV standards, and incorporating strings of text or pieces of dialog that are longer in other languages. And to really maximize sales across different territories, the localization effort needs to be sensitive to local tastes and customs, and even legal restrictions and regulations.

CONVERTING FROM NTSC TO PAL

Perhaps the most important part of localization is to ensure it will play on its target hardware in the region in which it is released. It's a quirk of the historical development of television standards that Japan and the USA use a different system from that used in the majority of European territories, and it's this difference that produces the most technically demanding aspect of the localization process.

The NTSC standard that's used in the United States dates back to 1953, when it was created by the National Television System Committee. Today it is widely used across other parts of the world, including Japan. But while the NTSC standard is composed of 525 lines

FREQUENCY
Music-based puzzler *Frequency*, and its successor *Amplitude*, featured the same playlist across all territories. But how much more successful would it have been with tracks licensed specifically for certain regions?

and refreshes at 29.97 frames per second, most of Europe and Australia use the PAL (Phase Alternating Line) standard, which features 625 lines and 25 frames a second. In the days of the 16-bit and 32-bit machines, this discrepancy was typically overcome by using the redundant lines to create wide borders at the top and bottom of PAL conversions, which also ran slower than their NTSC counterparts.

INGENIOUS SOLUTIONS

Nowadays, the main console manufacturers don't allow developers to get away with such lazy conversions. Such games would be rejected during their approval process. By way of example, the main difference between NTSC and PAL modes for the PlayStation 2 is that in high-res mode, NTSC PS2s run at a resolution of 640x448, while PAL PS2s run at 640x512. One solution to this discrepancy is to fill the missing lines in by increasing the resolution, which would require art assets and fonts to be redrawn. But developers have come up with various other ingenious solutions. The team behind *Summoner*, for example, on the PlayStation 2, chose to design artwork in such a way that they could scale up just the back layer to the 512-pixel resolution, while leaving the rest of the screen centered and unscaled.

TRANSLATION Of course the real meat of the localization process is the actual translation, converting all written text and spoken words into various foreign languages. This presents its own difficulties, not least of which is the scope for mistranslations and proofreading errors.

Inexperienced translators might not notice the difference, in Spanish, between *cagar* (a vulgar term meaning "to defecate") and *cargar* ("to load"), while in Italian, *servizio* ("service") is only one letter away from *sevizio* (again, an offensive term, meaning something like "to torture"). Consequently, the translation process is now generally handled by a specialized team of individuals, who work closely with the rest of the production team to provide translated text that can be slotted into the game during development.

But the real problem is the scale of the undertaking, and the fact that different languages require a different number of words to convey the same meaning. A game like *Civilization II*, for example, features 330,000 words that need to be translated, and it's of crucial importance that the developer implements code that allows text boxes to vary in size, since languages such as German

Above: **ZERO WING**
An otherwise fairly obscure Japanese Mega Drive game, *Zero Wing* has the dubious honor of having kicked off an Internet movement dedicated to its hilariously poor translation, of which "All your base are belong to us" is typical.

Above right: **ANIMAL CROSSING**
Nintendo's GameCube title, *Animal Crossing*, required intensive localization, because the game was tied in to its local calendar, with real-world events, such as Thanksgiving in the USA, taking place in the game's user-created virtual world.

and French are approximately 25 percent longer than English. Languages such as Japanese are even more complicated to account for, since its intricate characters must be represented as graphics files or larger font files. The only way this can be addressed is by planning for the increased memory this demands at the outset of development. Replacing spoken dialog is just as thorny an issue, particularly now that lip-synching is such an important facet of animation. If animation tools are designed from the outset with localization in mind, however, it's a problem that can be eliminated.

CULTURAL DIFFERENCES

But localization doesn't end with textual translation. A good localization team will address issues that vary widely—everything from local regulations to variations in taste with regard to game design. In Germany, for example, it's forbidden by law for games to feature representations of Nazis, or "realistic" violence. *Return to Castle Wolfenstein* was famously localized by having all its Nazi regalia removed for the German market, only to be banned anyway for being too violent! Titles such as *Mortal Kombat* and *Wolfenstein 3D*

CASE STUDIES

Perhaps the most difficult territory to conquer for a western developer is Japan. In 2001 only five out of the 100 top-selling games in Japan were developed in the west. But it is possible to overcome this apparent hostility toward western titles with a focused localization process, as some high-profile successes have demonstrated...

TOMB RAIDER

Tomb Raider (below) was localized by Japanese publishing powerhouse, Enix, and underwent a pretty major overhaul to make it acceptable to Japanese sensibilities. Notably there were no grisly death sequences: instead of dying, Lara would be whisked back to the beginning of the level by a mysterious aura. More significantly, levels were actually redesigned to alleviate the sudden-death difficulty spikes that characterized the game's western release.

CRASH BANDICOOT

Crash Bandicoot (bottom) achieved sales of one million copies in Japan, thanks to a series of major revisions. Whereas western gamers were treated to green eyebrows, these were gone in the Japanese versions, alongside changes to the size of Crash's eyes and ears. Levels were once again redesigned, to make them less difficult.

have also fallen foul of the censors (the fact that an ostensibly violent game such as *Duke Nukem* didn't is because the violence in it is directed at aliens).

And there is also the local receptivity to particular licenses and brands to consider. While Codemasters' driving game is known as *Pro Race Driver* in the USA and Spain, in the UK it is better known as *TOCA*, while in Germany it is *DTM Race Driver*, and in Australia it is *V8 Supercar Race Driver*. Atari, then known as Infogrames, even reckons to have increased sales of one of its driving games by 20 percent as a result of switching the soundtrack from dance to hard rock. With a whole genre emerging around music in recent years, licensing music tracks now has to be done with a view to the broadest global appeal.

KNOW YOUR MARKET

Knowledge of foreign markets can pay off in other ways too. In the USA and Europe, hiring Hollywood actors to provide voices can give a game box-office appeal, but in Japan, voice-actors, or *seiyuu*, are well known in their own right. Indeed, fans of a particular voice-actor are likely to buy a game simply because their favored voice-actor appears in it. Meanwhile, understanding of English is so widespread in Scandinavia, that it might be more cost-effective only to undertake a partial localization for these territories—translating just the packaging and manuals.

Perhaps the most surprising element of localization is the global differences in taste with regard to the types of game played. Research undertaken at the University of Abertay, in Dundee, showed that Japanese players don't like to compete; by pitting players against each other in a game of *Ridge Racer V*, it emerged that whereas British gamers would attempt to beat their opponents at any cost, Japanese gamers would rather wait for their opponent to catch up with them than inflict a potentially humiliating defeat. Nevertheless even differences as significant as this can be overcome—demonstrated by the Japanese success of the *Tomb Raider* series.

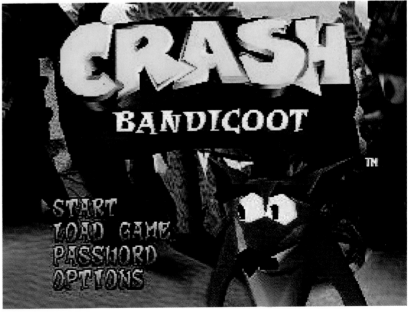

Q&A

ALGY WILLIAMS, MANAGING DIRECTOR, BABEL MEDIA

Algy Williams cut his teeth on a variety of positions across PR, sales and marketing, production, and management, across various media sectors before joining the videogame industry. He set up specialist videogame localization agency Babel Media in 1999 with Anthony McGaw and Ben Wibberley. The company now provides a variety of QA and localization services to clients across the videogame industry, including Nintendo, Microsoft, Atari, Sega, Sony, Konami, Capcom, and Activision.

What sort of skills and qualifications does someone need to be able to work in localization? Does the localization process demand technical skills, for example?
Working in games localization requires a combination of linguistic and technical skills. Whether on the publishing or localization agency side, it's important to have a sound understanding of how other languages work and the necessary provision that should be made for this at development stage.

Could you give a brief summary of the localization process and how it fits into the rest of the development process? Is it just a question of swapping text files, for example?
As an agency we usually work with text files that have been extracted from the code, and all the localization engineering is performed on the developer's side. Integration can be a lengthy process, and of course is related to other variables such as the volume of text in the game.

How many languages/territories are most modern games localized for?
Most of the games we deal with are created in English (U.S. or UK) and then localized into French, German, Italian, and Spanish for the European market. Manuals are often translated additionally into Dutch and sometimes Portuguese and the Nordic languages. Of course, many games are also developed in Japanese, and we also deal with this language on a regular basis.

How many people are involved in the localization process?
This can vary hugely, depending on how the developer and publisher are set up and whether they have localization specialists in-house, as well as the size and scope of the project in question. Typically our projects involve contacts from our client the publisher, a Localization Project Manager, and a team of in-house and in-country professional linguists working freelance. Furthermore there are the localized audio and manual elements to look after, not forgetting localization QA, and so the list of people continues.

Games such as *Forbidden Siren 2* (right) and *Far Cry* (opposite), both developed in Europe, are a testament to the emergence of new markets for videogames. Eastern Europe, Korea, and even China are increasingly home to talented development teams, and will become increasingly important videogame markets in the future—a fact that only increases the significance of a smooth localization process.

What points of contact and interaction are there between localization staff and the rest of the development team?

This varies from one project or client to another. Sometimes the development team take responsibility for organizing the localization, but usually it is the publisher who commissions this work from us, with the producer as point of contact for any queries that have to be relayed to the development team. On some projects we work simultaneously with the publisher and developer, allowing us direct access to the people most familiar with the text itself, which can improve efficiency of communication.

How much does the localization process add to the cost of developing a game?

This depends largely on the volume of text and the languages that a game is localized into. Some in-game texts are only 3,000 words whereas others can reach as high as 1,000,000 words—costs for localization and the subsequent QA will be in direct proportion to these volumes.

How well is the localization process usually integrated into the overall development process, in your experience?

In our experience this is improving as the games industry matures. However, the fact remains that localization often comes as an afterthought to the development process, particularly with U.S. developers. Add in the fact that it happens at the end of the development schedule when deadlines are already tight, and localization professionals

find they often have to work against the clock to provide a good-quality service. Localization can be highly complicated if the concept has not been borne in mind from an early stage in the development.

How important is outsourcing to the localization process?

Outsourcing is particularly relevant to games localization because it enables publishers to address the peak in demand caused by the industry's seasonal nature. There are other advantages that should not be overlooked, such as sourcing translators who live in-country and are therefore up-to-date with slang and colloquialisms, as well as using specialists in a particular genre, and having one Project Manager responsible to ensure consistency across multiple languages.

How much nonlinguistic localization typically takes place?

Tomb Raider is famous for being fundamentally altered for its Japanese debut, for example, while European titles need to be converted from NTSC to PAL playback.

Another typical situation where nonlinguistic localization is needed is to satisfy differing age-rating systems in the various territories. For the German market, displays of violence often have to be toned down, and there are other cultural sensibilities that must be taken into consideration as well. Usually those decisions are made at publisher level.

What can go wrong with the localization process, and why? Could you describe a best-case scenario that would minimize the risk of upsets?

There are many things that can go wrong in a game localization, too numerous to list here! The best-case scenario would be a well-written, locked-down source text supplied in a translator-friendly format, together with a full brief, glossary, and contextual references. Sufficient time would be allowed for the translation and ideally for a separate proofreading, with all queries answered promptly by the publisher or developer. Feedback is also always useful—good or bad.

Do you have any memorable experiences from your time working in localization?

Every project is different, which means there are many to choose from. One of the most rewarding experiences is for a client to come to us seeking professional advice with a particular linguistic issue, and helping them to find a solution to it. It's great when Babel is remembered for such things.

Videogame publishers can do their own localization in-house, or outsource to a localizing specialist such as Babel Media and its expert teams. *TimeSplitters 2* (left) and *Devil May Cry 2* (right and below), for example, both benefited from Babel's troubleshooting localization and functionality testers toward the end of their development cycles.

is a direct result of the compelling business case for focusing on the development of ongoing franchises. And while the decision to develop a sequel is not quite so straightforward from a creative point of view, as Warren Spector noted in his talk at GDC 2003, creating a sequel doesn't have to mean fashioning something unoriginal.

THE FINANCIAL IMPORTANCE OF SEQUELS

The financial case for developing sequels is compelling and clear-cut. Put simply, sequels generally outsell their originals, and if handled carefully are cheaper to produce. Likewise, expansion packs and add-ons elongate the shelf-life of any given title, as well as providing a revenue stream in their own right. It's no wonder then that the world's biggest videogame publisher, Electronic Arts, derives about half of its annual turnover from sequels or licenses that can be released on a yearly basis. The ongoing intellectual properties created by sequels are the lifeblood of many publishers and developers.

The alternative to creating original intellectual property (IP) is to buy it at exorbitant cost. As a measure of precisely how exorbitant, it's worth pointing out that the deal behind Atari's top-ten hit in 2003

PART 04. POSTPRODUCTION
CHAPTER THREE

SEQUELS AND EXPANSIONS

A BRIEF HISTORY OF THE SEQUEL

Videogame sequels have been around for almost as long as videogames have been in existence. It wasn't long after the first *Pong* cabinet broke down due to the strain on its jury-rigged coin collector in 1972 that Atari saw the merit in offering its customers something familiar but different. The game's followup arrived in the same year in the shape of *Pong Doubles.* Another sequel, *Quadrapong,* arrived two years later in 1974. Similarly, *Tank*, which also came out in 1974, spawned a sequel, *Tank II*, inside a year, with *Tank III* arriving just a year later (the series continued through *Tank 8*, in 1976, and *Ultra Tank* in 1978). And it wasn't just the Americans who were at it: Nintendo's *Donkey Kong*, which arrived in 1981, went on to spawn a series of sequels starring the game's protagonist, Mario (originally known as Jumpman), that stretches through to this day.

Today, sequels are a ubiquitous and (sometimes begrudgingly) accepted feature of the videogame landscape. Indeed, of the 800 console titles released in North America in 2003, only one of the top ten best-selling titles wasn't a sequel of some sort (although that game, Atari's *Enter the Matrix,* was based on a blockbuster movie). Similar statistics could be wheeled out for any recent year. This proliferation

is estimated to have valued *The Matrix* videogame brand at around $47m. A similar deal saw videogame developer 3D Realms sell its *Max Payne* brand to Take 2 Interactive in a deal that valued it at around $40m. But apart from saving money, IP creation can actually create money for cash-strapped developers. It provides the opportunity to establish additional revenue streams from merchandizing, and the sort of cross-promotional opportunities embodied by the appearance of *Tomb Raider's* Lara Croft on the cover of British style-bible *The Face* at the height of her fame (not to mention the spin-off movies starring Angelina Jolie).

Opposite: **Few videogame series have demonstrated such a prolific commitment to sequels as (the inappropriately named)** *Final Fantasy.* **Here's just a selection:**
Top row, left to right:
Final Fantasy, NES, 1987
Final Fantasy II, NES, 1988
Final Fantasy III, NES, 1990
2nd row, left to right:
Final Fantasy IV, SNES, 1991 (confusingly, released in the USA as *Final Fantasy II*)
Final Fantasy V, SNES, 1992
Final Fantasy VI, SNES, 1994
3rd row, left to right:
Final Fantasy VII, PlayStation, 1997
Final Fantasy VIII, PlayStation, 1999
Final Fantasy IX, PlayStation, 2000
Bottom row, left to right:
Final Fantasy XI, PlayStation2, 2001
Final Fantasy Tactics, PlayStation, 1997
Final Fantasy Tactics Advance, Game Boy Advance, 2003

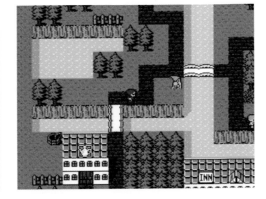

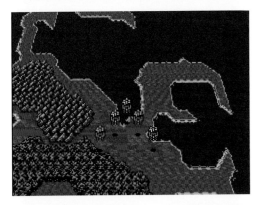

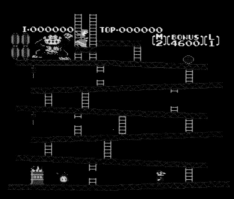
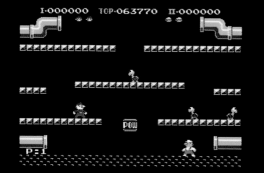

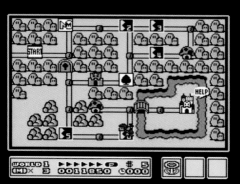

Perhaps the most well known
and enduring of all videogame
franchises, Mario just keeps
returning to save Princess:

Top row, left to right:
Donkey Kong, Coin-op, 1981
(NES version shown)
Mario Bros., NES, 1983
Super Mario Bros., NES, 1985

Above, left to right:
Super Mario Bros. 3, NES, 1988
Super Mario World, SNES, 1990
Mario Kart: Double Dash!!,
Gamecube, 2003

Above, left to right:
Super Mario: Yoshi's Island,
SNES, 1995
Super Mario 64, N64, 1996

Right, left to right:
Super Mario Sunshine,
GameCube, 2002
Mario Golf: Toadstool Tour,
GameCube, 2003

CREATING A SEQUEL From a financial perspective, the most important aspect of sequel creation is keeping costs down. There are a number of ways to do this, but the essence of all of them is forward planning. It might sound like stating the obvious, but it's essential to make sure that code is designed so that it's left in a reusable state.

This means designing code from the outset in such a manner that it's modular and scalable. Or, in other words, making sure that it's easy to add new components and features, and creating code that's capable of taking advantage of new, more advanced hardware in the future. This sort of programming philosophy is desirable in any case, but it's all too easy to compromise during punishing periods of "crunch time," and it's especially important for developers who harbor the ambition of creating a franchise.

British developer Creative Assembly has pioneered a novel technique for creating sequels over the course of its *Total War* series of realtime strategy (RTS) titles. Essentially, it consists of developing two titles concurrently. While one title is developed on the basis of existing technology in a fairly conventional timeframe, the second title (its sequel) is created in parallel from the ground up over a longer period to allow for the creation of an entirely new and more advanced engine.

Building a franchise is more than just a technical challenge; there are also several important creative decisions to be made too. What they generally boil down to is whether to opt for evolution or revolution. Do you try to keep your existing fanbase happy by giving them more of the same with higher production values and greater polish? Or do you make sure they don't get bored by giving them something different? It's the *Empire Strikes Back* dilemma; without the context provided by the original *Star Wars* movie and the narrative conclusion reached in the final part of the trilogy, the second movie made little sense. But many fans would argue that it was a better movie as a result. Likewise, videogame developers need to identify whether to keep their existing fanbase happy, or whether to try to attract new admirers.

Gary Penn, the producer of the original *Grand Theft Auto*, now at bijou development studio Denki, has perspicaciously approached this question by comparing videogames to golf. Just as golfers are quite content with playing the same game on new courses, he argues, gamers don't necessarily expect or demand the core mechanics of

USER MODS
Although it doesn't quite fit into the "expansion" category, shipping a PC game with easy-to-use development tools is another way that developers can enhance the attractiveness of their games. Aside from the long-term benefit of inspiring another generation of game creators, providing fan communities with tools gives them a vested and ongoing interest in the game, and allows them to create new content that has the potential to increase the audience. Perhaps the most obvious example of giving away tools is *Half-Life*, which spawned the massively successful user-created mod *Counter-Strike* and consequently benefited from an almost unprecedented retail longevity. More recently, titles like BioWare's *Neverwinter Nights* (below) have also benefited from fervent mod communities.

a game to fundamentally alter between an original title and its sequel. One of the advantages of this sort of gradualistic approach is that it can help minimize "feature creep"—a process that sees games delayed by developers who want to make time to include all those neat new features that they continue to create throughout the development process. With the knowledge that there will be a sequel, all these nifty tricks can be saved up for later use. Thus the development process becomes an iterative one over the course of a franchise, with each new episode carefully refining what's gone before.

But this isn't the only possible approach, and nor is it necessarily the best; there's no single way of appeasing everybody, and for every gamer who would like more of the same but better, the chances are that there's another who would prefer a fundamentally new experience. The opportunity to be free from the constraints of the iterative approach can be more creatively satisfying for developers, and consequently produce a better end product.

WHAT MAKES A SUCCESSFUL SEQUEL?

The question of whether to opt for an iterative approach or to adopt a more radical stance while creating a sequel is not one with a definitive answer, but developers could do worse than look at the precedents set by existing sequels:

FIVE SEQUELS THAT GOT IT RIGHT

Left: **GRAND THEFT AUTO: VICE CITY,** Rockstar Games (2002)
How do you improve upon one of the best-selling games of all time? How do you expand upon a living, breathing, sandbox-styled crime city? According to the *Grand Theft Auto III*'s sublime sequel *Vice City*, by providing bigger, better, and more; by increasing the scope for character and narrative development; and by giving it a nostalgic twist by dressing it all up in a shoulder-padded designer suit.

Below: **FINAL FANTASY VII,** Square (1997)
The seventh chapter in the massively popular Japanese role-playing game (RPG) series was the first in the series to feature 3D graphics. Indeed the decision to utilize the massive capacity and fast access provided by the PlayStation's CD-Rom media ensured this was the first title in the series not to appear on Nintendo hardware, since the N64 simply couldn't handle the lustrous rendered backdrops and acclaimed audio score. In keeping with its predecessors, the game featured a memorable cast of characters: Cloud and his nemesis Sephiroth, and the tragic figure of Aeris Gainsborough are still firm fan favorites.

Above: **MS. PAC-MAN,** Namco (1981)
Although the original *Pac-Man* was a pretty elegant and pure maze puzzle, *Ms. Pac-Man*, the first in a long line of sequels, still managed to find scope to improve upon the formula laid down by its predecessor. Alternating the action across four different mazes removed the repetition, while allowing fruit and bonus items to wander around the screen increased the game's variety. Indeed it even managed to introduce some semblance of a storyline by punctuating levels with rudimentary cut-scenes.

Above: **BALDUR'S GATE II: SHADOWS OF AMN,** Interplay (2000)
Demonstrating the effectiveness of an iterative approach to sequelitis, BioWare's *Baldur's Gate* followup was a case of careful refinement and gradual technical enhancement. This steady and surefooted approach allowed the developer to build on the solidity of its Infinity engine and the *Dungeons & Dragons* ruleset upon which the game was based, and afforded a greater freedom to toy with the scope and structure of the game's even more epic narrative.

Below: **AMPLITUDE,** SCEA (2003)
A clear case of revolution over evolution, *Amplitude* didn't even share a name with its precursor, *Frequency*. There was a certain thematic continuity though: the same focus on snappily hip music acts, and similar fluorescent visual stylings. But the core mechanics marked a fairly fundamental departure. Sure, they still charged the player with the task of constructing tunes by rhythmic button-pressing, but they did so in a wholly novel, and yet equally satisfying manner.

FIVE SEQUELS THAT GOT IT WRONG

Right: **TOMB RAIDER: THE ANGEL OF DARKNESS,** Eidos Interactive (2003)
In spite of the monumental success of the *Tomb Raider* series, its developer, Core Design, demonstrated the downside of trying to introduce too many changes with the *Angel of Darkness*. Bringing the game out on PlayStation 2 required the creaking PSone game engine to be drastically rewritten, but the decision to introduce new (and incongruous) gameplay elements such as stealth and elements borrowed from the RPG genre, just overextended the developer's resources. The result was a bug-ridden, unsatisfying rush job, in spite of a prolonged development duration.

Below: **FINAL FANTASY VIII,** Square (1999)
After the apogee of the series in *Final Fantasy VII*, *Final Fantasy VIII* divided the critics. Most, though, erred on the side of disappointment. Although it maintained the technical wizardry and visual splendor of its predecessor, it toyed unsuccessfully with a number of core game mechanics, and introduced a cast of inconsequential and unsympathetic characters to compound the sadness felt by its fans across the globe.

Right: **MARIO KART: DOUBLE DASH!!,** Nintendo (2003)
This was another update that suffered under the weight of expectations raised by the sheer and utter brilliance of its predecessor. Nintendo was unable to capture the essence of the original SNES title in this GameCube update. Dispensing with the sublimely intuitive powerslide and nuanced handling of previous versions, *Double Dash!!* opted instead for the novelty of a cooperative multiplayer mode.

Right: **DEUS EX: INVISIBLE WAR,** Eidos Interactive (2003)
It was unfortunate for developer Ion Storm that *Invisible War* was the followup to such a groundbreaking, genre-defying title as the original *Deus Ex*, because the second installment in the series was a competent title by any standard. It's just that the paradigmatic brilliance of its predecessor had so elevated expectations that the decision to simplify elements of the game and limit the size and scope of the game ended up disappointing fans—not least because the emergent possibilities presented by the original were not realized in the sequel.

Below: **DEVIL MAY CRY 2,** Capcom, (2003)
An example of the all-too-common overcautious approach that characterizes many contemporary followups, *Devil May Cry 2* was more of an upgrade than an outright sequel. Granted only a brief spell in development in a bid to capitalize on the success of the original, the game suffered as a result. Compared to its forerunner it was much less exhilarating, too brief, and offered no new features to distinguish itself.

Q&A

YANNIS MALLAT, EXECUTIVE PRODUCER, UBISOFT ENTERTAINMENT

Yannis Mallat didn't join the videogame industry until after he'd spent three years in West Africa providing humanitarian aid to developing countries. He also found time to earn a Master's Degree in International Agronomy and Economic Development in Paris before turning his hand to videogames.

Mallat's career has encompassed *Prince of Persia 2, Prince of Persia: The Sands of Time*, and *Rayman Advance*; as well as working on production for *Little Nicky*, Disney's *The Emperor's New Groove* and Disney's *Dinosaur*. Based in Ubisoft's Montreal development since January 2000, he was recently appointed Executive Producer for the *Prince of Persia* franchise.

Below: The *Prince of Persia* title screen from 1990.

Opposite page: Scenes from *Prince of Persia: The Sands of Time.*

How important are sequels and expansions to the way videogames are developed today? Is there any value in trying to create a standalone game?

When a successful standalone game is created (and we purposely use the phrase "original creation" to define it), the sequel is considered as soon as the commercial success of the first game is guaranteed. The same goes for movies, TV shows, etc. Although this mercantile view of the phenomenon is a reality, it still leaves room for highly creative content to be produced. In fact, with the industry becoming more and more mature, and more competitive on the demand side (consumers now have the choice of an incredible numbers of games that hit the market year after year), sequels are less a safe bet than ever. Developers still have to provide a fair amount of creative value to satisfy the consumers.

How far does the modern phenomenon of creating franchises (as opposed to creating a single game) affect the traditional development model? Does it simply elongate the process over several games, or is it more complex than that? Does the fact that you can amortize development costs over the whole process make it more likely to generate publisher interest?

I think it all depends on the kind of game you want to produce, but we can definitely find some rules of thumb, which are emphasized strongly by the franchise creation phenomenon: A) in the videogame industry, marketing does not create franchises, production does: the game you're creating needs well-above-average review scores (quality). From this first rule, we can derive several others: B) an original creation needs a longer preproduction because you want to validate your core gameplay and mechanics before a resource-intensive production phase (expensive). C) You have to stay focused on what the game is (or will be) before exploring new gameplay territories or ideas. D) Perennial technology is key.

In a sense, the franchise creation phenomenon is stimulating the rules of success of videogame development. That's one positive view of the phenomenon.

Does it simply elongate the process over several games? I think it mainly depends on how much creative value publishers want to put in their franchises' sequels. Some franchises may require a very small amount of original content; we can think of many sports titles based on actual sports leagues. In those cases, a few more features, up-to-date stats and teams players, new skins customization, etc. are often enough for consumers to be satisfied by buying the 2003, 2004, and 2005 version of the game. Thus, after the first game is produced, the development model is untouched until technology reaches its limit (the need for a new engine to develop new features on, for instance). But in the case of an action adventure game, such as *Prince of Persia*, we would never think of repackaging the previous title with some updated characters' textures. Instead we come up with a heavy dose of original content that revisits all the original aspects of the game: story, game features, game mechanics, art direction, etc. We can definitely say it's a choice and a more complex one than elongating the process over several games because it's iterative. On one hand, we pretty much know what to do well and what to enhance based on the previous title. On the other hand, we want to listen to consumers telling us how they perceived the experience, the game, the brand. There is a fine line between what could be addressed by elongating the development process and what needs to be adjusted on the fly. It's art, isn't it? On the technology side, you're absolutely right, we can definitely profit from cost amortization. There is much less amortization on data than on technology. It's not only a question of money, but a question of quality and scope. With a proven engine, tools, and a trained team, you can spend more on new data, and produce more and more efficiently.

How important is it to plan for sequels from the outset of the development process?

It actually depends…. There are two possible scenarios. First, in the case of an original creation and a new property, it's not important at all to plan in my opinion. The priority should go to unleashing creativity instead of planning. Planning a sequel would sound like thinking of a plan B just in case the initial plan is not working. By doing that, you naturally tend to create conditions for the initial plan to fail. There is always room for a sequel to happen if the game is a success. An original creation will not be a success if it's not good. The development process should support the creation of high-value content for the first game of what could become a franchise, nothing else. Not planning for sequels is the best way for them to happen because they will happen only if your first game deserves one. Trying not to kill your main character at the end of the first

game is enough planning! What I mean here is that eventually, the market (consumers) decides. The only thing you can do is come up with the best game you can create at any time.

Once you have a brand though, it's another story. Planning for sequels is good. On the one hand you pretty much know what the consumers like about it and you know how to do it. On the other, it gives you this extra time to build the franchise through the sequels, make it evolve, work on coherency, explore new gameplay territories, etc. But here again, the common thing is providing high-value content.

Are there different ways of creating sequels? I've heard of some developers who work on the original and sequel concurrently, for example, or of developers who outsource a substantial amount of work on the sequel to enable them to focus on adding new features.

There is definitely a multitude of ways of creating sequels. Some developers can start both game and sequel at the same time (high risk related to how successful the first game is) whereas some others will outsource part of the sequel data (high risk in quality and technology). We used another way to make *Prince of Persia: Warrior Within*. We decided to do 100 percent of the work internally but with some overlap between the two productions (*Warrior Within* began before

Above and opposite: **Scenes from the *Prince of Persia* sequel, *Prince of Persia: Warrior Within*.**

Sands of Time was over). This scheme allowed us to react to the consumers' feedback while giving us enough time to create high-value content. The reason why we kept the whole work internally was for productivity matters: in any game development process, the time where you produce high-quality content in the fastest way is at the end of production, when the team knows the tools by heart, when the tools and engine are working perfectly. This means that, at the beginning of *Warrior Within*, we were producing high-value content as fast as during the end of *Sands of Time*. Outsourcing a sequel, or even a part of it, would make me freak out!

One much-vaunted advantage of developing sequels is that code can be reused. How far does this happen in practice in your experience?

That's true but dangerous. It happens a lot actually. Once again it depends on how much high-value content you want to put into your sequel (or how cheap you are!), how refreshing you want your sequel to be. Reusing code is necessary because we're talking about proven code, code that works and supports cool features, game systems, and the like, which allow the sequel to be made. But here, we need to differentiate what code we are talking about. Bottom-layer code, such as routines, 3D display code, collision physics system, etc., can be reused without compromising the refreshing aspect you're looking for, because this kind of code doesn't carry the most

obvious game mechanics and core gameplay. The advantage is that using an already proven technology allows you to provide consumers with an expected sequel in less than two years. As soon as you're reusing AI code for example (main character or NPC behavior), you have to be cautious, because this code is supporting the most obvious game system. As I said earlier, most sports game sequels maintain a strong reuse of such code because the game mechanics are the same (you pretty much play hockey the same way in 2004 as in 2003, right?) From my experience on *Prince of Persia*, we had to get rid of the whole enemy AI code to start a new one allowing us to provide a really refreshing experience. The basic Prince behavior system was kept only to build new behaviors on top of it (environment and Free-Form Fighting system for example).

So, to summarize: keep 80 percent of the "invisible" code to allow you to make a sequel on the technology side, and keep 20 percent of the "visible" code to allow you to make a really refreshing experience. That's the model that appeared to me to make the most sense.

Does the knowledge that there will be a sequel make it easier to complete development of the first title in a series? It must make it easier to pin down the feature set, for example.
Maybe, but in theory only. Practically, when finishing a game, you don't think about anything other than finishing the game! What I mean is that people who complete the games are not the same as people who start games. It's a different skill set. People who are left in a rush to ship the first one may not want to hear about their friends having a good time conceiving a new one!

How far does the pressure to create franchises compromise creativity?
You cannot let this happen! That would be the death of your (nonexisting yet) brand. Although I know there are a lot of mediocre franchises that sell well (although these are mostly based on movies), they're not a guarantee of commercial success anymore. Videogame franchises are born from creativity, and they should be kept alive and evolve the same way. Anyone who sacrifices creativity, rejuvenation, refreshment, or innovation within a franchise is burying its tomb, with no interest in raiding it after....

On the market side, consumers sometimes miss very good games by going with existing well-known franchises that often deliver a less interesting play experience. In that sense, the pressure to create franchises can compromise creativity, inviting developers to build a game based on a formula that seems to work. Producers, developers, and publishers have a role to play in this. There is no better recipe to follow than the one that suits the game you're working on.

What are the most common mistakes that developers make when creating sequels?
Lack of creativity is definitely the biggest mistake developers can make. It's difficult to keep the same team on the same brand over time. The *Devil May Cry 1* team went to *Chaos Legion*, leading to a disappointing *Devil May Cry 2*. Examples like this are to be found everywhere in the industry. However, managing the talent is one of the few things that can help a brand evolve positively. Not listening to the market and the consumers' needs is also potentially damaging. The core values of a brand need to evolve, it cannot stay young forever. Whatever the brand, whatever the past successes, consumers have things to say about it. If they're not heard, someone else will listen to them and the risk is that you'll lose your fans.

BUSINESS AND FINANCE

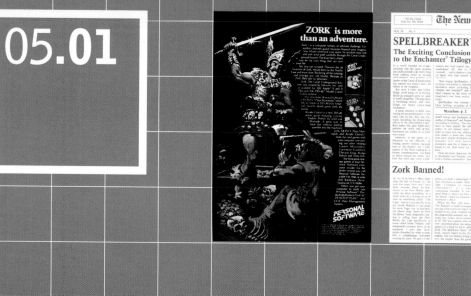

05.01

MARKETING AND PR

ABOVE THE LINE VERSUS BELOW THE LINE

The advertising and marketing industries are notorious for their jargon. Often, terms are invented and repeated without thought for their origin, with seemingly the sole purpose of baffling those outside of the business.

Common terms heard in the PR and Marketing industry are "Above the Line" (ATL) activity versus "Below the Line" (BTL).

Simply, ATL spend is attributed to advertising, in the print press, on television, radio, in movie theaters, and outdoors (with posters)—marketing that tries to tell consumers what they should think (far left). BTL spend deals directly with those consumers, through PR, direct marketing, or viral campaigns, and aims to change how they think by forging a closer relationship with them. The direct-mail flyer for *Zork* (left) is an early example of BTL marketing.

ATL activity tends to be the most expensive, as it has an immediate and tangible benefit. BTL is much more speculative—but when it works, it's immensely beneficial.

From politics to pornography, every sector boasts an associated Public Relations business—and the videogame market is obviously no exception. However, specialist PR is in its infancy. The earliest PRs appeared in the industry in the late 80s, usually handling other roles such as writing the manual and bug-testing. Over time, the profession has matured alongside the publishing community—it's not unusual for larger games publishers to have teams of up to seven internal PR professionals responsible for liaising with the editorial teams of print and Internet publications, with each one looking after a specific sector of the market.

In recent years PR has become more sophisticated, with large agencies eyeing the sector as a lucrative source of business. Their arrival has met with a mixed reception as PR heavyweights from other industries struggle to meet the demands of such a specialized sector.

It goes without saying that a PR professional working in the videogame industry should have a broad understanding of the market. Good videogame journalists boast a degree of expertise that can intimidate even the most competent communicator—and one slip-up can often tarnish the reputation of the PR and, by association, the titles they are promoting.

Unlike PR professionals, marketing managers and directors are used to paying for advertising coverage, so they rarely understand the intricacies of working with editorial teams. Far more used to throwing money at the problem in order to promote their titles, they can't comprehend the difficulties of persuading journalists to feature games for free.

Marketing and PR budgets tend to be rolled into one. They are set in two ways: either as a proportion of what the game is estimated to sell, or as a fraction of what the game needs to sell. Either way, they are set at the start of the project—or when a publisher signs—with, as all fixed costs, very little leeway once agreed.

Naturally, marketing budgets vary significantly, and from format to format. PC titles can benefit from a higher proportion of projected revenue as there are no hardware licensing fees to pay on

Above: Billed as the first "fun" computer magazine, *CVG* lasted some 25 years before its undignified closure. Launched in the UK in November 1981, it is widely regarded as the world's first specialist gaming press magazine—beating American rival *Electronic Games* by two weeks. In keeping with the hobbyist ethos of the time, the magazine combined news and reviews with program listings readers could type into their computers in order to play simple games. Although a tortuous and often futile endeavor (the tiniest error and the game would not work), it offered an insight into the development process, sparking an interest in its readers that prompted some of them to take up development positions in the industry.

Right: Unsurprisingly, the media's online presence offers the most regular coverage of computer and videogames. In the UK, the *Guardian* launched its "Games Blog" in the middle of 2004, drawing on a pool of writers who've plied their trade in the business for some years—and it's the only British national newspaper resource that offers dedicated daily games coverage. Print coverage across the other news titles is more sporadic and based mainly around the weekends, in specific review sections, although occasionally "real" news stories break into the main paper.

MANHUNT WITCH HUNT

"Ban These Evil Games" screamed the hysterical *Daily Mail* in the summer of 2004, as the game was linked—although not by the investigating officers, judge, defense, nor prosecution, it's worth noting—to the horrific murder of Stefan Pakeerah by Warren LeBlanc. LeBlanc was 17 at the time—below the legal age required to play *Manhunt*—and the link was tenuous at best (indeed, the game was actually found in the possession of the 14-year-old victim). But the escapade demonstrated the attitude of the press to videogames.

Sweeping aside the broader issues of censorship, the media concentrated on the fact that a teenage market exists for games rated for adults only. In a witch hunt that mirrored that of so-called "video nasties" in the 80s, newspapers demanded that games be removed from our shelves in order to protect our children. The furor soon died down, thanks to the solid defense provided by trade association ELSPA and Barrington Harvey, its PR agency. However, the industry does need to consider its attitude as it moves forward, as this issue is likely to raise its ugly head again in the future.

every unit manufactured. However, given the generally inferior sales performance of the average PC title, its total budget is usually less than a console equivalent.

Over recent years, the industry has seen a worrying trend develop as publishers compete for the attention of a public bewildered by the astonishing volume of games released. The peak selling period of October through December frequently sees dozens of games published on the same day.

EA's recent dominance of the charts has over the past few years been mainly down to its smart marketing as, in truth, its games have historically often left something to be desired—although this is improving. Huge advertising spends—occasionally outweighing the actual development budget—have nonetheless convinced consumers to stick with the brand.

The industry has learned to mirror the activity of other associated media. Avenues for promotion—either through PR or Marketing—are similar to those used by music and movies. Without

the charismatic star personalities of either (even *Time* magazine cover star Hideo Kojima doesn't have quite the same appeal as the lowliest Hollywood star, for example), coverage is typically restricted to the reviews columns, although creative ideas can occasionally result in editorial outside of these channels. Endorsements from outside of the industry obviously help here, with sportsmen and women happy to discuss how much they love the game they're promoting—in return for a share of the spoils.

This pigeonholing is a challenge to the PR industry. Being creative with relatively modest PR budgets is the order of the day—and there has been some limited success with stories designed to break into the wider media.

However, irresponsible ideas can have serious repercussions. Games are still considered to be the domain of children—despite a number of statistics claiming the average gamer is aged in their mid-twenties. Given the unsympathetic attitude of some sectors of the media, the industry as a whole has a fine line to tread.

PR AND MARKETING PROCESSES
Given the tendency for games to miss their scheduled release dates, it's impossible to plan a PR and marketing campaign from the outset of the development cycle. However, an approximate timeline can be drafted at the early stages, with the months initially proposed moved back as the game experiences inevitable delays.

It's commonly accepted that the most efficient specialist press campaigns run for nine months, working back from the month of issue. Additionally, nonspecialist media campaigns will run for three months—two prior to release, one after. Of course, there are exceptions, but they are usually for higher-profile titles that are all but guaranteed to sell.

BE PREPARED
In PR terms, the amount of coverage you generate depends on the assets available. Making things difficult for the media you are targeting—withholding information, for example, or only issuing a handful of screen shots—will greatly reduce the amount of space offered. Ensure materials are of the highest standard, and that everything is organized prior to its being requested. For example, don't wait until you are asked for photographic images of key staff to suddenly decide to grab a cheap digital camera and rattle them off.

USE A PROFESSIONAL
It is natural for a developer to assume he knows his game better than anyone else. But it's important to work with a PR professional you trust. They will know what the media wants, and when they want it. A good PR office will be able to negotiate coverage that best fits with the projected release date, in turn liaising with the development team to ensure everything reaches the journalist in time and with the right image. Let them concentrate on the dirty business of publicity; it's important for the development team to remain focused on the project in hand.

STRATEGY AND TACTICS
There is a broad range of media available to the videogame industry, but each requires a different approach. Indeed the full range of PR strategies and tactics could occupy an entire book themselves. The following paragraphs give an overview of the main categories and tactics worth considering when marketing a videogame:

TRADE
From inception to release, the trade media (aimed at those working within the videogame industry) is usually the first and last specialist sector to offer relevant editorial to an individual game.

Right from the start, there are opportunities here. The trade is interested in new developers springing up, the titles they are producing, and which publishers are potentially interested in signing their games. Unlike other media, the trade sector does not insist on in-game graphics to accompany stories, preferring instead to concentrate on personality and photography. Many developers use this approach to announce which titles are currently ripe for publishing deals, assisting their efforts at finding funding.

As development progresses, so the trade's interest typically wanes. As the trade covers the business of games rather than the quality, professionally it is not concerned with how well each title plays. Its major interest is: How many will it sell? So, outside of any feature- or issue-based coverage that may be planned, the trade media will forget about individual games until a couple of months prior to release.

Then, it becomes of paramount importance, although coverage will usually be negotiated by the publisher rather than the developer. Retail buyers need to know how the game is being received, and how much marketing money is being spent on the campaign. Release dates need to be publicized, along with any other special retail or consumer activity. This final push is all

Above: *FIFA Football 2004*, from Electronic Arts. EA reaches heights the rest of the industry can only aspire to. Its domination of the charts is in no small part down to its clever—and inescapable—marketing, working alongside its PR. Almost every game it releases tops the charts. The secret is in the timing of its activity, which reaches a crescendo in the week prior to launch. From TV to national press activity, those with an interest in the medium cannot fail to miss an EA release. It's reached the point where the industry may as well not bother releasing games on the days EA chooses to.

about ensuring the retail channel understands how much a game is worth to them. After all, if they're not interested from a business perspective, it's unlikely they'll stock a title in any significant numbers. And if nobody can buy it, it will obviously not sell.

SPECIALIST COMPUTER AND VIDEOGAMING PRESS

While the specialist media only communicates to a fraction of the potential audience—hardcore gamers who will happily shell out for a magazine every month—these are the consumers who have the potential to buy first and excite others about it. Encouraging these devotees onside first can reap tremendous benefits.

The downside? Every other developer is attempting the same tactic—particularly as retail stocking decisions are additionally based on what certain publications are saying about particular games.

There are ways of gaining an advantage. Typically, magazines are broken down into rigid sections that cover games at their relevant stages: news, previews, features, and reviews. It is reasonable to expect coverage in each of those sections at least once—more, depending on the reputation of the developer or the anticipation for the title. One tactic is to work specifically with individual magazines to boost pagination. Give some magazines assets early, and ensure that there are enough materials to give each publication an exclusive of sorts. Demos are crucially important for PC games, often bumping up coverage when a deal is agreed.

PR: ENTER THE MATRIX

Given the price Infogrames (now Atari) paid for the *Matrix* license—and the subsequent royalties due to the Wachowski Brothers—the game itself needed to sell in an incredible amount in order to break even, let alone make money.

Infogrames' job was made more difficult by the scathing reaction of the specialist press, so the success of its marketing campaign was of even more importance. Like everything else to do with the *Matrix* sequels, the objective of the Wachowski brothers was to extend the world into associated media—be that an animated series, graphic novels, and indeed, the videogame.

Impressively—or cynically—the *Matrix* movie sequels provided only a fraction of the tale; fans were encouraged to purchase the associated media in order to get the full picture. The game itself boasted around an hour of custom-made footage, directed by the Wachowskis, and a plot that ran in parallel to the movies.

The *Matrix* PR team worked together to promote all facets of the franchise, with, most impressively, *Time* magazine running a cover on the movie and game (above right). TV and cinema spots were ever present. The campaign utilized the prerelease hype for *Matrix Reloaded* to brilliant effect, and the game went on to sell over 2.5 million copies worldwide.

The flipside is that those magazines outside of any exclusive agreement can often be less likely to offer significant coverage if they consider their good prepublicity will help a rival when the demo is released.

Review scores are critical, and there's often little you can do to ensure a bad game gets a good mark. However, during the campaign you should be able to build up an idea of which publications are fans, and it is vital that they receive review code first. Then keep those fingers crossed.

SPECIALIST INTERNET SITES

The Internet press likes to think of itself as particularly important. The speed with which it can react and distribute media—and the breadth of sites with a videogame slant—can obviously ensure that millions of consumers have access to information a few seconds after it is published.

However, in an effort to carve out a niche for themselves, Internet news sites are often responsible for some bizarre and extreme rumors, some of which are simply hysterical, and others plain damaging. And the nature of Internet news reporting—copying editorial from others, in many cases—can mean that one stupid news posting can have widespread implications.

While it is impossible to know each of these journalists individually, it's important to maintain a dialog with the editors and reporters on commercial sites. Their authority can often dismiss inaccurate reporting in an instant.

CONSUMER PRESS

Over recent years, the consumer magazine sector—particularly those aimed at males—has covered games alongside music and movies. This is partly because games have become an integral part of the modern lifestyle. But it's also because videogames provide a chunk of the advertising revenue.

Space in the consumer press is at a premium. Typically, console games are preferred—obviously a consumer journalist has less time to appraise each title, so the plug and play

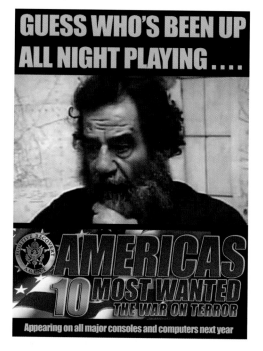

PR AND MARKETING:
AMERICA'S 10 MOST WANTED

System 3's controversial adventure game—which charged players with the task of hunting down real-life terrorists—was actually a variant of *Fugitive Hunter*, a game released a few months before to a generally poor reception. Despite improvements made during an extended period of development, it was felt the specialist press in particular would automatically dismiss it, given its already tarnished reputation. Therefore the decision was taken to implement a marketing campaign that raised awareness without specific editorial comment.

Two agencies were employed: notorious UK PR Max Clifford—more used to handling large Sunday tabloid revelations—alongside a dedicated games firm. While Clifford took care of whipping up controversy in the national papers, the games agency managed a nationwide competition in which players could win £10,000 by submitting the highest score.

The PR plan was shifted back a month. A high-profile advertising campaign—one strand capitalizing on the capture of Saddam Hussein—caught the attention, as did the lure of the prize fund. Reviews did not appear prior to launch.

It worked amazingly well. The game spent a significant time at the top of the charts, enjoying success through word of mouth and curiosity. While not technically an illustration of how to develop a game, it's a good example of how to sell one.

PR: *RESIDENT EVIL: ZERO*

The agency in charge of generating awareness for Game Cube rerelease *Resident Evil: Zero (below right)* used the notoriety of the series to pull off a cheap yet effective launch story.

Plenty of ideas were suggested—some that involved sending in soiled clothes—but the one that really worked was the helpline aimed at those scared witless by the content of the game.

A local rate line was bought for around $450. Professional voice talent was employed for around half of that. The script was written in-house, and recorded by the actress remotely.

A press release was issued over the wires, incurring an additional fee of around $300. A specialist radio company was also employed to organize radio interviews. While not necessary for the success of the campaign, it did result in an additional 20 live and prerecorded editorial spots for the $4,500 fee.

The crowning glory was the appearance of the story across the BBC News services, resulting in millions of people around the country hearing about the game's launch. Not bad for a total budget of under $6,000.

It's worth noting that tactics such as this are never guaranteed to succeed. That's the risk you take. Had there been a major news event on that day, it's unlikely it would have received any coverage at all. Knowing when to take these calculated risks is one of the real skills of PR and marketing.

element is welcome. They will also often only cover games that have been receiving rave coverage in the specialist press, making that sector of even more importance. Timing is an issue—the men's lifestyle journalists can often be working on magazines that hit the street two months ahead, and they want to cover games that will be on sale then. For this reason, incomplete, preproduction versions have to be supplied, with details explaining known bugs and unfinished sections.

The PR Holy Grail is breaking free from the standard reviews section and into regular editorial. Endorsements make this relatively straightforward: offer the magazine, for example, an interview with a celebrity, and expect the game to be mentioned at the end. However, more imaginative ideas without big names can often work—for example, features in which journalists learn the real-life skills presented in games.

BROADCAST

There are very few TV shows dedicated to games these days—broadcasting execs rarely understand the medium, resulting in presentation which is clichéd at best and insulting at worst. And those that do exist are typically relegated to satellite channels, targeting audiences that are committed but relatively small in TV terms.

Lead times play a major part for the broadcast media, too and for that reason they will tend to feature the games the specialist press is raving about at the time. However, broadcast demands a completely different set of assets—unedited Betacam video, and lots of it. While this can prove expensive to generate and distribute, the value of the coverage will significantly exceed the cost.

The videogame industry boasts few stars who are able to command a presence outside of these specialist shows, and even fewer who will attract the interest of a typical TV producer. Although general magazine TV shows will often carry interviews with anyone plugging a book or movie, few game developers will ever make it onto the set.

It is sometimes possible to generate "news-led" coverage. Radio talk shows will often cover games if they're controversial or different. Ensuring the spokesperson comes from the developer is a good idea—many shows are so misinformed on the subject of gaming, it is vital an expert is on hand to correct any inaccuracies.

VIRAL OR WORD OF MOUTH

It's impossible to guarantee the success of a proposed viral marketing campaign. Predicting public taste, and guaranteeing the marketing message is passed from individual to individual—the definition of the process—is difficult in the extreme. However, when it works, it's one of the most effective forms of advertising.

Viruses are at their most effective when they're easy to transmit, which is why most examples of viral marketing these days are Internet based. Many "humorous" attachments from friends and colleagues are thinly-designed marketing messages. Yet if they are genuinely amusing, recipients usually have no qualms about passing them on.

The videogame industry has been quick to embrace the viral marketing message. The proliferation of tools to build fan sites is not an example of a sudden sense of compassion on behalf of the publisher. They know that when a kid builds the greatest fan website using assets they have provided, that kid will tell his immediate network of friends in order to brag about his handiwork. They'll then visit and see the materials explicitly provided.

Other means of viral marketing include mini-games and video clips. It's difficult to track the success of them once they're released. They require enormous confidence on the part of everyone involved, because, if they fail, they're an utter waste of money. When they succeed, however, they're immensely valuable.

ABOVE THE LINE: CONSUMER SHOWS

One way of getting straight to your consumers is through consumer shows. From a purely accounting point of view, it may seem expensive. With floor space, stand build, equipment rental, and staffing costs, it can all mount up.

However, as well as building a direct relationship with consumers, which has other associated benefits such as being able to watch them play and listen to their feedback, these shows tend to attract a huge degree of media attention. Add the millions of readers and viewers who will subsequently digest the press reporting of the show, and you have a significant audience. Factor in the various show awards—awarded for the best games on display—and there can be a huge benefit in attending.

Germany (Leipzig Game Convention) and the UK (Game Stars Live) have large-scale consumer events in the summer; the USA prefers a series of regional tours, mainly of student campuses. In the UK, Sony has taken the unusual approach of launching its own exclusive show. PlayStation Experience 2004 was the third iteration, and took place over a few weeks at theme park Alton Towers. While undoubtedly a huge expense, the hardware manufacturer was able to guarantee itself a wholly attentive audience.

MARKETING

Of course, the easiest way to guarantee coverage is to pay for it. Advertising rates can vary from a few hundred dollars online, to tens of thousands in the national press and on TV.

And although research—from PR professionals, of course—claims that editorial is many times more effective in the minds of the reader or viewer than advertising, the videogame industry is spending an increasing amount of money on marketing. There's a valid argument for doing so: typically, coverage of videogames is very much compartmentalized, meaning that only those reading about games end up reading about games. Advertising can increase awareness across a wider demographic, but at a price.

For some, this price is worth paying. Licensed or big-budget games often need to sell millions of units across the globe, or risk bringing down the publisher, developer, and many other associated companies. In these cases, the marketing budget can far outweigh the development costs. It's a high-risk strategy, but can reap tremendous financial rewards, given the potential income from million-sellers.

The most important thing to remember is to be original without being intrusive. Web advertising has the ability to infuriate, as clever popups and animations wrest control of the screen. While there's no doubting that this is an effective way to grab the attention, it can often generate frustration and bad will.

Q&A

DAVID WILSON, HEAD OF PR, UK, SONY COMPUTER ENTERTAINMENT/PLAYSTATION

David Wilson's first industry job was editorial assistant on *Your Sinclair* magazine—one of the earliest specialist games publications in the UK. After roughly four years at Dennis Publishing, Wilson was eventually promoted to the position of editor of multiformat magazine *Zero*. His first move to the "dark side" of PR was when EA recruited him to look after its affiliated labels.

A move to overall European responsibility followed during his eight years at the firm. Wilson was poached by Sony Computer Entertainment Europe in early 2000 to head up the UK PR for PlayStation, a position he has retained since. He was instrumental in promoting the launch of PlayStation 2.

You've been involved in the industry for many years, first as a journalist and then in the PR profession. How has PR improved during your tenure?

The budgets required and offered to do the job have increased significantly—both out of necessity and also because more opportunities exist.

I think that the acceptance of gaming as viable subject matter for serious column inches has obviously improved as well, which is a good thing. There's still a degree of progress to be made, but we're no longer automatically relegated to the so-called "gaming ghetto," such as the specific games page of *FHM* or whatever. We're able to move more into the mainstream body copy, which is clearly indicative of the acceptance of videogaming as a normal entertainment pastime.

The games PR industry has reflected the growth of the business in terms of it being a bedroom industry initially. Back then was very hands-on—whereas now it's much more creative. While there's more

space available, there's more competition for that space, so you need to be more imaginative in terms of how you place those stories and the angles you seek in order to make it more compelling subject matter.

The standard's also improved. It used to be very formulaic. I shouldn't really name the person responsible, but there was a situation where a certain publisher used to send a very attractive young lady into our office to demo the games, and he actually told us after one or two drinks too many that the worse the quality of the game, the shorter her skirt would be. Those days are long gone, thankfully.

How much difference can PR really make to the overall sales of a game?

It can make a huge difference. It's all amplifying awareness and amplifying sales. Those sales can be better if it is supported by a really good PR campaign.

However, it's not the be-all and end-all. Clearly if a product sucks and the PR is great, it isn't necessarily going to sell, unless there's a massively expensive license attached to it.

What you're trying to achieve is awareness. Yes, you want positive exposure. But fundamentally at the outset, especially if it's not a franchise, you want people to be aware that it exists and that it has merits. And, basically, you want them to go to a shop to buy it. And if they aren't aware of it, they aren't going to buy it. Clearly there is some element of spontaneity in terms of someone going to a shop and liking the packaging. But what contributes to the success of a product is that awareness and people championing it.

A really good product can actually sell through word of mouth from early adopters on the forums. They are still a really influential sector of the gaming community. There are casual gamers who will know a friend who's hardcore, from whom they'll seek recommendations.

Is it possible to implement a really good campaign for a really bad game—and can you increase sales significantly by doing so?
I would argue in such cases it's not good PR. If you're doing good PR on a bad game, it's a really short-term investment. It depends what your aspirations are. If you're trying to create a new series you can do yourself a lot of damage by overpromoting something that doesn't deserve it.

However, it can work if you make a connection with the audience. At the end of the day, that's all you're doing. If something has a redeeming feature, that's what you play to. But if those redeeming features are not that significant you can damage your brand, and product name, and indeed any chance of that franchise succeeding. While you may be able to encourage people to buy it the first time, they're not going to make the same mistake twice.

That said, you know when you've got a "triple-A" product. It's a better use of time to spend all of it on that, and enjoy the benefits of the incremental revenue rather than spending the same amount of time on a product that nobody likes. You're not getting a good return on your own time. And you risk damaging your relationships. The next time you go and sell something that's good, you'll find people won't believe you. It's not exactly rocket science.

Mmm I got - ta have faith
Be- cause I got - ta have faith faith faith

Above, left to right: *PSOne*, *PS2*, *Singstar Party*, all published by SCEA.

So what kind of budgets are you playing with these days? Can money make a difference?

It's not just about the amount of money so much as the smart way you employ it.

You can throw as much money as you like at a title, but there's a level where you can only do so much. After a certain point, the more money you throw at something, the less return you get on that money.

Maybe you bring in external help—and there's a cost associated with that. Maybe you cofund things in the media, which have costs as well. You can end up spending a huge amount of money on competitions and promotions. What's more valuable from our perspective is editorial rather than advertorial.

There will always be someone who is willing to spend more. But it's not purely about that. It's about being creative with your budgets. A clever idea will garner so much more coverage; one that's disproportionate to what you'd spend paying for that space.

How important is the specialist press these days?

It is hugely important. I often come across the argument where PRs imply they "own" the specialist press, with the implied rationale that they should put all their efforts into the nonspecialist press. I really think that's foolish. The truth is, you're not the sole person making games for that media. You're competing for space. It's not guaranteed you'll get the cover, or win the pagination. That's down to who makes the best pitch to the magazine.

We've done research and reviews still rate incredibly high in terms of what influences consumers. The specialist press talk to an audience of gamers—it may not be the total audience, but that's not to say that the wider audience isn't influenced by those readers.

And the elusive wider media?

It has a strong part to play. The challenge is arguably different for us. Being the brand of choice is part and parcel of being a constant presence in lifestyle media where casual gamers or gift purchasers are more likely to turn. You still need front of mind presence. They need to know if PlayStation should be the format they're buying.

Explain how games such as *Ico*, *Rez*, and *Prince of Persia: The Sands of Time* can fail to sell particularly well, given the adoration of the games press and the associated wider PR campaigns.

It's one of the great imponderables. I don't have the magic formula. It's a great travesty that products I really love—and clearly the specialist media love—don't catch the imagination of the buying public to the extent that commercially justifies their existence.

A lot of extraneous factors can hamper games like this. Maybe they're ahead of the time. The original *Populous* or *Tetris* at the outset took a little bit of time to come to the boil commercially. It's also quite a hard sell in terms of explaining in simple terms how these games operate. Take *Ico*, for instance. It's beautiful, in its execution and interpretation. But all the casual gamers see is you're a little boy with horns leading a spectral girl by the hand through a castle… it's not an easy sell.

With *Ico*, the guys we showed it to bought into the vision of how good we knew it was, and that's evident in magazines such as *Edge* repeatedly rating it as one of their top five PlayStation 2 games. But for whatever reason that didn't connect. That may have been about when they shipped; what they were up against. You're competing for a finite amount of budget that people have to spend on games. Factors like that won't help.

But the *Ico* experience wasn't wasted. It's still lauded and championed by the specialist press. People still believe in it. They feel a sense of injustice that a title they gave such a high score didn't light up the charts. Games like this form a basis of original and strong products in our portfolio. When stories appear about the merging of cinema and art styles in our games, then these are the titles that are discussed. And that benefits PlayStation as a whole.

How can developers help make their games more "PR-friendly"?

With *The Getaway*, the guys created 19 square miles (48 sq km) of central London. It took them three years to do so, taking 150,000 digital photos of shop fronts. It was a massive technical achievement. But the team had to take a few negligible liberties to close off some of the minor roads in the interests of gameplay.

But the first thing people do when they play *The Getaway* is ignore the mission and drive to where they know, which is invariably their office. In the first game, we didn't have the *Time Out* building, for example. So this time round, we've worked with the team to ensure all our key journalists can drive to their offices. The game is a different experience if you're seeing what you know, and can say: "Hey, that's my office." And the media is obviously a section we need to specifically impress.

Developers need to be smart in terms of working with PR and marketing people to produce assets that will gain them additional coverage. What might be a great rendered image from the game might not work as front cover, for example. At the most simplistic level, that's where they can work together.

I worked on a game a while back called *Little Big Adventure*. The artists produced an image of the central character sitting at a desk reading a magazine—a high resolution rendered image with the magazine blank. So every magazine you sent it to, you could simply add in the front cover. It flattered the publications we sent it to.

Is all press good press?

I don't adhere to that. We're not after a quick win. And we're not after something that will besmirch the brand. We don't deliberately court controversy. You get the odd controversial piece, but that's usually from a journalist with an agenda. The worst thing I battle against is inaccuracy. I don't like misreporting of fact.

Which is most important: marketing or PR?

In terms of return on investment, the feedback we get from consumers in terms of what influences buying decisions, PR, or objective editorial is more influential. Consumers aren't stupid. Something that's clearly paid for is less influential.

PR is usually cheaper. I wouldn't say that it is easier, but it is cheaper than paying for adverts or advertorial, both in terms of perception from the consumer and what you actually pay for it.

Below: *Getaway 2: Black Monday*, published by SCEA. This title includes the central London offices of all the journalists who were likely to review the game.

Left: Licensed properties, such as these Cartoon Network titles, dominate the cell phone games landscape and prove the easiest way to capture the attention of the platform's mainstream audience. While the benefit in brand recognition can prove useful, intellectual property holders have wised up to the market potential and now require a larger share of revenue and a substantial advance. One high-profile game licensed from one of 2004's most hyped PlayStation releases is rumored to have cost the mobile publisher $1.5 million. Ouch.

PART 05. BUSINESS AND FINANCE

CHAPTER TWO

ALTERNATIVE MODELS

The iPod is a lousy games machine. It's underpowered, has a black and white display, and its joystick or whatever you want to call that hideous, solid wheel, is as inappropriate for controlling games as operating a mouse in a boxing glove. But that didn't stop Apple from implementing a tedious *Breakout* clone, or the proliferation of software engineers from introducing home-grown text adventures and quizzes. Why? Because modern consumers associate technology—any form of technology—with gaming. The key is actually making money from alternative platforms.

The greatest strides have been made in the cell phone market. The popularity of *Snake* illustrated the eagerness of phone owners to find other uses for the technology in their pocket, aside from communicating in an inefficient language that shuns vowels. Cell phone users like games, as much as they like shouting on trains. Of course, you could never sell *Snake* in its original form. But as handset technology improved, so the opportunity to develop more advanced, and potentially sellable software emerged.

Games drive the relentless march of hardware. The introduction of DirectX was not compassion on Microsoft's part—it was to ease the installation of games across a broad range of hardware. Microsoft and the PC manufacturers recognized at the time that the way to encourage its users to continually upgrade—spending more money in the process, of course—was through gaming. After all, you don't need a Pentium 4 to send e-mails or use a word processor. Similarly, your cell phone doesn't need such sophisticated technology simply to make a call. And your TV Digibox? Those cheap games were no random discovery. They've been aiming to fleece you from the start....

You can, of course, turn the tables. Alternative platforms actually offer enormous opportunity to leaner development teams. The games tend to take less time to develop and are therefore obviously cheaper and less risky. The simple nature of many cell-phone and set-top box games has the potential to reach a more casual and lucrative mainstream audience. For example, in its first two years of release, *Tetris* on the Sky digibox was paid for a staggering

The current generation of consoles offer limited opportunities for alternative business models outside of selling the additional game feature for a few dollars. However, PlayStation 3 and its rivals may offer additional on-board storage, which opens up new possibilities. Electronic Arts' Steve Schnur (below) has suggested it may well seek to partner with music labels to directly distribute downloadable songs featured in its games; a further illustration of the potential consolidation of entertainment mediums.

MODDING

Ever since *Doom* was released with its own modification tools, hobbyist developers have been able to experiment with the tools and software development kits (SDKs) of the professionals. "Total Conversions" take an existing title and change everything about it, often drawing inspiration from contemporary movies and books. Perhaps the most famous Total Conversion is *Counter-Strike* (above). Released in beta form on September 19, 1999, it rapidly set new standards for team-based multiplayer games. It was based on the *Half-Life* graphic engine which, in turn, was licensed from the original *Quake*. The game was initially freely downloadable and required only a full version of *Half-Life* to run. However, its appeal resulted in a full commercial release the following year, from which the developers were able to take a cut. The subsequent console version was a full commercial release, although—in the spirit of the initial idea—the original PC version is still available for free for those that are patient enough to patch it to its current iteration. Minh Le and Jesse Cliffe, the original creators of *Counter-Strike*, now occupy full-time positions at Valve. And while this route into commercial development is interesting because it's rare, plenty of current level and map designers cut their teeth through modding.

Lara had appeared on TV many times prior to Christmas 2002, but her debut on Sky's interactive channel *Gamestar* was of particular interest to the games industry. *Tomb Raider: Apocalypse* (above) combined two of the business's biggest dreams: pay-to-play and episodic gaming. Released in three installments—which cost a dollar a session to play—it was a simple 3D platformer, owing much in its look and feel to the original *Prince of Persia* games.

5.4 million times. In the USA, sales of cell-phone games are estimated to hit $203.8 million in 2004, more than doubling the previous year's figure of $91.3 million.

While there has been some effort to take the cell-phone game to stores in a more traditional commercial manner—i.e. in packages you pick off the shelf and pay for with real money—by far the most popular method of distribution remains downloads. Games on standard cell phones currently can't exceed 256K, which makes them a perfect size for electronic distribution. Additionally, users can opt to add the cost of the game to their cell-phone bill—often masking the cost.

Another alternative business model is the monthly subscription, favored by massively multiplayer games. Here, players use client software—free or purchased—which they pay monthly to use, much like a premium TV channel. When the model works, it's lucrative. *Lineage*—the world's most popular massively multiplayer game—boasts more than four million subscribers, generating a monthly income that many standalone commercial releases could only dream of.

It's also possible to encourage users to pay as they play by making premium content available after initial release. This can vary from in-game equipment to additional levels. By keeping these charges relatively small, a great deal of incremental revenue can be generated. Players don't mind spending a few dollars here and there for the odd extra course—and when hundreds of thousands do, the additional funds can be most welcome.

Given the risks associated with green-lighting games for full development, alternative business models are a welcome option, particularly for smaller teams that can operate on reduced running costs. While many developers can be openly dismissive of TV- or phone-based games—considering them lacking in glamor or prestige compared to coding full-price titles—the fact these devices have greater penetration than most home platforms makes them a worthwhile area. Indeed, industry watchers predict an increase in publishers setting up their own in-house cell-phone and TV teams. The competition for the lucrative mainstream dollar is about to get much fiercer.

Building games for limited platforms such as cell phones or set-top boxes is a technical challenge. It's important to reign in ambition and concentrate on games that run within the limits set by the hardware. Usually, this results in games on these platforms being reminiscent of the earliest computer games—and for that reason few cell or STB games receive the prestige and recognition of home console titles. However, the colossal installed bases can make them extremely profitable.

While conventional games have budgets in the millions, high-quality cell and TV games can be produced for less than $150,000, typically by teams of three to five—although often by individual lone programmers. And whereas console games can take between two and three years to develop, cell or set-top box (STB) games are developed in a few months.

In every developed country apart from America, a higher proportion of the population owns a cell phone than a computer. There are well over a billion phones in existence now, and with each new generation the hardware specifications improve. The current wave of 3G phones offers a quality of gaming comparable with early PlayStation games—albeit on a smaller screen—although the market for these high-end phones is quite small at present.

On standard cell phones, it's a crowded market. There's currently no approvals process for games developers and publishers, so anyone can, in theory, produce and distribute a cell-phone title. Intellectual property abuse is rife. Hordes of unofficial games can be found advertised in the classified pages of teen magazines. There are over 3,500 companies publishing cell phone games within the EU alone.

Most phones run the Java 2 Micro Edition (J2ME) language, although games can also be developed in C++, which offer direct access to the phone's hardware and the associated increase in performance.

Cell-phone games are mostly downloaded across the network, although some are stocked in traditional retail outlets. This offers a one-time fee, which usually varies between $2.50 and $8.00, although titles considered "premium" can often cost more. Games are either accessed through operator portals—and are therefore subject to revenue share—or delivered via WAP or third-generation high-speed data services. They are either charged directly to the user's cell-phone bill via operator costs or premium text messages or by credit card via a website.

Interactive TV, for example, through Sky TV's "Gamestar" channel, requires a more formal partnership with the TV operator, which provides the sole route to market. These services charge varying rates depending on the type of game and whether it's offering the chance to win cash or prizes. Games can cost as little as 50 cents per play, although the most popular price brackets offer unlimited plays within a specific period of time. For example *Lemmings* can currently be played all day for less than $2.

If the game has not been commissioned specifically by the operator, the revenue is split between the developer and the channel. Deals are negotiated individually and rates can vary depending on the parties involved. Games available on independent channels increase the number of parties vying

Developers have been contracted to create a host of iTV games designed to promote a range of other properties. *Scuzzboarding* appeared on Sky's service around the launch of the Scuzz music channel in order to encourage the service's gamers to tune in. Naturally, this was a free offering. Surprisingly, the promo game for *Eight Legged Freaks* (left)—presumably designed to encourage players to head straight to the movies—was not, costing, at $3, four times more by cell phone than if bought through the set-top box.

Above: **Of course, the best way to top the charts is through licensed titles. EA currently uses Digital Bridges to distributed its titles to the cell format, having moved development of its titles in-house. Although EA's cell-phone games naturally lack the million-dollar polish of their console and PC titles, they provide a good enough approximation.**

German cell-phone developer Elkware has built a solid business creating and distributing games through its own website. Shrewd licensing deals have enabled it to bolt on celebrities and bands to existing games and remarket them cheaply. Pamela Anderson and Jordan (below right and left, respectively) titles offer simple gaming mechanics with the promise of naughty pictures if you successfully complete versions of *Qix* or *Breakout*. *Blue: Revealed* (bottom) is a simple number guessing game that offers little reward, unless gawping at a bunch of average-looking males is your thing.

In mid-2004, the Entertainment Leisure Software Association began compiling the official cell-phone Java chart by collating data from the four largest UK operators. Comprising a mix of casual games that can be played on and off and hardcore titles that require longer attention and traditional gaming skills, the chart is more diverse than its home counterpart, offering a wider range of opportunities for cell developers.

Top row, left to right: *Tetris*—ifone, *Pac-man*—Namco, *Racing Fever 2*—Sumea. Middle row, left to right: *Mafia Wars*—Sumea, *Pub Pool*—Iomo, *Street Soccer*—Sumea. Bottom row, left to right: *Collapse*—Jamdat, *Steve Davis Snooker*—Iomo, *Space Invaders*—Digital Bridges.

Vodafone is one of the more active operators in the games space. Its Vodafone Live service offers a range of downloadable games, from $2 to $8. Many are classic games ported as faithfully as handsets will allow, and the operator has been keen to tie up exclusive games in order to distinguish its platform from competitors. Some UK developers have negotiated contracts worth up to $150,000 to port licenses to the service, usually taking around three months in total.

for revenue share. While a few cents here and there may not be considered worth getting out of bed for, consider that over half of Sky's 15-million audience regularly access the interactive games channel. Pipemania, for example, generated over 1.4 million premium rate calls while it was hosted on the service. PlayJam, another interactive content area, has enjoyed 1.7 billion plays since it launched in 2000 and while the service does offer some free content, the vast majority of its games are charged at about $1 per play. Do the math.

The cell-phone industry in particular is wising up to the opportunities of working more closely with the wider games business, to the extent that titles are appearing on handsets closer to their home console release. Codemasters' *Colin McRae Rally '04* appeared through Vodafone Live! on launch day and analysts predict its sales through this cell-phone portal could top those of PS2, Xbox, and PC. Of course, the revenue generated will be significantly smaller, but it's a sign of a trend that will make the cell market of increasing importance to developers looking to further exploit their intellectual property.

ONLINE BUSINESS MODEL
Despite the fact it's widely regarded that the future of games is online, the industry is undecided about the way its gamers prefer to pay to play. Whereas traditional retail prices fit neatly into bands, online pricing varies considerably.

Broadly speaking, there are two main methods of revenue generation: "Free to Consumer" or "Pay to Play." But many titles, particularly successful ones, utilize elements of both in hybrid models.

Games distributed Free to Consumer are funded by revenue from advertising partners. This model requires a huge audience in order to attract a business-sustaining income, which means the game itself should avoid anything that will restrict any potential players from signing up.

For this reason, these games are usually browser-based, scripted in Java, Shockwave, or Flash—and so can, in theory, be enjoyed by anyone who can connect to the Internet. Often card, puzzle, or simple arcade games, they eschew sophistication in favor of attracting and entertaining a mainstream audience. These games can be developed by

Below: **Accessed more than 60 million times, RealArcade is a Pay-to-Play service with limited free content. It offers over 70 free online and over 200 premium games once users have downloaded a 6MB client. Its hook is the "Game Pass," which, for $7 a month, opens up a host of additional services and discounts designed to keep subscribers playing and spending. It's a sophisticated service, offering a mix of mainstream and hardcore titles, which cost up to $20 to download. The service also offers developers an affiliate scheme for which RealArcade will promote independent games—in return for revenue split, of course.**

almost anyone as the programming languages are relatively unsophisticated, making them the perfect platform for aspiring developers keen to hone their skills. However, without the power of a major portal behind them, they're unlikely to hit a widespread audience but can still be attractive to advertisers as part of viral campaigns.

The Pay to Play model can be divided into three main categories. Monthly subscriptions vary from a few dollars to an average of $15 a month, and offer unlimited play over the period. Like a broadband Internet subscription, which is usually required in order to connect at suitable speeds, these plans are perfect for heavy users or those who prefer to calculate their monthly outgoings in advance. This is by far the most popular model for massively multiplayer online games (MMOGs).

Metered subscriptions are the equivalent of the cell-phone pay-as-you-go scheme and are perfect for those not willing to commit to a longer contract, although they can often work out more expensively for habitual users. Some games, such as *Z-Opolis*, offer a sliding scale that makes playing for longer more economical by reducing hourly rates the longer a user is online.

The one-time fee is a model that is usually offered in conjunction with other revenue schemes. At its crudest, it's the distribution in a boxed, retail version, usually with playing time bundled as part of this cost. Credit card details are taken at registration, with the player asked to actively cancel and re-subscribe to a full subscription

Left: It's not all roses in the online world. The ruthless termination of a couple of high-profile massively multiplayer games such as *True Fantasy Live Online* during 2004 was an illustration that there are challenges achieving the numbers necessary to pay for development of an original title and its subsequent technical support.

(rather than upgrade) after the trial period. One-time fees can also be used as entry fees to special items, tournaments, or as payment for additional or episodic content.

It may be necessary to team up with a third party in order to meet the technical requirements of an online game. A partnership with an ISP such as AOL or MSN or a portal such as Yahoo will offer the necessary exposure to a large customer base. Additionally, dedicated gaming sites such as GameSpy and MGON can help in driving consumers to specific online games and often produce SDKs to enable developers to integrate their games with the site's infrastructure.

Dedicated server support can obviously add to the running costs and will usually fall under the remit of the publisher. However, more and more games are embracing peer-to-peer technology. This neatly sidesteps the need for dedicated servers, relying instead on surplus player processing power to host networked sessions.

The diverse methods of revenue generation from online gaming represent a tremendous opportunity for development teams to establish direct relationships with their customers, sidestepping current models that are unfairly weighted toward retail. As broadband penetration continues, more and more gamers will move toward Pay-to-Play services. The key is creating titles that will sustain and entertain a large number of players over a long period of time at a price players are willing to pay.

Above left: The Internet Gaming Zone—now part of the massive MSN empire—offers a vast range of free online games, some of which can be played for cash prizes. While there are premium games available to download and play any time, it's the advertising throughout that provides the vast majority of the income generated.

Left: *Z-Opolis*—a massively multiplayer online world aimed at kids and families—uses a sliding scale of charges to accommodate its diverse audience. The first eight hours of gameplay are free, after which the users pay between 15 and 25 cents an hour, up to a maximum of $15 per month. A standard monthly subscription costs $7.95.

ROBERT GARRIOTT, NCSOFT AUSTIN

Robert Garriott is the brother of Richard, the founder of Origin Systems. Indeed, it was Robert who initially encouraged his sibling to set up his own company, convinced he could design games better than the developers of the time. Robert obtained his Masters Degree in Finance from MIT. He and Richard were decorated by *Inc. Magazine* in 1992 as "Regional Entrepreneurs of the Year" for the Austin, Texas area.

In April 2001, Richard and Robert merged their then company Destination Games into NCSoft Austin, a subsidiary of Korean giant NCSoft. The NCSoft Austin development team's goal is to provide the next generation of massively multiplayer role-playing games. The focus of their products is on fun, accessibility, and rich content, and having pioneered the online game industry, the brothers are currently intent on revolutionizing the marketplace with their future products. Their most recent title *City of Heroes* has won numerous accolades.

What is it that particularly interests you in the Massively Multiplayer genre?
I am tired of traditional games, and don't see myself moving back. I find Massively Multiplayer Online Games (MMOGs) to be exciting and dynamic.... It's the place to be!

How do player numbers typically change throughout the game's life, in your experience? For example, do tens of thousands of players sign up immediately, or is it a more gradual process than that? What are the typical churn rates, and is there anything a developer can do to limit them?
Usually, player numbers grow rapidly for six months to one year, then they stay somewhat level or increase fairly gradually over the next several years.

On average, online gamers stay with a game for 10 to 12 months, which means that about 10 percent churn out of a game in any given month. Developers continually update their games, and add upper level depth in order to reduce churn.

Often, new players find it difficult to find their feet in a game world that has existed for a significant period of time. What can be done to ease the introduction of newbies into an established game and ensure they are converted into long-term subscribers?
In my opinion, new Massively Multiplayer Online Games have about 20 minutes to attract a new user into a game. In that 20 minutes, a new user should be able to do many things. They should be able to create a character. They should be able to take that character on a mission, and not be killed. Indeed, they should win the mission—and be told how great they are, and given awards and honors, etc. They should then be sent on an additional mission. Most MMOGs today do not allow the above, but the newer-generation products we are working on currently will be designed this way.

Do you think we'll ever see real estate or in-game items traded properly?
As you know, currently there is lots of item selling and trading, but it is not sanctioned by the companies publishing the products. This is a legal limitation, not a technical limitation. If publishers acknowledge that these items have real-world value, then they also have real-world liability if any of the items are lost or stolen in the game, and the publisher does not replace them. This type of legal liability is unacceptable to most publishers, and therefore they do not allow buying and trading as part of the game. For this to change, the legal atmosphere would need to change first.

Left and right:
Guild Wars, from NCSoft.

Below right:
Lineage 2, from NCSoft.

The players who enjoy MMOGs tend to be hideously stereotyped. Is this fair? What is your experience of the demographics of your players? What can we do to broaden the appeal of MMOGs?
The way to broaden the appeal is, simply, to create games with broad appeal. The main problem so far is that 99.9 percent of online games are medieval fantasy role-playing. We need to publish games in many different gaming genres in order to broaden the appeal, and their acceptance by the general public.

With a "typical" singleplayer (or even standard, networked multiplayer) game, the developer more or less has an idea of any potential player actions. However, whenever large numbers of gamers exist in a persistent world, there are often unpredictable outcomes—sieges, demonstrations, that kind of thing. What mechanics must exist within a MMOG to deal with random player behavior given the difficulty of switching off the world without causing further uproar?
The main difficulty with controlling player action comes with too many people gathering in one place at one time. When this happens, it stresses a couple of things: the graphics-generating capability of many home computers, and the processing power of the single server that is hosting the large group.

In order to overcome this issue, many games are designed to spread people out among the many servers by starting people at different locations, and having many different paths to complete a mission. In *City of Heroes,* we also have the ability to create multiple copies of the same exact area when too many people want to be in a certain place at one time.

Is the decision to greenlight such a project more difficult for an MMOG given the expensive backend and support system that needs to be in place whether it's commercially successful or not? What other financial considerations are there?
MMOGs are three to five times as expensive as singleplayer games, and take three to five times as long to develop. This means that a decision to "greenlight" is taken less frequently,

and needs to be considered more carefully. You can't afford many mistakes in the MMOG business, as a number of companies have found out.

The incremental revenue possible from a successful MMOG is an obvious reason why developers/publishers cater for it. However, given that a monthly subscription would encourage its users to play as frequently as possible, doesn't this commitment prevent those players from buying more titles a month, therefore damaging the games market as a whole? Should you care?

The goal of the "free market" is to provide as many options and opportunities to the consumer as possible. The consumer will decide which method of game play and business model finally wins in the long term. In our business, the consumer is king.... Business caters to wherever consumers are spending money.

Obviously it's not easy to predict how players will discover ways in which to cheat the system—but what are the general restrictions one should try and place on players in order to level the playing field?

Cheaters hurt the game for everyone, and all game companies try to stop cheating in some way. In general, this is a losing battle, just as stopping illegal product copying was a losing battle. However, we do what we can, and the honest players are very appreciative of our efforts.

How have you found global tastes have differed within game worlds that should, in effect, have no such boundaries? Do players from different continents prefer different types of games? Can one game ever appeal to everyone?

Just like one shoe style will not appeal to everyone, no single game will ever appeal to all gamers. Tastes are a mixture of culture, age, and millions of other details that vary within families, countries, and continents. While everyone is basically the same inside, and enjoys having fun, the way the fun is "expressed" creates an exciting variety. And changes in this "expression" create new and unique opportunities for game growth and development over time.

You can obviously gather a huge amount of information about your players—what they do, how frequently they play, that type of thing. How have you used this information to develop subsequent titles? Are there trends emerging now which suggest how the next generation of MMOGs will evolve?

Most of the trends I have seen in MMOG gaming say, more fun, more frequently. Gamers want action and excitement, combined with depth. Old-style MMOGs gave only one or the other.... Next-generation MMOGs will deliver both.

Given that the future consoles will become networked-enabled, how can games ensure they stand out from the crowd? Are persistent worlds the way forward, or do modern gamers—with an increasingly shortening attention span—prefer games they'll be able to dip in and out of? Should designers of MMOGs stick rigidly to PC development, or is there an opportunity on console?

Good games are good games independent of what platform they are on. The platform allows for different types of interaction and interface, but the game itself needs many of the same characteristics to be enjoyable on any platform. We are platform agnostic, and, as such, will follow the MMOG gamer onto whatever platform he or she chooses to play on.

All images from *City of Heroes*, from NCSoft. This MMOG deals with the problem of too many players in one place at one time by creating multiple copies of the same area.

RESOURCES AND BIBLIOGRAPHY

Although there are too many books about videogame development to list here, the following should provide a useful starting point for further research:

HISTORY
The Ultimate History of Video Games, by Steven L. Kent, (released in the USA as *The First Quarter : A 25-year History of Video Games*)

Trigger Happy, by Steven Poole

Game on: The History and Culture of Videogames, edited by Lucien King

Supercade: A Visual History of the Videogame Age 1971-1984, by Van Burnham

Game over: How Nintendo Zapped an American Industry, Captured Your Dollars, and Enslaved Your Children, by David Sheff

From Barbie to Mortal Kombat: Gender and Computer Games, by Justine Cassell

DESIGN
Game Architecture and Design, by Andrew Rollings and Dave Morris

Gameplay and Design, by Kevin Oxland

Andrew Rollings and Ernest Adams on Game Design, by Andrew Rollings and Ernest Adams

Rules of Play: Game Design Fundamentals, by Katie Salen and Eric Zimmerman

More Than a Game: The Computer Game as Fictional Form, by Barry Atkins

A Theory of fun for Game Design, by Raph Koster

Game Design, by Robert Bates

Designing Virtual Worlds, by Richard Bartle

Game Design Workshop: Designing, Prototyping, and Playtesting Games, by Tracey Fullerton

The Indie Game Development Survival Guide, by David Michael

Postmortems from Game Developer: Insights from the Developers of Unreal Tournament, Black and White, Age of Empires, and Other Top-Selling Games, edited by Austin Grossman

PROGRAMMING
The Pragmatic Programmer, by Andrew Hunt and David Thomas

Game Coding Complete, by M. McShaffrey

C++ for Game Programmers, by Noel Llopis

Game Physics, by David H. Eberly

AI Game Programming Wisdom, edited by Steve Rabin

Artificial Intelligence for Computer Games: an Introduction, by John David Funge

Programming Game AI by Example, by Mat Buckland

Physics for Game Developers, by David M. Bourg

Essential Mathematics for Games and Interactive Applications: A Programmer's Guide, by James M. Van Verth

ART AND ANIMATION
The Art of Game Worlds, by Dave Morris and Leo Hartas

Creating the Art of the Game, Matthew Omernick

The Animator's Survival Kit: A Working Manual of Methods, Principles and Formulas for Computer, Stop-motion, Games and Classical Animators, by Richard Williams

The Art of 3-D Computer Animation and Effects, by Isaac Victor Kerlow

Maya Character Development: An Anatomical Approach, by Chris Maraffi

Designing Arcade Computer Game Graphics, by Ari Feldman

The Dark side of Game Texturing, by David Franson

Animating Real-time Game Characters, by Paul Steed

Game Modeling Using Low Polygon Techniques, by Chad Walker and Eric Walker

SOUND
Audio Programming for Interactive Games, by Martin Wilde

Game Audio Programming, by James Boer

Audio for Games, by Alexander Brandon

The Complete Guide to Game Audio, by Aaron Marks

Sound Design: The Expressive Power of Music, Voice and Sound Effects in Cinema, edited by David Sonnenschein

NARRATIVE
ScreenPlay: Cinema/videogames/interfaces, edited by Tanya Krzywinska and Geoff King

Chris Crawford on Interactive Storytelling, by Chris Crawford

Videogames, by James Newman

First Person: New Media as Story, Performance, and Game, edited by Noah Wardrip-Fruin and Pat Harrigan

Character Development and Storytelling for Games, by Lee Sheldon

Pause & Effect: The Art of Interactive Narrative, by Mark S. Meadows

INTERNET RESOURCES

The Internet is teeming with websites that are dedicated to videogames and their development. Some of the following may be useful:

AboutAI.net—http://aboutai.net/DesktopDefault.aspx
A site dedicated to general AI principles, including videogame AI

Blitz Research—http://www.blitzbasic.com/
A simple programming language aimed at those learning to code, or experienced coders who want to quickly prototype a game design

Botman's Bots—http://www.planethalflife.com/botman/MOD_FAQ.shtml
An FAQ about creating mods for Half-Life

C/C++ Reference—http://www.cppreference.com/
Aimed at experienced programmers, to provide a reference for C/C++ syntax

Everything You Always Wanted to Know About Becoming an Independent Game Developer—http://www.superxstudios.com/services/article/everythingyouever.htm
Some advice for would-be developers

ExtremeTech—http://www.extremetech.com/article2/0,1558,594,00.asp
Game engine creation article

Flipcode—http://flipcode.com/
Likewise contains a series of resources for game development, including articles and forums

Gamasutra—http://www.gamasutra.com/
The online website of US periodical *Game Developer Magazine*, Gamasutra features industry news and job listings as well as fascinating articles written by industry insiders, ranging from technology reviews to project post-mortems.

Gamedev.net—http://www.gamedev.net/
Contains a variety of columns, articles, forums and job listings related to game development

GIGnews.com—http://www.gignews.com/index.html
Various articles and columns offering advice about working in videogame development

Grumpy Gamer—http://www.grumpygamer.com/
A blog written by industry veteran Ron Gilbert, the brains behind the *Monkey Island* series

Ludology.org—www.ludology.org
A site dedicated to the culture of play

Makegames.com—http://www.makegames.com/
Another site offering various resources for would-be developers, including advice about which software to use

The Making of GoldenEye—http://www.europeandevelopersforum.com/martinhollis.doc
An interesting insight into the creation of one of the greatest games ever made can be found here

MSDN—http://msdn.microsoft.com/library/
Microsoft's MSDN Library contains various reference materials and information about developers using the company's tools and technology

Sloperama—http://www.sloperama.com/advice.html
Various articles offering advice about working in the videogame industry

Technicat—http://www.technicat.com/index.html
A good list of Internet resources for game developers can be found here

GLOSSARY

Artificial Intelligence (AI) In the context of videogame development, artificial intelligence is less concerned with authentically modeling behavior, as it is with convincingly depicting conduct. So although there is some overlap with cutting-edge academic research, it's more important to use smoke and mirrors to make in-game entities behave plausibly.

Alpha stage Although the precise point at which a game enters alpha can vary, it's essentially the point during development at which most, or all, of the assets and functionality are implemented. It should be possible to gain a pretty good idea of what the finished game will be like from the alpha version.

Beta stage Again, the precise definition of the beta stage can vary, but in general it refers to a nearly-complete version of the game, prior to final debugging, tweaking, and polishing. Often, it's the beta version that gets sent to journalists so that they can produce reviews to coincide with the launch of the game.

Bug Some sort of unforeseen glitch that arises within the game due to programming errors or poor design: bugs are the bane of developers' lives. They can vary in magnitude from irritations to major and debilitating crashes, and their occurrence needs to be minimized before a game can be released.

Cut-scene Usually a non-interactive sequence of animation book-ending interactive stretches of play, and generally used to provide a game with some sort of narrative, and/or to provide the player with information.

DirectX Microsoft's suite of multimedia APIs (Application Programming Interfaces) are built into its Windows operating system to provide a standard development platform for PCs. Consequently it's easier for developers to ensure compatibility across various hardware configurations and they can access specialized hardware features without having to write hardware-specific code

Emergence Emergent systems are complex systems and behaviors that arise out of the interactions between simpler components, frequently in unexpected ways. It's commonly used to refer to AI, but, more recently, has come to be used to describe a form of systemic game design. So, for example, where traditional game design might put a player in a room with a door that can only be destroyed with a rocket launcher, systemic or emergent design would give every material in the room a series of properties, and allow the player to come up with their own solution (e.g. repeatedly shooting the door with a less effective weapon, finding a key, or even escaping through a window).

Engine A game engine is essentially non-game-specific technology which facilitates the creation of a videogame. They can typically be reused across the development of several titles.

Intellectual Property (IP) The lifeblood of any publisher, IP is essentially abstract artistic creations that are treated by the law as if they were tangible entities. Thus, a publisher who owns the right to make games based on a particular fictional character or world would be said to own it as IP.

Middleware Middleware is a broad term that encompasses off-the-shelf development tools and technology created by a thirdparty. It can be acquired by developers to allow them to create games.

Milestone Contracts between publishers and developers typically require developers to allow publishers to assess their development progress by stipulating various milestone dates, at which the developer will submit certain contractually stipulated assets in return for payment.

Mod A mod is some sort of user-created modification applied to a commercially available game or piece of game development technology. *Counter-Strike* is a mod of *Half-Life*, for example. The "mod scene" is the community which arises around the creation of such modifications.

Software Development Kit (SDK) The SDK is a collection of software utilities, documentation and special development versions of hardware that developers purchase from manufacturers to enable them to build software for that particular piece of hardware.

Stock Keeping Unit (SKU) Each different released version of a game is known as a SKU (pronounced "skew"). Thus, if a developer creates one disc which contains several foreign language versions of the game, it represents one SKU. If those language versions were divided across several discs that were released separately, it would represent multiple SKUs.

Technical Requirements Checklist (Sony) or Technical Checklist Requirements (Microsoft) (TRC/TCR) Each console manufacturer requires developers and publishers to put their titles through internal approval systems which are known as TRC or TCR checks. This allows the manufacturers to prevent questionable material from appearing on their hardware, and to provide a consistent approach to usability and interface.

Thirdparty In the context of game development, a thirdparty entity is typically used to denote a developer or publisher that is independent of the console manufacturers (known as firstparties).

INDEX

the art of producing games

ACKNOWLEDGMENTS

Simon would like to thank Charles Cecil, for his eternal sunshine and sound advice, David Wilson for illustrating that not all PR professionals are work-shy fops, Richard Garriott for his patience and co-operation and Richard Joseph for his assistance and Into The Wonderful. It's clichéd to thank your friends and family: but he would like to, genuinely.

Ste would like to thank the Triforce, Jonathan Smith, Jennie Kong, Nancy Gatehouse, Doug Lombardi, Warren Spector, Lisa Forrest, Ben Cousins, Tim Sweeney, and Dario Casali.

David would like to thank Jennie Kong and Vanessa Wood, Lidia Stojanovic and Kerry Martyn, Stefan McGarry and Gary Rowe, Jeremy Chubb, Andy Beveridge, Algy Williams, Asad Habib. And Simon's friends and family. Okay, and his own.